# THE SHORTEST HISTORY OF ANCIENT ROME

**Other Titles in the Shortest History Series**

*The Shortest History of China* by Linda Jaivin
*The Shortest History of the Crown* by Stephen Bates
*The Shortest History of Democracy* by John Keane
*The Shortest History of Economics* by Andrew Leigh
*The Shortest History of India* by John Zubrzycki
*The Shortest History of Israel and Palestine* by Michael Scott-Baumann
*The Shortest History of Music* by Andrew Ford
*The Shortest History of Sex* by David Baker
*The Shortest History of the Soviet Union* by Sheila Fitzpatrick
*The Shortest History of the Universe* by David Baker
*The Shortest History of War* by Gwynne Dyer

# THE SHORTEST HISTORY OF ANCIENT ROME

ROSS KING

PICADOR INDIA

First published in Australia in 2024 by Black Inc.
First published in India 2025 by Picador India
an imprint of Pan Macmillan Publishing India Private Limited
707 Kailash Building
26 K. G. Marg, New Delhi 110001
www.panmacmillan.co.in

Pan Macmillan, The Smithson, 6 Briset Street, Farringdon, London EC1M 5NR
Associated companies throughout the world
www.panmacmillan.com

ISBN 978-93-6113-247-6



1 3 5 7 9 8 6 4 2



Printed and bound in India by Thomson Press India Ltd.

MIX
Paper | Supporting responsible forestry
FSC® C010615
FSC
www.fsc.org

# Contents

*To Christopher Sinclair-Stevenon*

| **PREHISTORIC ROME** | c. 1000 BCE | Evidence of early settlement on the Palatine Hill. |
|---|---|---|
| | c. 800–750 BCE | Formation of small villages around the Tiber River. |
|  | 753 BCE | Traditional date for the founding of Rome by Romulus. |
| | 753–509 BCE | Rule of the seven legendary kings of Rome (Romulus, Numa Pompilius, Tullus Hostilius, Ancus Marcius, Tarquinius Priscus, Servius Tullius, Tarquinius Superbus). |
| **THE ROMAN REPUBLIC (509–27 BCE)** | 509 BCE | Establishment of the Roman Republic after the expulsion of Tarquinius Superbus. |
| | c. 450 BCE | Creation of the Twelve Tables, Rome's first codification of laws. |
|  | 396 BCE | Conquest of the Etruscan city of Veii, significant expansion of Roman territory. |
| | c. 390 BCE | Sack of Rome by the Gauls and the construction of the Servian Wall. |
| | 343–290 BCE | The three Samnite Wars, including the Battle of the Caudine Forks (321 BCE) in the Second Samnite War. |
| | 264–241 BCE | First Punic War against Carthage, leading to Roman control over Sicily. |
|  | 218–201 BCE | Second Punic War, highlighted by Hannibal's invasion of Italy. |
| | 146 BCE | Destruction of Carthage and Corinth, establishing Roman dominance in the Mediterranean. |
| | 133–121 BCE | The Gracchi brothers' attempted reforms and subsequent social unrest. |
| | 107–86 BCE | Military reforms and the rise of Gaius Marius. |
| | 91–88 BCE | Uprising of the *socii* against Rome in the Social War. |
|  | 82–81 BCE | Dictatorship of Sulla and subsequent constitutional reforms. |
| | 60 BCE | Formation of the First Triumvirate (Julius Caesar, Pompey, Crassus). |
|  | 49–45 BCE | Caesar's civil war, leading to Julius Caesar's dictatorship. |
| | 44 BCE | Assassination of Julius Caesar. |
| | 43–33 BCE | Second Triumvirate (Octavian, Mark Antony, Lepidus). |
| | 31 BCE | The Battle of Actium, Octavian defeats Antony and Cleopatra. |

## THE ROMAN EMPIRE (27 BCE – 476 CE)

| | |
|---|---|
| 27 BCE | Octavian becomes Augustus, marking the beginning of the Roman Empire. |
| c. 20 BCE | Construction of the Ara Pacis, an altar to Peace. |
| 9 CE | The Romans suffer a devastating defeat to the Cherusci at the Battle of the Teutoburg Forest. |
| 14 CE | Death of Augustus, Tiberius becomes emperor. |
| 37–41 CE | Reign of Caligula, known for his cruel and erratic behaviour. |
| 41–54 CE | Reign of Claudius, who expanded the Empire and built the Aqua Claudia. |
| 54–68 CE | Reign of Nero, known for the Great Fire of Rome and his artistic ambitions. |
| 64 CE | St Peter executed in Rome. |
| 69 CE | Year of the Four Emperors (Galba, Otho, Vitellius, Vespasian). |
| 70 CE | Destruction of the Second Temple in Jerusalem by Titus. |
| 79 CE | Eruption of Vesuvius, with the destruction of Pompeii and Herculaneum. |
| 98–117 | Reign of Trajan, who expands the Empire to its greatest extent. |
| 113 | Trajan's Column erected to commemorate his victories in Dacia. |
| 117–138 | Reign of Hadrian, known for Hadrian's Wall in Britain and the Pantheon in Rome. |
| 161–180 | Reign of Marcus Aurelius, known for his philosophical work *Meditations*. |
| 180–192 | Reign of Commodus, whose rule marks the beginning of the Empire's decline. |
| 212 | Caracalla's edict granting Roman citizenship to all free men in the Empire. |
| 235–284 | Crisis of the Third Century, a period of military, political and economic turmoil. |
| 271–75 | Construction of the Aurelian Walls. |
| 284–305 | Reign of Diocletian, who introduces the Tetrarchy to stabilise the Empire. |
| 303 | Beginning of the Great Persecution, with thousands of Christians executed under the authority of imperial edicts. |

| | | |
|---|---|---|
| **THE ROMAN EMPIRE (27 BCE – 476 CE)** (*cont.*)  | 306–337 | Reign of Constantine the Great, who endorses Christianity and founds Constantinople. |
| | 312 | Battle of the Milvian Bridge, Constantine's conversion to Christianity. |
| | 378 | Battle of Adrianople, significant defeat of the Roman army by the Goths. |
| | 410 | Sack of Rome by the Visigoths under Alaric. |
| | 452 | Attila the Hun's invasion of Italy. |
| | 455 | Sack of Rome by the Vandals. |
| | 476 | Fall of the Western Roman Empire, deposition of Romulus Augustulus by Odovacar. |

# 1

# THE CITY ON THE HILLS: THE ORIGINS OF ROME

AFTER SUFFERING THROUGH HEAT SO INTENSE that the ground burned their feet and the solder in their drinking cups melted, an expedition of Roman legionaries exploring the Nile found themselves in an overgrown marsh. They had reached the vast Sudd swamp in present-day South Sudan, almost 2,500 kilometres south of Alexandria. Despite the impenetrability of these wetlands, which baffled even the local guides, the expedition somehow pushed upstream for another 800 kilometres, ultimately reaching a waterfall thundering between two immense rocks – what is now known as Murchison (or Kabalega) Falls in Uganda.[1]

This was the remarkable tale that two centurions who took part in the expedition in about 60 CE told the philosopher and statesman Seneca the Younger following their return to Rome. The party had been sent by the Roman emperor, Nero, to discover the source of the Nile, and possibly also to gather information for Nero's planned invasion of Ethiopia. Although Nero's death precluded any further progress in this African odyssey, elsewhere around the known world the Roman imprint, the result of comparable struggles and endurance, was much deeper and more lasting. The Roman Empire stretched enormous distances across both time and space. It lasted for more than 500 years, from the reign of Augustus (begun in 27 BCE) until the fall of the Western Empire in 476 CE. At its peak, it would extend from the Irish Sea all the way round the Mediterranean Basin to the shores of both the Caspian Sea and the Persian Gulf. It encompassed all or part of what are today more than twenty-five different countries, including such remote (from Rome) places as Azerbaijan, Saudi Arabia, Iraq, Ukraine and England, the latter of which was, according to an incredulous Roman historian, 'outside the limits of the known world'.[2] Archaeologists have found Roman coins and artifacts scattered from the north of England, south to Timbuktu and east to the hoard of coins discovered in al-Madhāriba in Yemen, at the very bottom of the Arabian Peninsula. Pots that once contained a favourite Roman condiment, the fermented fish sauce known as *garum*, have been found in Tamil Nadu, in the hinterlands near the coast of the Bay of Bengal. Here, the Tamils knew the Romans as 'Yavanas'.

Evidence for the scale and reach of ancient Roman commercial, cultural and industrial activity has been found in many other places, from the top of the world to the bottom of the sea. Scientists studying core samples from the ice sheet in Greenland and other locations in the High Arctic have found that, in Antiquity, lead pollution – produced by smelting ores in clay furnaces – peaked during the height of the Roman Empire. Meanwhile, more shipwrecks dating from between 100 BCE and 100 CE have been discovered (no fewer than 600 of them) than for the thousand years that followed the fall of the Roman Empire in the West. These abundant wrecks are testament not to poor Roman navigational or shipbuilding skills but, rather, to the massive amount of seaborne trade conducted during the glory days of the Empire.[3]

The Romans left behind much more than air pollution, silver coins and sunken treasure. They also bequeathed us their politics, their laws, their philosophy, their architecture and – in many countries – the underpinnings and vestiges of their language. They gave us Roman numerals, the days of the week, the months of the year, aqueducts, underfloor heating and concrete. Along with the Greeks, with whom they enjoyed a cultural symbiosis, they laid the political, intellectual and artistic foundations of Western civilisation. They were skilled engineers and brilliant military tacticians. Their physicians, accustomed to dealing with the wounds of gladiators and victims of plagues, were medical pioneers. Their invention of hydraulic concrete – made with the ash from volcanoes such as Vesuvius – allowed them to raise magnificent, shock-and-awe buildings as well as to construct harbours and ports that enabled and expanded trade in far-off lands.

But what was Rome, and who were the Romans? The beginnings of Rome were, as we shall see, a mixture of mystery and myth. All that can be said for certain, thanks to archaeological finds, is that the Romans arose more than two and a half millennia ago from among a group of Iron Age communities scattered through central Italy. Although they eventually conquered their enemies on the battlefield, their greatest feats were not military but political and cultural, as they assimilated and absorbed the diverse tribes of peninsular Italy. They created for their conquered foes, no less than for themselves, an identity as 'Romans'. This pattern would be repeated as their legions spread inexorably – and often brutally – outwards in a conquest of the far-flung territories that became known as the *orbis Romanus* (the 'Roman world'). By the first century CE, the phrase *civis Romanus sum* ('I am a Roman citizen') had become a boast heard from Rome to Jerusalem. In 212 CE, Roman citizenship would be extended to virtually all free people across the Empire, making 'Romans' out of much of the known world. Indeed, by the third century, as much as 20 per cent of the world's population (possibly more) counted as Roman – at least 65 million people, slightly more than the population of Italy today.

How this astonishing domination came about is one of history's greatest stories. As the ancient historian Polybius asked in the second century BCE, long before the Romans had reached their dizzy peaks of conquest and supremacy: 'For who is so indifferent or indolent as not to wish to know by what means and under what system of polity the Romans ... succeeded in subjecting nearly the whole inhabited world to their sole government – a thing unique in history?' His question is surely every bit as pertinent and compelling today.[4]

*

In both ancient legend and the popular imagination, the story of Rome often begins with Romulus and Remus. The outlines of this foundation myth are familiar to many of us. Romulus and Remus were the twin sons of Rhea Silvia, the daughter of Numitor, king of an ancient city in central Italy called Alba Longa. On orders of their great-uncle, Amulius, who had usurped Numitor, they were taken away as infants to be drowned in the Tiber. The men forced to carry out this deed were either compassionate or less than conscientious, merely placing the basket containing the boys into a sluggish stretch of water, which, as it ebbed, left them high and dry. Suckled by a passing she-wolf, they were rescued and raised by a benevolent swineherd named Faustulus and his wife, Acca. As the boys grew to manhood they proved themselves courageous and strong, performing such heroic antics as chasing off robbers and foiling cattle thieves. After crossing swords with the usurper Amulius, they killed him and, their true identities triumphantly revealed, restored their grandfather to his rightful place. Leaving Alba Longa in his capable hands, the young twins set off to found a new city: one that, beginning in 753 BCE, would rise along the Tiber near the spot where the she-wolf had found them.

No details of this action-packed plotline are above suspicion. In the first place, the motif of castaway heroes suckled by animals and raised by kindly rustics is found in numerous foundation myths of the ancient world: from Babylon (where the infant Gilgamesh, thrown from a tower on orders of his grandfather, was caught by an eagle and then raised by a gardener) to Persia (where the infant Cyrus the Great, abandoned in the wilds by his grandfather, was suckled by a dog and rescued by a shepherd) and Greece (where Paris was suckled by a she-bear and rescued by a shepherd after his father, King Priam, left him exposed on a mountainside). Wolves sometimes came to the rescue, as in the case of Miletus, founder of the Greek city that bore his name. And often the story featured twins, such as Amphion and Zethus, the sons of Zeus who were raised by a shepherd after their abandonment; or Aeolus and Boeotus, the twin sons of Poseidon: they were nurtured by a cow and then discovered and raised by – what else? – a shepherd.[5]

The story of Romulus and Remus therefore bears all the hallmarks of a folktale of widespread diffusion. What's more, in ancient times it was not the only explanation of Rome's founding.

In fact, there were at least twenty-five different versions of how Rome was founded, who the founder was, and from whom or what it took its name.[6] The story of the outcast twins suckled by a she-wolf did not actually appear until around 300 BCE. Dubious as it must have seemed, the story quickly caught on. The image of the two babies suckled by a wolf thereafter became emblematic of Rome's beginnings. In 296 BCE a bronze statue of the she-wolf and the twins was placed beside the Tiber, and three decades later coins were minted showing the trio. Early historians of Rome such as Quintus Fabius Pictor developed the legend of Romulus and Remus over the course of the third century BCE. They were followed (albeit with some scepticism) by two of the most important historians of Ancient Rome: Titus Livius (or Livy) and Dionysius of Halicarnassus, both writing in the last decades of the first century BCE. Livy pointed out that the story of Rome's beginnings was 'adorned with poetic legends' that bore little relation to verifiable facts. But there could be no doubting, he noted,

A famous bronze statue depicting Romulus and Remus nurtured by a she-wolf. The wolf is probably Etruscan, from the fifth century BCE – before the Romulus and Remus story was popularised. The twins were added in the late 1400s.

that this city, however inscrutable its origins, had become 'the mightiest of empires, next after that of Heaven'.[7]

*

One of the few aspects of the Romulus and Remus story that rings true is the description in the sources of how Rome was laid out. The boundaries and streets of cities in the ancient world, such as those of the Greeks and the Etruscans, were plotted by means of important rituals. The first step was to establish a perimeter by ploughing a furrow, the boundary known to the Romans as the *pomerium* (from the Latin *post* and *moerium*, beyond the wall). According to the legend, Romulus chose a spot on the Palatine Hill, and accordingly began marking off his territory. We must imagine him using a bronze plough pulled by an ox (on the outside edge) and a cow (on the inside), moving anticlockwise along the slopes of the Palatine. When he came to places where he intended to raise a gate, he would have lifted and lugged the plough through the air: an act of carrying (*portare* in Latin) that is the root of the Latin word *porta* (gate or door) as well as the English words portable, portal and porter.

As Romulus went to work, these same rituals were being performed about 800 metres away on another hill. One constant of Roman history will be family squabbles and, indeed, familicide, especially fratricide. We have already seen fraternal strife in the rivalry between Romulus and Remus's grandfather and his brother. Now, at the very moment of Rome's foundation, internecine conflict re-emerges. While Romulus had picked the Palatine, Remus had decided on a location a short distance to the southwest, on the Aventine Hill, where he planned to establish the city of Remonium. In order to resolve their disagreements, the twins turned to auguries, which involved interpreting divine will through natural signs, such as the movements of birds (the term 'augur' seems to derive from the Latin *avis*, meaning bird). Remus was the first to receive a sign: six birds flying over the Aventine. However, Romulus, situated on the Palatine, then spotted a dozen birds. Which omen indicated the gods' favour: the sign received first or the one with more birds? Angry taunts led to a violent altercation in which Remus, after leaping over Romulus's freshly ploughed furrow on the Palatine, was struck and killed by his brother.

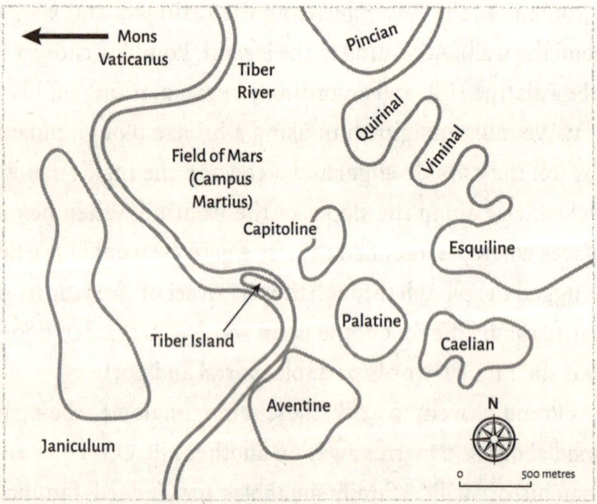


When the dust settled on this deadly skirmish, Romulus found himself the sole leader of the new city. The date was 21 April 753 BCE, still commemorated each year on the 'Natale di Roma' with parades and floats along Via dei Fori Imperiali and gladiatorial battles in the Circus Maximus. The date is, however, as fictional as the rest of the story: it was calculated in the first century BCE, during the time of Julius Caesar, by a mathematician and astronomer named Sosigenes.[8]

A new city needs people. Livy described how, having constructed his walls and other defences, Romulus set about populating Rome. He did so by operating an open-door policy that in the space of a short time attracted 'a miscellaneous rabble' – a ragtag band of runaway slaves and fugitives from justice.[9] Most of these new residents were male, which meant that Romulus, if he were to build and sustain the Roman race, needed to find women for them. He sent envoys to the nearby towns to extol the benefits of intermarriage with the Romans. These appeals fell on deaf ears. 'Nowhere', reports Livy, 'did the embassy obtain a friendly hearing,' for the people of the neighbouring towns were loath to offer their daughters in marriage to Romulus's band of outcasts and ruffians.[10]

Faced with this intransigence, Romulus hit upon a desperate and brutal strategy. He invited the people from nearby towns, as well as the Sabines, a neighbouring tribe, to celebrate a harvest festival in Rome. Eager to see what Rome had to offer, these neighbours arrived en masse, husbands, wives and children, in anticipation of a pleasing day out. They were hospitably received and suitably impressed. Then, at a prearranged moment, Romulus gave the signal for his men to unsheathe their swords and begin carting off any nubile females among the guests. After this mass abduction, war broke out between the Romans and the Sabines but ceased some nine months later when the bridenapped Sabines – many by now pregnant with, or even clutching in their arms, their Roman babes – pleaded for peace. The two communities, Roman and Sabine, thereafter struck an alliance, with Romulus and the Sabine leader, Titus Tatius, ruling jointly over the city of Rome.

This last part of the story – the political union of the Romans and the Sabines – no doubt reflects a historical reality. The Romans' act of fighting and then joining forces with another tribe, assimilating them into their own culture and identity, was to be repeated numerous times in the centuries that followed. It would become, indeed, one of the secrets of Roman success.

Such, then, were the foundations of Rome: abandoned children; a bloody brawl ending in fratricide; a population of bandits, slaves and renegades; a mass kidnapping; and a battle that tore families apart, pitting father against son-in-law, brother against sister. Taken as a whole, the story is so unedifying that Rome's enemies would later mock the Romans for it. One of Rome's greatest foes, Mithridates of Pontus, would claim that the 'wolfish spirit' of the Romans – their bloody and inexhaustible greed for empire and riches – could be explained by the fact that Romulus had been suckled by the she-wolf.[11] A historian writing in the 1960s even tried to argue that the story was so insulting to the dignity of the Romans that it could only have been invented as propaganda by their enemies.[12] This intriguing theory fails to explain why the Romans themselves should have so enthusiastically embraced various elements of the story.

Whatever the case, Rome got off, in these legends, to what might have seemed an inauspicious start. And yet, as Livy wrote, despite these 'lowliest beginnings' the city came to enjoy the 'favour of Heaven'.[13] For this community that included misfits, kidnappers and captives would become the forefathers of the greatest power the ancient world had ever seen.

*

So much for the mythology. Archaeology tells a story that often varies from the literary tradition. The truth is that Rome did not need founding in 753 BCE because by that time the slopes of its hills were already home to clusters of inhabitants. Archaeological relics (in the form of pottery) show a human presence on the Palatine Hill dating from roughly 1500 BCE. No evidence of permanent human settlement appears until around 1000 BCE, which, coincidentally or not, was the time when volcanic activity in the area ceased (there are fifty craters in the vicinity of Rome) after showering the landscape with a phosphate-rich ash that made for abundant agricultural opportunities.

If we could transport ourselves back to around 900 or 800 BCE, we would find a number of villages and hamlets perched on the hilltops and clinging to the slopes overlooking the Tiber. The villagers cultivated barley, spelt and millet, raised pigs, sheep and goats, and wove their clothes on looms. They buried their dead in graves after cremating them and then placing the ashes in urns shaped, charmingly, like the primitive wattle-and-daub, thatched-roof huts in which they lived. The departed were sent away on their voyages to the underworld with a few utensils

A bronze 'hut urn' from the sixth or seventh century BCE.

and storage containers for food and drink, as well as, for the women, loom weights and spindle whorls: women were evidently expected to continue performing their domestic chores in the afterlife.

The miniature swords and spears likewise found in these graves tell us that the villagers fought skirmishes with neighbours who may well have coveted this enviable location. The hills with their steep sides provided the villagers with natural protection, while the Tiber gave fresh water and access to the sea, 30 kilometres downstream at what would become Ostia. The site was located along natural arteries for trade and travel: not only the Tiber – the widest river valley in Italy, featuring forty tributaries along its 400-kilometre stretch – but also a series of roads that intersected at the site, including the one running north into Etruria, land of the neighbouring Etruscans.

These hill-dwelling villagers were the remote descendants of migrants who, centuries earlier, had arrived on the peninsula during the prolonged Indo-European migration out of eastern Europe and central Asia. They were Latini, or Latins, one of the many 'Italic tribes' (the Sabines were another) that had settled central and southern Italy by around 1500 BCE (possibly earlier). The Latins lived in settlements scattered through the territories south of the Tiber, in an area known as Latium that stretched some 100 kilometres along the coast and through the hinterland. Rome was at Latium's extreme northern edge, bordering the mineral-rich lands of the Etruscans on the north side of the Tiber and the Sabines to the east. The most important of the early Latin communities were south of Rome, in the Alban Hills. The Latin settlements that huddled on the future site of Rome were smaller, and included Velienses (occupying a ridge connecting the Palatine and the Esquiline hills) and

Querquetulanus (in effect, 'Oakville', found on the Caelian Hill).

Archaeology offers little evidence of anything as dramatic as the founding of the new community of Rome on the Palatine Hill in the middle of the eighth century BCE. However, in 2005 the archaeologist Andrea Carandini announced his discovery of the remains of a palace 10 metres beneath the pine-clad surface of the north slope of the Palatine Hill. Complete with a banqueting hall and courtyard, it appeared to be a regal dwelling dating from the middle of the eighth century BCE: the putative time, in other words, of Romulus and Remus. It was contemporary with, and close to, a dozen metres of an ancient wall (the course of the original *pomerium* ploughed by Romulus?) that Carandini had discovered in 1988. Although no one doubts their importance, archaeologists are divided over the meaning of these finds, which Carandini has controversially promoted as proof of the Romulus legend.[14]

However that may be, over the course of the eighth century BCE the Latin communities on the future site of Rome and elsewhere appear to have gradually become more populous and prosperous, with a wealthy elite emerging. By about 700 BCE the local Latins (or at least the elite among them) were burying their dead not with spindle whorls and eating utensils but rather with gold and silver jewellery, bronze shields, fine ceramics and even, in some cases, chariots – like a rich man today passing to his eternal reward in the reassuring company of his Rolex and Ferrari.

This prosperity and the ostentatious new aristocratic culture came about in large part because of contact between the Latins and recent immigrants who called themselves *Hellenes* but whom the Romans called *Graeci* (Greeks). Greek-speaking colonists had begun settling on the southern reaches of the

Italian peninsula from the beginning of the eighth century BCE, growing in number such that the south of the peninsula became known as *Megale Hellas* (or in Latin *Magna Graecia*) – that is, 'Greater Greece'. These Greek immigrants imported into Italy not only their pots, vases and the custom of burying their dead in elaborate tombs, but also the political and cultural values of their homelands. They brought their religion, by means of which gods from the Greek pantheon, such as Aphrodite, Hermes and Hephaestus, were translated into, or equated with, Latin ones, such as Venus, Mercury and Vulcan. Crucially, the Greeks brought the concept of the city-state, and for the bureaucratic regulation of these enlarging and increasingly complex political communities they brought something else the Latins would also adopt: their alphabet.

During the 600s BCE, political communities on the pattern of Greek ones therefore began developing up and down the Italian peninsula. The hills on which Rome was built, separated by valleys, initially obstructed an easy unification of the scattered settlements. But as the population increased, the people dwelling there coalesced into a more unified settlement with, in place of the primitive huts, more durable houses with stone foundations and tiled roofs. Public buildings were eventually constructed, squares laid out, temples and sanctuaries raised, and the Cloaca Maxima (a sewer carrying effluent into the Tiber) excavated. In about 625 BCE the Forum, the most important public space, was paved. At some point during this time – it is impossible to give an exact date – the Latins from villages such as Querquetulanus would have begun regarding themselves as Romans and their expanded political community as Rome. They may have taken the name of their new city from the Greek word ῥώμη (Rhome), which meant 'stronghold' or 'strength'.

Other possible origins of the name are the Etruscan word *rumon* or *rumen* (river), or else the Latin *ruma* (breast) – a possible reference to the she-wolf that suckled the twins or even, perhaps, the 'breast-like' shape of the Palatine and Aventine hills. What is certain, however, is that the name did *not* come from Romulus, who was much more likely to have taken *his* name – when it became necessary to invent a creation myth – from the burgeoning new city.

*

The ancient historians agreed that Rome between the eighth and sixth centuries BCE was ruled by a line of kings. These sources described the 'seven kings of Rome' who ruled before the establishment of the Roman Republic in 509 BCE. This lineage is suspect (and a number of the kings no doubt largely fictitious) because each reign must have lasted, on average, thirty-five years – suspiciously long at a time when life expectancy (if infant mortality is factored out) was fifty at most.[15]

Traditional accounts claimed that Romulus died – or, in some accounts, vanished into thin air during a fierce storm – after almost forty years in power. Kingship in Rome then passed, according to legend, to Numa Pompilius, a Sabine originally from the town of Cures, in Sabine territory some 40 kilometres northeast of Rome. Kingship in Rome was not hereditary. A new monarch was elected by constituent assemblies of both patricians – that is, the leaders of the wealthy and aristocratic clans – and those from the lower orders, the plebeians. Before the choice became official, the gods were consulted in a ritual known as the *inauguratio*, by which a religious dignitary, the augur, sitting on a special stone with a hood over his head and a staff in his hand, appealed to the gods for signs that the candidate put forward was the right one. If a flock of birds appeared from the proper and reassuring direction, the new king was 'inaugurated'.

Numa Pompilius evidently came to power in such a manner. But even if he never existed, the fact that Roman legend would happily cast a Sabine as the second king of Rome shows, even at this early stage, the permeable margins of what it meant to be Roman. Nor would Numa be the last 'foreign' king of Rome. Besides the Sabines, the Romans had close (and occasionally combative) relations with another neighbour, this one to the north. The Etruscans occupied ancient Etruria, the beautiful and fertile lands in central Italy that by and large are present-day Tuscany. They were known for their expertise in crafts, metalworking and navigation. Preoccupied with social status and indulging in luxury and enjoyment, they practised elaborate burial customs, adorning their tombs and sarcophagi with intricate decorations. Like the Greeks, with whom they did brisk business trading copper and tin in return for pottery, they were an urban people whose autonomous city-states featured fortified walls, stone temples and houses with courtyards and tiled roofs laid out along grids of stone-paved streets.

According to legend, the last three kings of Rome were Etruscans. Over the past century, historians have debated whether Rome, during the 500s BCE – the period, in other words, of its formation as a city-state – was an 'Etruscan' city. The Etruscans were certainly expanding their influence on the peninsula during this time, though the theory of an Etruscan conquest and decades-long domination of Rome lacks supporting evidence. The Etruscan kings appear to have come to power in Rome not as conquering invaders but as immigrants. Notably, the fifth king of Rome and the first of the three 'Etruscans', Lucius Tarquinius

Priscus, whose reign began (according to the traditional chronology) in 616 BCE, was actually Greek rather than Etruscan: he was the son of a trader from Corinth who had fled political turbulence in his homeland and set up his business in the Etruscan city of Tarquinii (a story made plausible by the strong trade links between Etruria and Corinth). Tarquinius Priscus in turn emigrated from Tarquinii to Rome with his wife, Tanaquil. She encouraged the move after she saw an eagle pluck the cap from her husband's head and then replace it – an omen that she believed (correctly, as it happened) foretold how Tarquinius Priscus would become king.

Tarquinius Priscus's successor, Servius Tullius, may or may not have been Etruscan. Some sources claim that Servius was actually an Etruscan adventurer named Mastarna, others that he was the son of a former slave in the household of Tarquinius Priscus. The name Servius references *servus*, Latin for 'slave' – which seems to indicate a remarkable upward mobility. Regardless, like Numa he was a character that, largely invented or not, represented an outsider, perhaps a foreigner, who rose to power in a city that valued ability over both bloodlines and ethnic origins. Alas for him, his reign was cut short when he was murdered by his successor, Lucius Tarquinius Superbus, or Tarquin the Proud.

The spectre of Tarquin the Proud, a brutal autocrat, would haunt Roman history for many centuries as an example of a rapid and perilous descent into tyranny. The son of Tarquinius Priscus, he married one of Servius Tullius's two daughters. In Ancient Rome, a daughter was given the feminine version of her father's name (Marcia for Marcus, Gaia for Gaius). The system was simple enough unless there were multiple daughters – in which case, as with Servius Tullius's girls, they were known as

Tullia Major (Tarquin's first wife) and Tullia Minor (wife of Tarquin's brother). The latter sister, ruthlessly ambitious, encouraged the equally merciless Tarquin to – in what was to become a familiar and ghastly motif in Roman history – carry out familicide: she urged him to kill her father, her older sister and her husband, then to marry her and make her queen. Tarquin obliged, and the slaughter ended with Tullia Minor running over the murdered corpse of her father in her chariot, splashing her clothes with his blood. The narrow lane where the savage episode took place subsequently became known as Vicus Sceleratus, or Evil Street.

Tarquin was successful as a king insofar as he conquered various Latin towns in the vicinity of Rome. He also constructed great buildings such as the temple to Jupiter Optimus Maximus, a massive building that stretched more than 60 metres along the Capitoline Hill and featured columns measuring 2.5 metres in diameter. However, Tarquin made himself odious to his subjects by centralising power in his own hands and dealing harshly with political opponents. The final straw came when Sextus Tarquinius – his son by Tullia Minor – raped Lucretia, the virtuous wife of a Roman named Collatinus. Lucretia told her husband about the rape, along with his friend Lucius Junius (who had earned the nickname Brutus, or 'stupid', because he had been feigning idiocy to survive Tarquin's tyrannical rule). As Lucretia plunged a dagger into her own heart, Roman history reached a turning point. Brutus displayed her corpse in the Forum, calling on the people of Rome to avenge her suicide and expel the tyrants. Tarquin was duly overthrown and the monarchy abolished. It was, according to legend, 509 BCE. For the next 482 years, Rome would be a republic, with the powers of the kings devolving onto, and shared by, a pair of annually elected consuls (Brutus and Collatinus supposedly served as the first pair) who could command the army and summon a 300-strong advisory body, the Senate. The name of this institution, which would survive for the better part of a millennium, derived from *senex*, 'old man', because it was staffed, in theory at least, by wise, grey heads.

Lucretia prepares to plunge the fatal dagger in this 1627 painting by Artemisia Gentileschi. Political change in Rome was often connected, at least in myth, to violence against women.

The date of 509 BCE, the rape of Lucretia and the ousting of the Tarquins: all stand on the same uncertain foundations as the Romulus myth. In fact, the transition from kingship to republic may have taken a more orderly, prolonged and even peaceful course whereby the powers of the king were gradually assumed, through a series of reforms, by the consuls and magistrates. But such a sedate narrative makes for bad box office, and Rome's history, in the usual telling, was to feature many further block-buster storylines. According to the legend, familial rivalries continued unabated into the new regime, and the Republic survived its infancy thanks to yet more bloodshed. In another example of fractured families and divided loyalties, Brutus was the nephew of Tarquin, the man he overthrew. When his two sons sided with the deposed king, Brutus had them beheaded, even watching the gory spectacle himself – a steely act that later impressed Niccolò Machiavelli, for whom 'to kill the sons of Brutus' became the catchphrase for the unflinching brutality that political leaders needed in order to make tough decisions, maintain their power and preserve the state. The pages of Roman history would fill with many examples – for good or ill – of this kind of murderous resolve.

# 2

# 'THE FAVOUR OF HEAVEN': THE RISE OF THE ROMAN REPUBLIC

AT THE TIME OF THE FOUNDING of the Roman Republic, the Italian peninsula had an estimated population of about four million people. Rome itself ranged over some 800 square kilometres (roughly the same surface area as the five boroughs of New York City today) and counted around 35,000 people. Over the next five centuries the population of the peninsula would double. What's more, it would be transformed from a land of Greek and Etruscan cities and scattered settlements, populated by tribes speaking dozens of languages and dialects, practising different customs and forging shifting alliances, into more of a political, cultural and linguistic unity as the Romans gradually subjugated the surrounding peoples.

One of the first conquests made by the new Roman Republic was over the neighbouring Latin League, an alliance of people who shared their language, religion and customs. The Romans had established military authority over them during the regal period, but in 499 BCE the Latins rebelled, led by the exiled Tarquin the Proud in his latest bid to regain power. They were defeated by the Romans when, according to legend, a pair of giants, the twins Castor and Pollux, heroically intervened on behalf of the Romans.

Rome steadily expanded its territory over the course of the following century. One of its greatest acquisitions came in 396 BCE with the capture and subsequent destruction of a long-time rival, the Etruscan city of Veii, only 15 kilometres to the north. Veii was the wealthiest, the most southerly and, in terms of surface area (almost 350 square kilometres), the largest of the Etruscan cities. Following various battles and truces, the Romans began a long siege of the city in 407 BCE, ultimately sacking it in 396. They slaughtered much of the population, sold the remainder into slavery and helped themselves to plunder so astonishingly copious that a 'vast throng' of Romans greedily made their way to Veii to claim their share of the spoils.[1] Among the plunder was a statue of the goddess Juno, 'Queen of Veii', who was taken to Rome and given new lodgings in a purpose-built temple on the Aventine Hill.

The fate of the Juno statue from Veii matched that of the rest of Etruscan culture, likewise commandeered by the Romans. Over the next century and a half, the great Etruscan civilisation would steadily be absorbed into the Roman one. Many of their ceremonial trappings were taken over by the Romans, from the purple-trimmed robe and ivory-inlaid throne of the Etruscan kings to their triumphal chariots and eagle-topped sceptre. The Romans likewise adopted the *fasces*, the axe bound in a bundle of rods that was carried before the Roman magistrates: the rods represented their power to inflict chastisement, the axe their authority to behead. The Etruscan language would disappear apart from certain words adopted by the Romans, such as *autumnus* (autumn), *catamitus* (catamite), *ferrum* (iron) and *idus* (ides, as in the ides of March).

One recurring feature of Roman history, as we'll see, is a stunning reversal of fortune – a dramatic victory following a crushing defeat or (as in this case) vice versa. Recently victorious over the Etruscans at Veii, Rome soon suffered a shocking setback when the city was sacked by a renegade band of Gauls. Numerous Celtic tribes inhabited northern Italy, having migrated across the Alps from their middle and eastern European homelands as early as the thirteenth century BCE. They settled in areas such as the Po Valley and along the Adriatic coast, and founded settlements such as Mediolanum (Milan). The Romans called them Gauls, a catch-all term for Celtic tribes such as the Boii, the Cenomani and the Insubri (whose name meant 'ferocious'). By about 400 BCE they occupied most of the lands east of the Apennines once controlled by the Etruscans. This area became known as Gallia Cisalpina, or Cisalpine Gaul – Gaul on 'this side' of the Alps (as opposed to Gallia Transalpina, or Transalpine Gaul, on the other side of the Alps, in what is now southern France).

The gradual Gallic drift southwards and the Roman expansion northwards inevitably brought the two cultures into conflict. According to legend, around 390 BCE a Gallic tribe, the Senones, defeated the Romans at the Battle of the River Allia, then marched the 15 kilometres to Rome, which they sacked and burned, slaughtering many of the inhabitants. The sack persuaded the Romans to prolong and enhance the fortification (the Servian Wall, named for Servius Tullius) constructed in the sixth century BCE. Parts of this fortification, originally more than 10 kilometres in circumference and in places more than 10 metres high and 3.5 metres thick, still survive. One short stretch of these sturdy blocks can be seen outside Rome's Termini railway station; another is inside the station itself, beneath platform 24, where passengers disembark after arriving from Fiumicino Airport on the Leonardo Express.

The other legacy of the sack was a lingering terror that in 1985 a German scholar called a *metus Gallicus*, or 'fear of Gauls'.[2] This irrational, paralysing panic would last for centuries and encompass any sort of invader coming from the north – of which there were destined to be many.

*

The sack by the Gauls did little to check Roman expansion. Two years later the Romans attacked Tarquinia, a flourishing Etruscan city 95 kilometres north of Rome. Then in 381 BCE they captured and annexed Tusculum, an important Latin settlement 25 kilometres southeast of Rome. Many other cities in Latium, often allied to Rome but increasingly uneasy about its expanding influence, rose in rebellion in 340 BCE. Livy claimed that the conflict, which lasted two years, amounted to a civil war, 'so little did the Latins differ from the Romans'.[3]

The war ended with the Romans and the Latins coming even closer together as the inhabitants of a number of defeated Latin cities were granted Roman citizenship, earning them the right to vote and hold office in Rome, as well as, crucially, the obligation to provide military service. The inhabitants of more distant defeated cities, such as Capua and Cumae, received partial citizenship (known as *civitas sine suffragio*, or 'citizenship without a vote'), whereby they provided arms for Rome but – as the name suggests – enjoyed no political rights. All were known as *socii*, a word derived from *socius*, or partner (the root of our words 'society' and 'associate').

The Romans therefore developed a system of alliances with

these erstwhile foes in cities and ethnic communities up and down the peninsula, creating a kind of federation of tribes and city-states with Rome at its head. The main obligation of the *socii* was to provide manpower to Rome in times of warfare, for which they received protection as well as a share of booty and plunder. Roman territory expanded dramatically to encompass almost 8,000 square kilometres and an estimated population of 484,000. Over the following decades, and then centuries, Rome, already the supreme military power in Italy, enjoyed the benefit of formidable military reserves thanks to the large contingents of *socii*, who in some campaigns outnumbered the troops fielded by the Romans themselves. This coalition forged between Rome and its allies was one of the most important reasons for its success. By increasing its manpower pool and gaining access to skilled soldiers and diverse military tactics, Rome quickly developed a formidable fighting force, vital for both conquest and defence.

The Romans still faced stiff challenges and suffered defeats, sometimes spectacular ones. By the middle of the 300s BCE their most implacable foe had become a tough, mountain-dwelling, Oscan-speaking people known as the Samnites, an offshoot of the Sabines. The Oscan-speaking tribes had gradually spread through the central and southern lands of the peninsula thanks to a ritual known as the *Ver Sacrum* (Sacred Spring). In times of crisis, most likely due to famine or overpopulation, a tribe would sacrifice to a deity, usually Mars (known in Oscan as Mamers), all their newborn livestock. Even more extreme, they would also consecrate to the god all the children born that same springtime: once of age, the children were led to the border and, armed to the teeth, sent forth to find new lands for themselves, if necessary wresting them by violence from an incumbent population. These *sacrani* ('devoted') were often guided to their new homeland by a bird or an animal, a kind of totem from which they and their community then took their names.

The Sabines, for example, sent forth a group of *sacrani* from their heartland to the north and east of present-day Rome. These *sacrani* crossed the Apennines to the Marche, following a woodpecker (*picus* in Latin) from which they took their name: the Piceni. (The flag of the Marche region today proudly features a woodpecker.) Another offshoot of the Sabines likewise moved eastwards, following an ox until it halted in the mountains. Here the *sacrani* founded Bovianum, named for their bovine pathfinder. They became the Samnites and their mountainous homeland, Samnium, comprised a large chunk of central Italy. Another group of Samnites, in time, migrated south, following a wolf (*hirpus* in Oscan) from which they took the name Irpini – sons of the wolf. Affirmed by various ancient authorities, these legends may nonetheless be retrospective constructions to explain migration patterns brought about by warfare, crop failures and unsustainable population increases.

A fresco of Samnite warriors dating from the fourth century BCE.

The Romans fought the Samnites over the course of many decades. In 321 BCE they suffered a disastrous defeat at the Caudine Forks, a narrow pass through the Apennines some 225 kilometres south of Rome. The victorious Samnites humiliated the Roman soldiers by forcing them to pass through a yoke (*sub iugum* – from which comes 'subjugate'). The Samnites' ferocity, as well as their splendid arms and armour, inspired one of the gladiator 'types' that (as we shall see) began appearing in Roman arenas: the 'Samnite', a warrior armed with a rectangular shield, a lance and a short sword (the *gladius*).

The Samnites finally surrendered and, in 290 BCE, became *socii*. Three decades later the Piceni – the people of the woodpecker – were likewise conquered and became allies. Thus, by the middle of the third century BCE, through a series of conquests followed by alliances, virtually the entire peninsula had been incorporated into the Roman federation. Roman territory itself comprised more than 25,000 square kilometres, and adult male Roman citizens numbered almost 300,000.[4]

Besides the Gauls in the north, the Etruscans and Latins in the centre and the Oscan-speaking tribes such as the Samnites and Piceni, the Romans also controlled Magna Graecia. One of the few Greek cities to resist Roman overlordship had been Tarentum, since the fifth century BCE the most important city in Magna Graecia. In 280 BCE, fearing Roman encroachments, the Tarentines appealed for help to Pyrrhus of Epirus, the king of the Molossians on the Ionian coast of Greece (and the cousin of Alexander the Great). Pyrrhus responded with an army of 25,000 men and twenty war elephants. Despite the ordeal of a shipwreck on his way across the sea, he defeated the Romans in two costly battles. The first was near Heracleia, a Greek colony in league against the Romans with nearby Tarentum. The second was on the plain below Ausculum Apulum (modern-day Ascoli Satriano), where the elephants – creatures never before seen by most Romans – were deployed to devastating effect. However, Pyrrhus sustained such losses among his own troops that Plutarch quotes him as saying: 'If we are victorious in one more battle with the Romans, we shall be utterly ruined'[5] – the origin of the expression 'Pyrrhic victory'. In 275 BCE he returned to the Greek mainland, his mission a failure. He died in Argos in 272 BCE, by which time Tarentum had fallen to the Romans and become their latest ally.

A marble bust of Pyrrhus of Epirus.

*

The incursion by Pyrrhus was only a foretaste of what was to come as, over the following decades, the Romans fought a series of long and costly wars against the great Mediterranean superpower, the Carthaginians.

Carthage was a colony founded on the north coast of Africa (in present-day Tunisia) in 814 BCE by Phoenicians from Tyre;

its name in Phoenician simply means 'new town'. Quickly becoming one of the wealthiest and most powerful colonies on the Mediterranean, it controlled sea routes to the west and extended its influence along the top of the African continent (across present-day Libya and Morocco) as well as into Sicily, Sardinia and southern Spain. Along the way the Carthaginians came into conflict with the Greeks, Etruscans and Syracusans. However, they maintained good relations with the Romans until the latter's movement into Magna Graecia in the middle of the third century BCE upset the equilibrium.

The flashpoint was a tribe from southern Italy called the Mamertines, or 'Sons of Mars'. An offshoot of the Samnites, they had fetched up in Sicily after a Ver Sacrum and, in 288 BCE, taken by force the city of Messana (Messina) on the northeast tip. The neighbouring Syracusans, hoping to oust the Mamertines, asked both the Romans and the Carthaginians for help. The latter sent a small garrison, at which point the Romans 'were in great apprehension', in the words of Polybius, because they could foresee the day when Carthage, taking control of Sicily, would become a troublesome and dangerous neighbour, 'hemming them in on all sides and threatening every part of Italy'.[6] This fear of Carthaginian expansion prompted the Romans to borrow boats from the Tarentines and other allies, and then, for the first time in their history, send an army over the waters – across the Strait of Messina. And so began the Punic Wars, known as such because the Roman name for the Carthaginians was Poeni, adapted from what the Greeks called the Phoenicians, Phoinikes. The three Punic Wars – lasting intermittently from 264 to 146 BCE – would present Rome's greatest challenges so far. As Polybius wrote, 'It is not easy to name any war which lasted longer, nor one which exhibited on both sides more extensive preparations, more unintermittent activity, more battles, and greater changes of fortune.'[7]

The Romans rescued the Mamertines besieged in Messana, then moved south to attack Syracuse, which swiftly came to terms and allied itself with Rome. It was now Carthage's turn to take fright, especially after the Romans, pressing south across the island, attacked and brutally sacked Acragas (Agrigento), a Carthaginian ally. In 262 BCE the Romans defeated the Carthaginians in battle on Sicilian soil, but to truly vanquish this enemy, who commanded the Mediterranean, they would need a navy. The only problem was that, as Polybius wrote, they had never 'given a thought to the sea', so they had no ships. What they did have, he noted admiringly, was 'incredible pluck' and, undaunted, they built a hundred warships in sixty days, having reverse-engineered and then copied plank-for-plank a Carthaginian warship that fell into their hands after running aground in the Strait of Messina.[8] As the fleet was under construction, the novice Roman sailors, in an early example of dry-land training, sat on benches, gripping oars and honing their rowing techniques.

These efforts paid off handsomely. The Romans won naval battles off both the north (260 BCE) and south (256 BCE) coasts of Sicily. But they also suffered various setbacks in the decade that followed, including one at the hands of the great Carthaginian general Hamilcar Barca (whose surname in Phoenician meant lightning). Finally, after more than two decades of warfare, the Romans and Carthaginians were exhausted both financially and militarily. The Romans managed to raise a new fleet and, in 241 BCE, defeated the Carthaginians off the west coast of Sicily. Hamilcar grudgingly made peace with the Romans, one condition of which was his complete withdrawal from the island. Sicily became the first of what, over the centuries, would be more than forty provinces of Rome – that is, regions outside of Italy governed by officials appointed by the Senate.

Hamilcar had a six-year-old son whom, after this defeat, he made swear at an altar an oath never to be a friend of Rome. The boy's name was Hannibal, and he would prove true to his sacred vow.

*

Hannibal was taken to Iberia by his father in 237 BCE, at the age of ten. By 221 BCE, still only in his mid-twenties, he had become a formidable soldier and tactician with supreme command of Carthaginian forces on the Iberian peninsula. 'By no hardship', claimed Livy, 'could he be physically exhausted or mentally cowed.'[9] But Hannibal was also, according to Pliny the Elder, treacherous, pitilessly cruel and devoid of integrity, scruples and fear of the gods. Such was the terrifying opponent about to unleash himself on Rome.

This time the flashpoint was Saguntum, a fortress city on the Balearic Sea (now Sagunto, 320 kilometres south of Barcelona) that some years earlier had placed itself under Rome's protection. Hannibal regarded this Roman ally in Iberia as an impediment to Carthaginian interests. He therefore engineered a crisis, claiming that a band of Saguntians had mistreated a neighbouring tribe of Carthaginian subjects. Rome dithered in its response (leading to a phrase about time-wasting used in Italy today: *mentre a Roma si delibera, Sagunto viene espugnata* – 'while Rome debates, Sagunto is conquered'). Taking advantage of the situation, Hannibal besieged Saguntum in the spring of 219 BCE, convinced, according to Polybius, 'that by this blow he would inspire universal terror' – not only among the Iberian tribes whom he was trying to conquer but also, more to the point, among the Romans.[10]

Saguntum fell to Hannibal's forces after an eight-month siege. Hannibal then plotted his next move, destined to be even more audacious. In the early spring of 218 BCE he began a march that would take him from southern Spain through the Pyrenees and then via the Alps into Italy – a distance of some 1,500 kilometres. Hannibal chose this difficult overland route partly to avoid superior Roman sea power, and partly because once in northern Italy he hoped to rally the Gauls, who had recently renewed hostilities against the Romans in the Po Valley. He had been assured of the bravery of the Celtic tribes in warfare, 'and above all', reported Polybius, 'their hatred of Rome'.[11]

The long and incredibly arduous march presented massive logistical problems. Hannibal's army at the outset numbered more than 100,000 men, with a cavalry of 12,000 horses and, famously, a battalion of thirty-seven war elephants. Elephants could be tremendously effective and intimidating on the battlefield, but a 1,500-kilometre march must have seemed daunting given that adult male elephants need to eat more than 100 kilograms of vegetation each day – a task consuming at least ten hours, and one made difficult by the lack of vegetation in the high Alps.[12] Even for a week-long march the elephants would have required 200 pack animals to carry their food.[13] Then there were the tens of thousands of soldiers also needing provisions. When Hannibal contemplated how he might supply his troops with food, one of his lieutenants proposed an alarming solution: Hannibal would need to persuade his men to eat human flesh. According to Polybius, 'Hannibal had nothing to say against the boldness and usefulness of this suggestion.'[14] But it would be the Italians, not the Carthaginians, who resorted to such desperate measures.

So began one of the greatest feats in the history of warfare. The astonishing campaign witnessed Hannibal's troops fighting their way through the hostile tribes in southern France, using special rafts to transport the elephants across the Rhône. The beasts panicked in the middle of the river, almost 800 metres wide, upsetting the rafts and drowning their drivers. They survived by walking along the riverbed with their trunks raised like snorkels.

Then came the crossing of the Alps. The exact route has been much debated and will probably never be known, despite the fact that Polybius, during the course of his research, not only spoke to survivors but even paid a visit to the Alps. Whatever the route, it proved a horrific ordeal of panicked horses, disordered

This sixteenth-century fresco by Jacopo Ripanda shows Hannibal astride one of his elephants – probably Surus, the last survivor of the doomed battalion.

columns, pack animals tumbling down ravines or starving to death, ambushes by hostile local tribes who tried to roll boulders onto them, elephants moving at a snail's pace through the trackless terrain and, of course, the cold and heavy snowfalls that left the hungry and disgruntled troops wet and weakened. The journey from Cartagena to the Po Valley took five months and came at a cost – by Hannibal's own reckoning – of 36,000 men and almost all his elephants. He managed to get a few of them across, albeit in, as Polybius noted, 'a wretched condition from hunger'.[15]

Hannibal's achievement is all the more stupefying considering that his exhausted and depleted army went on to defeat the Romans in a cavalry skirmish near Pavia and then, with the help of the Gauls, in a larger engagement near Piacenza. In June 217 BCE, despite having lost an eye and all but one elephant, Hannibal destroyed a Roman army at Lake Trasimeno: his troops appeared out of the morning mist and, in a devastating ambush, killed 15,000 soldiers and captured 10,000 more. The Roman commander, the consul Gaius Flaminius, died on the battlefield. So desperate were the Romans following this shattering loss that they adopted the Oscan practice of the Ver Sacrum, pledging to sacrifice to Jupiter all animals born the following springtime.

Jupiter was evidently unappeased. Hannibal's victories were a mere prelude to his next and most famous triumph, in August 216 BCE, at Cannae, which a Roman poet over a century later called 'the grave of Italy'.[16] The battle was fought during a windstorm against a numerically superior Roman army, whose troops Hannibal encircled in a tactically brilliant manoeuvre and then mercilessly slaughtered. Estimates of Roman losses ranged from 55,000 to 70,000. Casualty figures in ancient battles are notoriously exaggerated, but it was still perhaps the greatest loss of life in a single day's fighting ever suffered by a Western army. Several ancient historians report the dead were so numerous that Hannibal, ever resourceful, built a bridge using their corpses. The panic and chaos in Rome grew so intense that measures even more extreme than a Ver Sacrum were implemented to pacify the wrathful gods: two couples, one Greek and the other Celtic, were entombed alive in an underground chamber in the Forum Boarium, the city's livestock market. It was one of the rare instances when the Romans engaged in human sacrifice. Later Roman historians were taken aback by these ritualistic killings: Livy wrote that such 'extraordinary sacrifices' were 'very alien to Roman religious observance'.[17] Hannibal had plunged Rome into an existential crisis.

Hannibal appeared poised to march on Rome, some 400 kilometres away. The commander of his cavalry, Maharbal, predicted that in four days he would dine in triumph in Rome. When Hannibal replied that he needed time to think, Maharbal retorted: 'You know how to win a battle, Hannibal; you do not know how to use the victory!'[18] It's far from certain, however, that Rome would have fallen despite Hannibal's supremacy in land warfare. He lacked siege equipment, which meant that Rome, with its robust walls, would have been virtually impossible to capture. Indeed, it took eleven months for Hannibal to take the small town of Petelia (in present-day Calabria), where conditions became so grim that after their food supplies were exhausted the population first ate leather, then the shoots and branches of trees, and finally (if we can believe a later writer, Petronius) each other. Furthermore, he lacked a permanent supply base from which to provision his army, which he did largely through plundering the local communities. Limited to devastating the countryside, he ultimately destroyed some 400 towns and villages. *Hannibal ad portas* ('Hannibal is at the gates') subsequently became a phrase expressing fear of an impending disaster.

Hannibal achieved surprisingly little during what became some fifteen years on Italian soil. He understood that his success relied not only on the support of the Gauls but also – if he could appear as the saviour of the Italian people from Roman domination – on the desertion of Rome's allies across the peninsula. He enjoyed some success in this regard. Polybius and Livy both speak of the 'rebellion of Italy' during Hannibal's invasion. Certainly there were defections in the South: his victory at Cannae meant virtually all of Magna Graecia rallied to his side, as did some Oscan-speaking peoples. Capua, the most populous and important city in Italy after Rome (and connected to it by Via Appia, the first of the great Roman roads), likewise revolted after Cannae. Hannibal could also count on the Gauls, one tribe of which ambushed two Roman legions in northern Italy in 215 BCE. They decapitated the commander, Lucius Postumius Albinus, then used his skull as a drinking cup.

However, Rome still enjoyed support from other allies on the peninsula. Most of the Oscan people, on whom Hannibal had pinned high hopes, stayed loyal to Rome, putting at its disposal a huge population of conscripts (sometimes estimated at half a million men). Meanwhile, Roman naval superiority prevented Hannibal from receiving provisions and reinforcements or – despite his attacks on Neapolis and Cumae – from capturing a port. The result was that he was confined to the south of Italy until 203 BCE when, with the Romans under Publius Cornelius Scipio taking the fight into Africa, he was recalled to Carthage. There, a year later, at the Battle of Zama, he suffered a comprehensive defeat at the hands of Scipio, subsequently known for his famous victory as Scipio Africanus. Hannibal's tactic of unleashing eighty war elephants backfired when many of the beasts, panicked by blasts from Roman trumpets, turned around and stampeded into the Carthaginian cavalry.

The war against Hannibal was momentous in the formation of Rome's sense of itself and its destiny. As Livy stated regarding the aftermath of Cannae: 'There is surely no other people that would not have been crushed by such an overwhelming disaster.' Rome's recovery from one of history's heaviest military defeats, and its ultimate victory over such a formidable warrior, became the stuff of legend – Rome's 'finest hour'.[19] Despite many difficulties and adverse events to follow, the path to a worldwide empire lay open.

*

Rome faced the Carthaginians once more, in the Third Punic War, which culminated in 146 BCE, following three years of conflict, with the obliteration of Carthage. The buildings were demolished, the streets ploughed and the land ritually cursed (although the fields were never, as a modern legend claims, sowed with salt).[20] This victory marked the end of the great Carthaginian civilisation, altering the geopolitical landscape of the Mediterranean and solidifying Rome's dominance in the region for centuries to come. Rome created a huge new province, Africa, which covered more than 12,000 square kilometres of present-day Tunisia, Libya and Algeria.

Soon after they destroyed Carthage, the Romans devastated another great and ancient city: Corinth. In 214 BCE they had begun a series of wars against the Macedonians following Philip V's support of Hannibal in the Second Punic War.

Having defeated the Macedonians, by the middle of the second century BCE the Romans were battling their former allies in the Achaean League, a confederation of Greek city-states in the central and northern Peloponnese. In 146 BCE they defeated the league in battle before the walls of Corinth, Greece's wealthiest city. With the Senate having decreed that Corinth should be burned and all valuables taken as booty to Rome, the victorious army sacked the city in a horrifying display of savagery witnessed by Polybius himself.

The subjugation of Greece, with the mainland and then the Aegean Islands becoming a protectorate of Rome, was accomplished in just a few decades. The Macedonian phalanxes, renowned under Alexander the Great, proved inferior to the Roman legions. The legions' tactical units, the maniples – consisting of around 120 soldiers arranged in three lines or ranks – allowed Roman soldiers to respond more swiftly and dynamically to the changing battlefield than did the rigid phalanxes.

Although superior on the battlefield, many Romans considered themselves culturally inferior to the sophisticated Greeks (who, taking a similar view, regarded the Romans as 'barbarians'). Their first real inkling of the grandeur of Greek culture came following their conquest in 212 BCE of Syracuse, the greatest city in Magna Graecia, and one that had been supporting Hannibal. (This 212 BCE conquest witnessed a Roman soldier killing the brilliant engineer and mathematician Archimedes, whose catapults and other weapons had been wreaking havoc on the Roman invaders.) According to Plutarch, when the beautiful spoils were brought from Syracuse to Rome and paraded through the streets, the Romans realised that they lacked such 'elegant and exquisite productions' of their own, and that their city was devoid of the 'graceful and subtle art' of the Greeks.[21]

An even more chastening demonstration came in 167 BCE, when for three days hundreds of wagons triumphantly transported through Rome the plunder from Macedon and Epirus: Greek sculptures, paintings, objects in gold and silver, and even works by Phidias, the greatest sculptor of the ancient world.

Produced by a Greek sculptor in Asia Minor in about the fourth century BCE, *Lion Attacking a Horse* was brought to Rome as war booty. For the Romans, who valued strength and martial prowess, it represented raw power, dominance and the natural order, becoming an icon of the might of the Roman state and its ability to conquer and control.

The Romans were already well acquainted with Greek cultural products. Greek words had found their way into Latin, Greek pots into Italian homes, Greek gods into Italian temples, Greek plays into Roman theatres, and Greek legislation into Rome's legal code, the Twelve Tables. Fabius Pictor composed his history of Rome in Greek. Even the Sibylline Books were written in Greek – a collection of oracular utterances about the fate of Rome that, according to tradition, were purchased from a sibyl by Tarquin the Proud, housed in the Temple of Jupiter Capitolinus and consulted by special officials in times of trouble. But the plunder from the conquest of Greece revealed the splendours of Hellenistic civilisation on a new scale. The Roman ruling class – made wealthy through overseas conquests – eagerly embraced Greek art, language, medicine, literature and philosophy. They hired Greek tutors for their children, ate from Corinthian dishes, and hired Greek artists to decorate their villas. They imported bronze statues from Greece: the Riace Bronzes, discovered by a snorkeller off the Calabrian coast in 1972 and now the stars of the Museo Nazionale della Magna Grecia, were no doubt destined to adorn the home of a Roman aristocrat before a shipwreck intervened. Greek statues were copied by the thousand. One statue of Hermes in Athens was perpetually covered in pitch, according to Pliny the Elder, as each day plaster moulds were prepared in order to cast bronzes or carve marble versions for Roman clients.

This admiration for Greece and its cultural artifacts alarmed and offended certain Romans. The poet Horace later famously wrote of the relationship that 'Greece, the captive, made her savage victor captive, and brought the arts into rustic Latium'.[22] Although Horace regarded this as positive, others believed that honest, rustic Latium had been corrupted by its contact with a decadent, frivolous Greek civilisation. One of the most vocal advocates of this position was a red-haired, grey-eyed politician named Marcus Porcius Cato, who as a young man had fought against Hannibal before going on to enjoy a long and distinguished career in the army. He was known as Cato the Censor because in 184 BCE he served a term as one of Rome's censors, an office in charge of both the census and the supervision of public morals: a censor would place a black mark of censure against the name of anyone whose conduct was disreputable. Cato's censuring continued long after his term of office expired.

He found especially reprehensible the Roman adulation of the Greeks, whom he called 'utterly vile and unruly'.[23] He agitated for the expulsion of Greek philosophers from Rome, believing that 'Rome would lose her empire when she had become infected with Greek letters'.[24] Rather than Greek statues or philosophy, he admired the simple Roman virtues of military vigour and honest toil.

Cato died in 149 BCE, after the destruction of both Carthage (for which he had agitated ceaselessly in the Senate) and Corinth. He therefore lived to see the Philhellenism (as this passion for all things Greek is known) that took hold of Rome in the decades that followed. By then others agreed that Rome had lost its way, that the old virtues had been eroded and that the Republic was in grave danger.

# 3

# 'MEN OF VIOLENCE': THE DECLINE OF THE ROMAN REPUBLIC

BY THE MIDDLE OF THE SECOND CENTURY BCE, the Romans were masters of the known world. They had defeated formidable foes such as Pyrrhus and Hannibal, and ravaged the great civilisations of the Greeks and Carthaginians. Roman power flowed outwards, seemingly unstoppable, with the city-state becoming an empire of far-flung possessions. This growth meant, however, that serious internal problems – the cracks of which had been opening for decades, if not centuries – would lead to a series of crises and, ultimately, the destruction of the Roman Republic.

In the middle of the fifth century BCE, long-running conflicts between Rome's social and political elite (the patricians) and the less wealthy or privileged people (the plebeians) culminated in a serious crisis. In 451 BCE the two consuls abdicated in favour of a special commission of ten men, the *decemviri*, tasked with governing the state and, crucially, collecting and publishing its laws – something for which the plebeians (who did not wish Roman law to remain the secret preserve of the patricians) had been agitating. These *decemviri*, most if not all of whom were patricians, had a year-long tenure during which they produced the Ten Tables (so called because they were engraved on ten panels of either wood or bronze). This first commission was then replaced by a second group, who proved more conservative, adding two further tables of law to make up the Twelve Tables. One of these new laws controversially banned marriage between patricians and plebeians – a clear attempt to close the ranks of the patriciate.

The members of this regime began behaving despotically and, at the end of their tenure, refused to step down. Their overbearing conduct was highlighted by the actions of one *decemvir*, a patrician named Appius Claudius, who began showing an unhealthy interest in the beautiful and chaste daughter of a plebeian named Lucius Verginius. Appius planned to murder Verginius and abduct the girl, Verginia. Powerless and despairing, Verginius saved his daughter from Appius's brutal scheme in the only way possible: he stabbed her through the heart. Verginius's supporters (including the girl's betrothed) paraded Verginia's lifeless body through the marketplace 'and showed it to the people, bewailing the crime of Appius'.[1]

Roman history began with a mass kidnapping of women, and its subsequent developments were often likewise linked to the violation of women. If the death of Lucretia led to the fall of the Tarquins, the outrage caused by that of Verginia – another virtuous young woman sacrificed on the altar of tyranny and lust – resulted in the overthrow of the 'ten Tarquins' (as the *decemviri* became known). The fall of this oppressive regime catalysed a series of political reforms that led to a more representative and inclusive political system, in which the plebs enjoyed greater participation through elected officials and a popular assembly where they could cast their votes (in what were known as plebiscites). By 367 BCE a law was passed decreeing that one of the two consuls should be a plebeian, and a generation later, in 342 BCE, it was even agreed that both consuls could be plebs.

Social mobility meant that some plebs eventually became wealthy and prominent, and by the middle of the 300s BCE the plebs enjoyed equal legal footing with the patricians. The wealthier among the plebs began forming a new aristocracy of their own, the *nobilitas*, so named because its members were *nobiles* (from *nobilis*, 'well-known' or 'famous') thanks to pleb forefathers who had achieved political or military renown. These departed ancestors were an important part of family lore: wax masks (known as *imagines*) of these illustrious forebears adorned the entrances of their family homes. It was rather like the descendants of a rags-to-riches railroad tycoon displaying his bewhiskered portrait in the hall of their Gilded Age mansion.

A proud Roman carries two portrait masks of his deceased ancestors in a funeral procession. Polybius wrote that sculptors paid close attention to making the masks as lifelike as possible.

However, the Romans took the veneration much farther, hiring actors to wear their forebears' death masks during important public festivals, and to don a ceremonial toga and tour the streets in a chariot. The Romans found these reverential displays edifying. 'For who would not be inspired by the sight of the images of men renowned for their excellence?' asked an approving Polybius. 'What spectacle could be more glorious than this?'[2]

While some plebeian families emerged triumphantly from among the lower orders, most of the poor remained in a wretched condition. In Rome itself, the urban poor were crowded into *insulae* – cramped apartment blocks rising a dozen floors above the narrow streets. The *plebs sordida* ('great unwashed'), as they were pejoratively known, became ever more disenfranchised as their political representatives effectively joined the ranks of the patricians. But by the end of the second century BCE, the poor found champions in the grandsons of Scipio Africanus: Tiberius and Gaius Gracchus, two brothers from a distinguished plebeian family who, to improve the lot of the poor, attempted to reform how land was shared.

Land distribution was one of Rome's perpetual problems. Rome had begun (and for many of its citizens it continued) as an agricultural community. Romulus supposedly gave each of his followers a plot of land measuring 2 *iugera*, roughly an acre and a quarter (an area slightly larger than a football pitch). A *iugerum* (from *iugum*, 'yoke') represented the amount of land an ox could plough in a single day. Although an acre might seem a generous chunk of real estate today, Roman methods of farming meant the amount of land needed for a family's basic subsistence was 15 *iugera* (a little less than 10 acres). To survive, a family therefore needed access to additional lands, especially for grazing livestock. This need was traditionally met by the communal lands known as the *ager publicus* (*ager* being the root of 'agriculture'). But large portions of these so-called public lands had been expropriated by the wealthier classes for their private use. Despite a law from 367 BCE that had set the limit on private ownership at 500 *iugera*, some of the wealthiest Romans expropriated far larger tracts of the *ager publicus*. Theoretically they paid rent to the state, but often, for lack of an efficient fiscal apparatus, it was never collected. Labour on these vast estates, known as *latifundia* (large farms), was provided by slaves, whose numbers had been bolstered by Rome's military conquests. Deprived of access to arable land, the smallholders lived an increasingly hardscrabble existence, many of them leaving the land and moving to the city, where they eked out an equally meagre living among the urban poor.

Landownership was crucial not just for Roman citizens, who needed to eat, but also for the state, which needed troops. The poor and landless were not eligible for military service because Roman soldiers were required to pay for their own food and weapons. The proliferation of the *latifundia* at the expense of the smallholders meant a great many peasants, who had once formed large parts of the citizen militia, failed to meet the property requirement for military service. The poor and propertyless were classified in the censuses as *proletarii*, or 'producers of offspring', for they produced and owned nothing but their children.

Various efforts at reform were mooted. In 140 BCE a consul named Gaius Laelius made noises about land redistribution. However, he faced vigorous opposition in the Senate, many of whose members were themselves large landowners and therefore ill-disposed towards reform. Forced into a swift rethink,

Laelius was given the nickname Sapiens, meaning 'wise'. The next would-be reformer, Tiberius Gracchus, was not so wise. In 133 BCE he proposed a law that would have enforced the long-ignored 500-*iugera* limit. His law made provisions for confiscating the *ager publicus* from the wealthy usurpers and allotting units of land to the poor – not least to increase the supply of soldiers. Tiberius's efforts at reform ended abruptly after he made his way to the Senate one morning despite a series of unfavourable omens: he stubbed his toe on his threshold, spotted a pair of ravens squabbling on his neighbour's rooftop and then, to top it off, discovered a family of snakes living in his old army helmet. The day did indeed prove inauspicious for Tiberius: he was clubbed to death with a chair leg by enraged senators, then tossed into the Tiber with the corpses of 300 of his slaughtered supporters. It was Rome's first explosion of political violence and murder for many centuries.

Roman senators respond unfavourably to Tiberius Gracchus's proposals for land reform.

More blood was shed a few years later when Tiberius's handsome and fiery younger brother, Gaius, pressed for similar reforms. His enemies in the Senate promptly put out a bounty, promising that anyone bringing them Gaius's head would be rewarded with its weight in gold. The prize was claimed by an unscrupulous fraud named Septimuleius: he stole the severed head from the assassin who had slain the fleeing Gaius, then removed the brain and filled the cavity with lead. When the ghastly trophy was placed on the scales, he received 8 kilograms of gold.

Greed, violence, fraud, factions, mass slaughter, a severed head – the murders of the Gracchi would set the stage for much that was to follow.

*

One of Gaius Gracchus's other ambitions had been to extend Roman citizenship more widely across the peninsula. We have already seen how Rome adopted an effective strategy of forming military alliances whereby the *socii* retained their autonomy while complying with Rome's demands, first and foremost by providing soldiers. These alliances meant that Rome had united under its rule the disparate ethnic groups – Gauls, Greeks, Etruscans, Samnites – inhabiting the peninsula. Yet the alliances faced severe challenges due to the invasions of Pyrrhus and Hannibal, both of which witnessed defections to Rome's enemies and exposed the fragility and variability of these coalitions. The greatest challenge to this unity, as well as to Rome's supremacy, came with the Social War (that is, the war of the *socii*).

The Social War (91–87 BCE) featured a coalition of Rome's Italian allies rising in rebellion. It erupted partly because of the allies' demand for Roman citizenship – entitlements and privileges long withheld from the *socii* (apart from allied soldiers who were sometimes enfranchised as a reward for service). Roman citizenship conferred numerous advantages, such as legal protection, access to political offices and tax exemptions. As the ancient historian Appian observed, Rome's allies 'did not think it right that they be classed as subjects rather than partners', especially since they had been instrumental in Rome's military successes.[3]

The demand for citizenship intensified following the reforms initiated during the time of the Gracchi, when land distribution was to be restricted to Roman citizens. Roman statesmen, however, were reluctant to grant citizenship more widely. A law passed in 95 BCE aimed to address the supposed abuse of the privileges by non-Roman Italians, some of whom were alleged to have gained citizenship without proper qualifications. The rigorous scrutiny of these citizenship claims exacerbated existing tensions, culminating in a devastating conflict.

The fuse for the uprising was lit in 91 BCE when a politician named Marcus Livius Drusus, a prominent supporter of the enfranchisement of the *socii*, was stabbed to death with a shoemaker's knife in Rome. The *socii* immediately began preparing for rebellion. When the Romans caught wind of these subversive activities, they sent out representatives – one of whom, in the town of Asculum Picenum (modern Ascoli Piceno), some 200 kilometres northeast of Rome, unwisely threatened the locals during a festival. They responded by killing him, then slaying all of Asculum's Roman citizens and looting their properties. Appian enumerated the huge coalition that rose against Rome: the Marsians, the Paeligni, the Vestini, the Marrucini, the Picentines, the Hirpini, the Iapygians, the Lucanians and the 'people of Pompeii'. Also joining the rebellion were the Samnites. 'These had proved troublesome to the Romans before,' wrote Appian in a splendid understatement.[4]

Both sides sustained massive casualties. The corpses of legionaries arrived in Rome in such alarming quantities that senators began fearing that young Roman men would be deterred from military service. The Senate therefore decreed that the dead should be buried where they fell, a policy soon also adopted by the *socii* due to their own heavy losses. Some 18,000 Samnites, for example, were massacred at Pompeii – a larger death toll than the city would suffer with the eruption of Vesuvius more than 160 years later.

After a bloody stalemate, the Romans 'restored the tottering power of the Roman people' (as the historian Velleius Paterculus put it) by submitting to the allies' demand for citizenship.[5] Thus the Romans finally addressed longstanding grievances and promoted unity on the peninsula. All people south of the Po River (excluding slaves) shared equal rights and privileges and, increasingly, a common language. Latin became ever more dominant, leading to the decline in subsequent decades of Oscan and its dialects. The conflict therefore gave birth to a new Italy, one that gathered together the peninsula's scattered cities and diverse ethnic groups. As so often, Rome's former enemies had themselves become Romans.

*

Unity on the peninsula, as well as within Rome itself, remained fragile, with political violence ever present. The decades that followed the Social War witnessed what Appian called a descent from wrangling and competition into civil conflict, from civil conflict into murder, 'and from murder into full war'.[6]

This civil strife was triggered by a power struggle between two statesmen and military commanders, Gaius Marius and his one-time deputy, Lucius Cornelius Sulla. Born about 157 BCE, Marius had been one of the greatest soldiers of his generation, improving the army's organisation and leading Rome to victory against the Gauls in 102 and 101 BCE. His reforms had been far-reaching. Rome's war machine had formerly served the needs of a city-state waging short seasonal campaigns, staffed by citizens conscripted to fight. Troops were raised by levies, and indeed the word 'legion' comes from *legio*, 'levy'. The levies consisted of the consuls mustering all men of military age to assemble on the Capitoline Hill, where various officials selected them for service. However, Rome's acquisition of overseas territories in Africa and Greece required long campaigns and a permanent military presence: an unrealistic onus on the conscripts in a citizen army who needed to return to their homes, farms and businesses. Further, the poor and landless were excluded from service, as we have seen, since the soldiers needed to pay for their own food and weapons, receiving only a small stipend (and the prospect of booty).

Marius therefore introduced reforms by which military service was opened up to the poor, who would be paid not only in booty but also, at the end of their service, in parcels of land (often in the territories captured in battle) given to them by their generals. What followed, then, were armies of increasingly professional, privately funded soldiers who owed both their financial welfare and their allegiance to their generals rather than to Rome. Meanwhile, their commanders, to fulfil their troops' expectations of land and plunder, were compelled to engage in perpetual military campaigns.

Marius soon experienced, directly and personally, the consequences of his reforms. As the Social War ended, both he and Sulla wished to lead the upcoming military expedition against Mithridates VI of the Hellenistic kingdom of Pontus. Ruling vast territories that encompassed most of modern Turkey and encircled the Black Sea, Mithridates was Rome's most redoubtable foe since Hannibal: a man who reputedly spoke twenty-two languages and made himself immune to poison by daily ingesting small doses of lethal toxins. His soldiers – armed with square shields and a curved sword called the *sica* – inspired, like the Samnites, one of the fearsome gladiator types that appeared in Roman arenas: the 'Thracian'.

The Senate offered the commission – with its splendid opportunities for glory and plunder – to Sulla. A ruthless operator, Sulla had distinguished himself during the Social War with excessive brutality (he was behind the slaughter of the Samnites at Pompeii). However, at the behest of a corrupt and scheming politician named Publius Sulpicius Rufus, the choice commission was soon revoked in favour of Marius. Sulla's troops, encamped outside Rome, responded to this unwelcome news by stoning the messengers, to which Marius retaliated by killing many of Sulla's supporters inside Rome. Sulla then turned loose on the city the legions whose fidelity was to him rather than to the state (although many of his officers, to their credit, resigned). The soldiers crossed the *pomerium*, the boundary laid out by Romulus, and began launching burning arrows at a mob pelting them with stones and roof tiles. Marius fled the city, hijacking a boat (the great commander overpowered an old fisherman) and sailing to Africa. Having taken Rome by force, Sulla finally claimed his prize, sailing off to fight Mithridates. 'From this moment on,' Appian bitterly reflected, 'it was armies that now decided political conflicts.' The 'men of violence', he lamented, had taken charge of the state.[7]

Sulla returned from Asia a few years later to find his enemies in control of the city – so he and his troops invaded Rome for a second time. He assumed the powers of dictator, a temporary emergency magistracy intended to deal with a specific crisis. 'Sulla now busied himself with slaughter,' as Plutarch wrote, 'and murders without number or limit filled the city.' Names of his foes, the 'proscribed', were posted in the Forum, with the rewards for their capture set out along with the punishments for anyone who sheltered them. The properties of the proscribed were confiscated, and Sulla decorated his palace with their severed heads. Appian put the death toll at fifteen former consuls, ninety senators and 100,000 soldiers on both sides.

Sulla resigned his dictatorship a short time later, having carried out reforms that, among other things, strengthened the powers of the Senate by restoring prerogatives that had been undermined during political upheavals. Having given a measure of order and stability to Rome – albeit with extreme violence – he retired to his country estate at Cumae. But old habits die hard: a year later he suffered a fatal haemorrhage while screaming at his men to strangle a local magistrate.

*

Rebellion, civil war, slaughter, private armies, invasions of Rome, ruthlessly ambitious strongmen, the spectre of one-man rule: the terrible crisis triggered by Sulla in the 80s BCE was, like the murders of the Gracchi, a grim portent of the decades to follow.

One of the architects of Rome's subsequent civil war was a former henchman of Sulla: Gnaeus Pompeius, or Pompey.

Few men in history have entertained such lofty dreams of personal grandeur, and then, seemingly effortlessly, realised them. In 81 BCE, when he was only twenty-five, Pompey had added 'Magnus' (the Great) to his name in emulation of Alexander, whose cloak he later claimed to own and whose hairstyle (a swept-back middle parting) he imitated. He became known for his brutal military exploits in Sicily, Spain and Africa, where, on behalf of Sulla, he eliminated supporters of Gaius Marius and earned another nickname: *adulescentulus carnifex* (teenage butcher). When he besieged Calagurris in Spain, the inhabitants ate all their quadrupeds before, in desperation, they made a 'nefarious meal' of their wives and children.[8] He enhanced his reputation for brutal efficiency in 71 BCE by crucifying thousands of fugitives along Via Appia following the revolt of the gladiator Spartacus. Tasked with ridding the Mediterranean of pirates, he was given such extraordinary and unprecedented powers and resources that the Senate feared Rome was on a fast-track to one-man military rule. He rendered the pirates

Gnaeus Pompeius Magnus, aka Pompey the Great. Born in 106 BCE, he distinguished himself at a young age with his ruthlessness.

impotent within months, inspiring such gratitude among the citizens of the island of Delos that some of them began worshipping him as a god.

Pompey's greatest success came in Asia, where he defeated King Mithridates, whose diet of toxins backfired when he tried to commit suicide by poison. (He was forced to appeal instead to one of his sword-wielding soldiers.) In addition, Pompey captured Jerusalem, made Syria a Roman province and founded thirty-nine cities across Asia, one of which, with a typical disregard for humility, he christened Pompeiopolis. He began glorying in a new title: Master of Earth and Sea.

Pompey's triumphs in Asia and his favour among the Roman people unsettled numerous senators, who were reluctant to endorse his Eastern settlements and provide land to his veterans. So Pompey formed a strategic alliance with another energetic and savvy commander: Gaius Julius Caesar. The two men combined outstanding leadership and military acumen with relentless personal ambition and merciless brutality. Their partnership would reshape the Roman Republic's balance of power and set the stage for decades of conflict.

*

Balding, slight, pale and suffering from a 'distemper in the head' (probably epilepsy), Julius Caesar was physically unprepossessing.[9] But he was also charming, vain and fanatically ambitious, and by the age of forty he had already cut a conspicuous dash both in Rome and abroad. He was born in the summer of 100 BCE, in the month of Quintilis (which after his death would be renamed Julius – whence comes 'July'). Few people can have contemplated their family tree with such satisfaction: Caesar believed himself descended, on one side, from Ancus Marcius, the fourth King of Rome, and on the other side from no less a figure than Venus. As he once declared in a speech, he possessed both 'the sanctity of kings, whose power is supreme among mortal men' as well as the 'reverence which attaches to the Gods, who hold sway over kings themselves'.[10] Belief in such a splendid lineage did little to enhance his limited stocks of humility.

The name Caesar (pronounced *KAI-zer*) came from a remote ancestor, Sextus Julius, who, according to legend, had killed one of Hannibal's elephants. All Romans used a personal name (in his case Sextus) followed by a family name (Julius). Many also took, or were given, a third name, a cognomen, which usually referred to a personal trait, place of origin or glorious deed. As we have seen, Lucius Junius acquired 'Brutus' (stupid), while Gaius Laelius became 'Sapiens'. The physical appearances of other Romans earned them names such as Strabo (squinty) or Barbatus (bearded). As for Sextus Julius, since the Punic word for elephant was *caesai*, and since the Latin verb *caedo* means to kill, he became, thanks to a clever pun, Sextus Julius Caesar: Sextus Julius the Elephant Killer. This cognomen, like many others, was passed down the generations, finding its way more than a century later to Sextus's distant descendant – and eventually to various kaisers, czars and shahs.

Caesar's father, also named Gaius Julius Caesar, had an impressive political career before retiring from the bloody fray and, in about 84 BCE, when his son was still an adolescent, dying in his bed (a rare feat in such fraught times). Soon afterwards, Caesar began enthusiastically pursuing a military career. He spent years soldiering in Asia, winning renown with acts of conspicuous bravery but attracting innuendo when his dalliances at the court of King Nicomedes of Bithynia (in modern Turkey) led to suspicions of intimate relations between him and the king (whom a poet named Licinius Calvus called 'Caesar's buggering boyfriend').[11] Tales of romps in purple bed-sheets earned Caesar the malicious nickname *Bithynica regina* (Queen of Bithynia). Later, Caesar would be taunted with the story by his own soldiers, something that left him so 'greatly vexed and manifestly pained' that he swore under oath that the alleged affair never took place – 'whereupon he incurred all the more ridicule'.[12]

Romans found nothing inherently unnatural or offensive in sexual relations between two men; the issue was rather the positions (quite literally) of the partners. The Romans, like the Greeks, judged sexual behaviour not by the gender of the participants but by their roles. It was emasculating for a free-born Roman man to submit to passive, receptive sexual relations (becoming what was called a *cinaedus*), whereas to be the dominant, penetrating partner was acceptable.[13] *Cinaedi* were viciously mocked in Roman literature (and no doubt in the streets of Rome) as soft and effeminate – associations that the thrusting, red-blooded Caesar would have shunned with horror.

Caesar's career took him to Spain, where in Gades (modern Cádiz) he came across a statue of Alexander the Great. The sight of the young commander made him regret that he had achieved so little by the age at which Alexander had already conquered the world. He therefore resigned his army commission with a plan of returning to Rome and launching a political career. However, he was troubled by a dream in which he bedded his own mother – though he was soon reassured by soothsayers, who informed him that the compliant woman embraced in his dream was, in fact, 'none other than the earth, the common parent of all mankind', and that the dream foretold 'that he was destined to rule the world'.[14]

First Caesar needed to get himself elected. Most political offices in Rome, including that of consul, were elected positions. Our word 'candidate' comes from the fact that electioneering was done in a whitened robe, the toga candida, from the Latin *candidus*, 'white' – the root of words like incandescent and candle. A political campaign became known as an *ambitio*, from which 'ambitious' derives. *Ambitio* stems from *ambire*, meaning 'to go around', reflecting the tradition of candidates, dressed in white, conducting walkabouts to meet voters – the sort of flesh-pressing familiar to today's politicians. Candidates often employed a slave tasked with memorising the names of influential voters, highlighting the meticulous nature of Roman campaigning.

Caesar's fluent oratory – and his willingness and ability to pay bribes – made him an excellent candidate. In 65 BCE, he was elected to the important role of Aedile, a kind of minister of the urban infrastructure (*aedile* comes from *aedis*, meaning a temple or dwelling – and the origin of 'edifice'). He was therefore in charge of the upkeep of Rome's temples, streets and water supply. He used the position to curry favour with the masses by laying out piazzas for popular entertainments such as athletics contests, the mass slaughter of wild animals and that reliable crowd-pleaser, gladiatorial combat.

Caesar's budding political career was not without intrigue and scandal. One of his political cronies was a former supporter of Sulla, a nobleman named Marcus Crassus who had become fabulously wealthy by helping himself to the lands and fortunes of the men whose severed heads adorned Sulla's villa. Crassus planned to continue this reign of terror, assisted by Caesar. The duo were suspected of planning a gory conspiracy in which they would turn up at the Senate and – when Caesar gave a secret signal by flapping his toga – fall upon the senators and murder as many of them as possible. Crassus would then declare himself dictator and appoint Caesar his right-hand man. This prospective carnage was abandoned when, evidently entertaining second thoughts, Crassus failed to turn up to the Senate on the appointed day.

Caesar furthermore found himself embroiled in a sex scandal thanks to Pompeia, his second wife (his beloved first wife, Cornelia, died in childbirth in about 69 BCE). Pompeia allegedly smuggled her lover, dressed as a woman, into a female-only festival. Although the amorous interloper was acquitted thanks to a hasty exchange of hush money, Caesar divorced Pompeia anyway. 'I maintain that the members of my family should be free from suspicion,' he pompously explained, 'as well as from accusation' – leading to the famous proverb that 'Caesar's wife must be above suspicion'.[15] This demand for exemplary moral behaviour must have been viewed with grim scepticism by those who hailed the follicly challenged Caesar, known for debauching the wives of his friends, as the 'bald adulterer'.[16]

Indeed, Caesar had slept with the wives of both Pompey and Crassus – one of the few things the two men had in common. They had been bitter rivals ever since the former offended the latter during their discordant year-long reign together as consuls, when Pompey claimed undue credit for defeating the slave rebellion led by the gladiator Spartacus in 73–71 BCE. Caesar, deploying his diplomatic talents, reconciled the pair, and the secret alliance became known (to us, though not to the ancients) as the First Triumvirate, a Gang of Three who combined the wealth of Crassus (by far the richest man in Rome), the military prestige of Pompey and the sharp political instincts of Caesar.

The partnership was sealed by Pompey's marriage to Caesar's thirteen-year-old daughter, Julia, and in 59 BCE, thanks to bribes doled out by Crassus, Caesar was elected consul.

Caesar's ambition, along with his popularity among the Roman people, earned him the abhorrence of many senators. Although Rome did not have anything remotely like the political parties of today, the orator and statesman Cicero used two terms – *optimates* and *populares* – to describe the 'two classes of men in this State who have sought to engage in public affairs'. The *optimates* were (in Cicero's biased opinion) the 'best men': those who were 'upright, sound in mind, and easy in circumstances'. These well-heeled, right-thinking men desired whatever was 'the best and the most desirable for all who are sound and good and prosperous'. The Senate, unsurprisingly, was top-heavy with these wealthy conservatives. By contrast, the *populares* aspired to be what Cicero called 'friends of the people' – rabble-rousers (as the Gracchi brothers had been) 'who wished everything they did and said to be agreeable to the masses'. While the *optimates* had succeeded in crushing the Gracchi, they faced a much more dangerous and daunting proposition in the populist Julius Caesar.[17]

Caesar's year as consul was predictably tumultuous, witnessing riots, mob violence, armed gangs, jailed opponents and Caesar maintaining such tight-fisted control that the two consuls were said, in a bitter jest, to be 'Julius' and 'Caesar'. In fact, Caesar's fellow consul, Marcus Calpurnius Bibulus, an ardent *optimate*, was forced to hole up in his house for fear of getting killed. Supported by Pompey and Crassus, Caesar forced through laws designed (as Plutarch sneered) to 'gratify the multitude', such as distributing land to Pompey's veterans and the poor.[18]

When his term ended, Caesar became governor of Cisalpine Gaul and then (when the incumbent died) Transalpine Gaul. By a stroke of good fortune, in 58 BCE a Celtic tribe began moving south from their lands in present-day Switzerland in search of new settlements, offering Caesar the chance to rush to the frontiers and do battle. He spent much of the next decade fighting the Gallic Wars, eventually bringing vast territories, including present-day Germany, northern France and Belgium, under Roman control. Along the way he conquered or set fire to 800 cities and towns, subdued 300 tribes, pillaged numberless shrines and temples, and killed (by Plutarch's reckoning) a million people, enslaving perhaps as many more. He crossed both the Rhine (where he skirmished with the barbarians) and the English Channel, the latter on two occasions in hopes of getting his hands on some pearls. He also composed his great treatise, *Commentaries on the Gallic War*, a first-hand propaganda account of his military achievements. In repeating the success of Pompey in Asia, he developed, like Pompey, kingly ambitions that unnerved many senators, who regarded him – justifiably – as a dangerous threat to their power.

The third member of the Gang of Three, Crassus, began dreaming of a glorious military triumph abroad that would match those of Pompey in Asia and Caesar in Gaul. He eventually received the governorship of Syria, from where he planned to attack the Parthians, whose empire sprawled across present-day Iran and Iraq. As he set off with seven legions at the end of 55 BCE, he had to force his way through a mob of Roman anti-war protesters, one of whom, greeting him at the gate with burning incense, cast 'dreadful and terrifying' curses on the expedition.[19]

Eager for passage across the Ionian Sea, Crassus launched his fleet from Brundisium in the middle of a winter storm that wrecked many of his vessels. The rest of the expedition proved even more spectacularly ill-judged. Crassus died in battle in Mesopotamia, and his disembodied head was sent to Armenia for use as a prop in a production of Euripides' tragedy *The Bacchae*. In the Parthian city of Seleucia (near modern Baghdad) he received a grotesque parody of a triumph: a Parthian soldier, who looked uncannily like Crassus, dressed up as a woman and led through the streets what Plutarch called 'a laughable sort of procession': musicians, prostitutes and a collection of disembodied Roman heads, accompanied by 'scurrilous and ridiculous songs about the effeminacy and cowardice of Crassus'.[20] The career of Crassus thus ended in both tragedy and farce.

*

Following the death of Crassus, battle between the two remaining triumvirs looked inevitable. Pompey's beloved wife (and Caesar's daughter), Julia, died in childbirth in 54 BCE, removing one of the strongest bonds between the two men. Caesar's success in Gaul brought him wealth and prestige, but also the envy and enmity of many senators, who began courting Pompey as a counterweight – Pompey, who was (as Caesar later wrote) 'jealous and critical of Caesar's renown'.[21] However, their first recourse was a legal one. Caesar's many critics in the Senate believed the laws passed during his consulship defied the Roman constitution. Planning to prosecute Caesar for his illegal conduct, they ordered him to surrender his command in Gaul, disband his legions and return to Rome to face the legal consequences.

As a private citizen, Caesar would lose his legal immunity and face prosecution. Entertaining no doubts about the outcome of a trial, he decided to return to Rome – though not as a private citizen. Sometime in early January 49 BCE, he performed one of the most notorious and momentous frontier crossings in history. He had spent the day in Ariminum (Rimini), watching gladiatorial battles, having a bath and then enjoying a banquet from which he soon excused himself, feigning illness before, in secret, setting off at sunset with his 13th Legion, veterans of murderous battles against the Gallic tribes. The historian Suetonius described how the expedition began inauspiciously: after harnessing to a chariot two mules taken from a local bakery, Caesar got lost when his torches extinguished. The great warrior found himself wandering aimlessly on dark paths until a local guide came to the rescue. Finally he and his men reached the boundary between Gaul and Roman territory, marked by a river named – because of its ruddy waters – the Rubicon.

Caesar was not without misgivings as he contemplated the bridge crossing the river. Plutarch wrote how he 'communed with himself a long time in silence as his resolution wavered back and forth'.[22] Appian described him staring for a long time into the dark waters before telling his men: 'My friends, if I do not make this crossing, it will be the beginning of troubles for me. If I do make it, it will be the beginning of troubles for the whole world.'[23] Then, with the words 'Let the die be cast' (*Alea iacta est*), he and his troops, armed to the teeth, marched across.

Caesar's reference to dice suggests he was aware that his action was an enormous gamble. However, Suetonius claimed Caesar's confidence was boosted by a comforting vision of 'a being of wondrous stature and beauty' playing a reed beside the river. So enchanting was the melody that Caesar's soldiers clustered round to listen. The mysterious figure then snatched a trumpet from one of the pipers, let loose a thunderous blast and strode across the bridge. 'Take we the course which the signs of the gods and the false dealing of our foes point out,' Caesar declared, then followed the giant.[24]

The *optimates* had gradually won over Pompey, not least thanks to his second marriage, following Julia's death, to the daughter of one of Caesar's most vehement critics, a senator and former consul named Metellus Scipio. Pompey grew bold after his recovery from a serious illness was celebrated up and down the peninsula with sacrifices, festivals, torchlight processions and adoring throngs who showered him with flowers. It was enough to make any budding autocrat dream of glorious despotism. As Caesar marched south down the peninsula, Pompey prepared to face him. Although his best legions were stationed in Iberia, he was confident of raising troops. 'In whatever part of Italy I stamp upon the ground,' he boasted, 'there will spring up armies of foot and horse.'[25]

These legions failed to materialise. Caesar, meanwhile, moved rapidly south, facing no resistance as city after city opened their gates to him, receiving him (as he later recalled) 'with the utmost enthusiasm'.[26] Two of his legions in Gaul likewise began descending into Italy. Rome was filled with 'tumult, consternation, and a fear that was beyond compare'.[27] Panic and confusion were such that Romans fled the city for the safety of the countryside while people from the countryside fled their villages for the safety of Rome. Pompey and many senators, as well as the two consuls, fled south to Capua and then to Brundisium, from where – with Caesar in hot pursuit – they crossed the Ionian Sea to Macedonia. As Plutarch reported, Caesar had become 'master of all Italy without bloodshed'.[28] Pompey began mobilising in Macedonia, raising troops as well as a fleet of 500 ships, thanks to his allies and clients in the East. Caesar turned round and marched to

Spain to fight Pompey's legions there, after which, in the late autumn of 49 BCE, having secured ships of his own, he sailed for Greece. He was full of confidence after a hawk circling overhead dropped a sprig of laurel onto one of his soldiers – clearly a favourable sign from Jupiter.

The decisive engagement took place in the summer of 48 BCE at Pharsalus in Thessaly. Caesar fielded 22,000 troops against double that number for Pompey. But while many in Pompey's legions were hastily levied and largely untested recruits, Caesar's were skilled and drilled veterans fiercely loyal to their commander. Caesar scored an overwhelming victory, even overrunning Pompey's camp, where, to his astonishment, he found tables laid for celebrating the anticipated victory. Pompey fled the field, spending the night in a fisherman's hut before hitching a ride on a merchant ship and eventually making his way to Egypt. Here he hoped to find refuge with the pharaoh, fifteen-year-old Ptolemy XIII, whose father Pompey had restored to his throne a few years earlier. Ptolemy feared that if he agreed to Pompey's request, he would make an enemy of Caesar, and if he refused the request, he would make an enemy of Pompey. He solved this dilemma by sending a boat to collect Pompey and then having him stabbed and beheaded on the beach. 'A dead man does not bite,' explained the young pharaoh.[29]

Caesar arrived in Egypt a short time later. His victory was not without poignancy, for Pompey had once been his son-in-law and close political ally. He therefore turned away in disgust when the disembodied head was presented to him, promptly murdering Pompey's killers. As for King Ptolemy, he died a year later, drowning in the Nile during a power struggle that pitted him against his older sister (and wife), Cleopatra, who was supported by Caesar. She took over the kingdom and a few years later began ruling jointly with her infant son, pointedly named Caesarion ('Little Caesar') – conceived on a sultry night in Alexandria after she had been smuggled into Caesar's presence, bundled in a rolled-up carpet.

Jean-Léon Gérôme's 1866 depiction of the moment when Caesar's studies are interrupted by the arrival of a beautiful visitor.

*

Caesar entertained lavishly on his return to Rome, staging gladiatorial spectacles and hosting a banquet featuring 20,000 dining couches (because, rather than sitting in chairs as they ate, the Romans reclined on cushions at low tables). He was full of plans for the future: to defeat the Parthians, to invade Scythia and to overrun Germany. His pretensions, like the frontiers of the empire, seemingly knew no bounds.

One of Caesar's boldest ambitions, and perhaps his greatest legacy, was reforming the calendar to address longstanding problems. The old Roman calendar, which, according to tradition, dated back to Romulus and Numa Pompilius, was based on the lunar year. While the lunar year is approximately 355 days long, the solar year, on which the seasons depend, lasts approximately 365 days. This ten-day discrepancy meant that, in time, the dates of festivals and other events failed to coincide with their proper seasons, leading to inconsistencies in agricultural practice and religious observance. As the historian Suetonius complained, 'The harvest festivals did not come in summer nor those of the vintage in the autumn.'[30] Attempts had been made to correct the situation by periodically adding an extra month called Mercedonius ('work month'), but this makeshift solution led to abuses since the officials in charge often manipulated the calendar for personal gain – to extend their terms in office, for example – further undermining its utility.

Julius tasked an astronomer from Alexandria named Sosigenes with solving the problem. Sosigenes' reset of the calendar meant that the year 46 BCE featured two extra months, respectively thirty-three and thirty-four days long, and lasted a total of 445 days. It became known, unsurprisingly, as the 'Year of Confusion'. But with the days and months synchronised to their proper seasons, the new 'Julian' calendar came into effect on 1 January 45 BCE. It established a solar year of 365 days divided into twelve months, with an extra day added every four years – the *annus bisextilis*, or leap year – to account for the extra fraction of a day in the solar year (which actually lasts 365 days, five hours and 48 minutes). This leap day fell on 24 February, which lasted forty-eight hours. A landmark in the history of timekeeping, Caesar's new calendar would be used for the next 1,627 years.

The Romans did not, of course, refer to the years as we do today – as '46 BCE', for example. Most ancient societies numbered their years according to the reign of their king or from the date of the founding of their city. Sosigenes (at Caesar's behest) calculated the date of Romulus's founding of Rome to 21 April 753 BCE. Subsequently, from Caesar's time onward, years were often identified as, for example, '707 AUC': 707 years *ab urbe condita* ('since the founding of the city') – equating to 46 BCE. But during the Roman Republic, years were traditionally referred to by the names of the consuls in office: events in 46 BCE, for example, took place 'in the consulship of Julius Caesar and Marcus Aemilius Lepidus'. Since many detailed chronological lists of the consuls and other officials have survived, historians have been able to use them to reconstruct the historical record.

Julius Caesar survived barely more than a year after the inauguration of his new calendar. His vast ambitions and the drastic shift towards one-man rule quickly became too much for many Romans to bear. He occupied a golden throne in the Senate, sported a purple toga and placed statues of himself in temples beside those of the gods. In one famous and controversial incident, while watching a festival from a throne in the Forum he allowed his relative and ardent supporter Mark Antony – 'naked, oiled, and drunk', according to Cicero[31] – to offer him a crown, which he made a show of rejecting only when the revellers displayed a distinct lack of enthusiasm for this attempted coronation. He did appreciate his right to wear a crown of laurel leaves – the *corona civica*, given to him for service to the Republic – because it allowed him to camouflage his balding pate, otherwise concealed by means of a comb-over.

Worst of all for Caesar's critics, early in 44 BCE he became *dictator perpetuo* (dictator for life) – a position that looked little different from that of a monarch. He rendered himself, according to Plutarch, 'odious and obnoxious even to the mildest citizens'. Plutarch speculated that some of the overweening honours were actually conferred on Caesar by his enemies, 'in order that they might have as many pretexts as possible against him and might be thought to have the best reasons for making attempts on his life'.[32]

The attempt came on what is now one of the most famous days in Western history, the Ides of March (15 March) in 44 BCE. The conspiracy was led by the men Caesar called 'those pale, thin ones': Gaius Cassius Longinus and Marcus Junius Brutus.[33] The former was a one-time supporter of Pompey, the latter supposedly a descendant of the Brutus who founded the Roman Republic. Brutus's wife, Porcia, also joined the conspiracy. She persuaded her husband to divulge the plot's details to her by imperturbably inflicting a deep gash on her thigh to prove that, if caught, she could withstand torture. Brutus was suitably

Elisabetta Sirani's 1664 depiction of an unflappable Porcia wounding her thigh. She insisted to her husband that she could withstand torture – and that 'to that extent I was not born a woman'.

impressed, raising his hands to heaven and praying that he might succeed in the plot and thereby 'show himself a worthy husband of Porcia'. He then, sensibly, applied first aid. He would later say of Porcia that although 'her body is not strong enough to perform such heroic tasks as men do, still, in spirit she is valiant in defence of her country, just as we are'.[34]

At least sixty senators also took part in the conspiracy, an indication of just how much Caesar had alienated the *optimates*. With the city teeming with alarming apparitions – lights and crashing in the heavens, birds of ill-omen flapping round the Forum, men on fire stalking the streets – he made his way to the Senate, temporarily housed in Pompey's magnificent theatre (the Senate itself had burned down eight years earlier during a violent factional dispute). Here Caesar was greeted by a soothsayer named Spurinna, who had often warned him in the past about the Ides of March. 'Well, the Ides of March are come,' Caesar taunted him that morning, to which the seer responded: 'Aye, they are come, but they are not gone.'[35]

Once inside, Caesar was approached by various petitioners. One began tugging at the neck of his own toga – the sort of signal, ironically, that Caesar had planned to give, years earlier, to trigger his and Crassus's own attack on the senators. The first assailant slashed at Caesar's neck; others leapt into the fray as the hemmed-in dictator desperately fended off the killers with his stylus. The sword, in this case, proved mightier than the pen: he received twenty-three knife wounds without, apparently, inflicting any damage on his assailants. The only assassin against whom Caesar made no show of defending himself was Brutus, who stabbed him in the groin. According to Suetonius, he uttered not the Latin phrase (*Et tu, Brute?*) made famous by Shakespeare but, rather, 'You too, my child?', which he spoke in Greek. (Rumour had it that Brutus was Caesar's illegitimate son.) He then slumped against the blood-spattered pedestal of a statue of Pompey, 'so that one might have thought', wrote Plutarch, 'that Pompey himself was presiding over this vengeance upon his enemy, who now lay prostrate at his feet, quivering from a multitude of wounds'.[36] His body was unceremoniously borne to his home on a litter by three slaves.

A statue of Pompey the Great presides over Caesar's assassination. Plutarch claimed the conspirators agreed that each of them should give him a wound.

The motives of the conspirators and the justification for their actions have been debated for more than two millennia. Shakespeare's play *Julius Caesar*, first performed in 1599, invites audiences to ask whether Caesar was a brutal dictator or the 'noblest man / That ever lived in the tide of times'. Was his murder a foul crime, or an idealistic and patriotic act performed by Brutus, 'the noblest Roman of them all'? The ancient sources report a wide range of motives among the killers, not all of them high-minded. Many were inspired by grudges, believing Caesar had impeded their careers. Whatever Brutus's principles, he too may have been spurred into action for a personal reason: Caesar's poor treatment of Brutus's mother, Servilia, his long-time mistress. Brutus may also have resented the fact that fourteen years earlier, his engagement to Caesar's daughter Julia had been broken so a more advantageous match could be made with Pompey. Cassius, meanwhile, was apparently motivated at least in part by the fact that Caesar had passed him over for various offices and had even expropriated some lions he was planning to bring back to Rome.

The varied – and in some cases petty – personal motives of the conspirators meant that, with Caesar gone, they possessed no unifying vision or principle, no single-minded commitment to, or plan for, restoring the Roman Republic. It is no surprise, then, that what followed was more than a dozen years of chaos and violence.

# 4

# *PAX ROMANA*: THE AGE OF AUGUSTUS

ROME CONTINUED ITS INEVITABLE LURCH towards one-man rule during the long power struggle that followed Caesar's death. Brutus and Cassius found it prudent to leave Rome following popular expressions of support for the murdered dictator, who had provided generous financial support for the poor. The pair fled to Greece where, having been defeated by the army of Caesar's long-time ally, Mark Antony, both committed suicide – Cassius apparently by means of the same dagger with which he had stabbed Caesar. Brutus's head was dispatched to Rome and cast down at the foot of a statue of Caesar. His wife, Porcia, committed suicide by swallowing hot coals.

Rome found itself, as so often, grappling with political instability and violent power struggles. In 43 BCE, to mitigate further conflict, a law was passed, the *Lex Titia*, ratifying a special magistracy called the triumvirate (known to us as the Second Triumvirate). Buoyed by Caesar's popularity with the people and the support of his followers, its three members had come together on their own accord to counter Caesar's enemies in the Senate and among the *optimates*. The three members, appointed to five-year terms, held emergency powers and reigned supreme over the two consuls, the provincial governors and even, if necessary, the due process of law. Two of the triumvirs were Caesar's most influential partisans: Mark Antony and Marcus Aemilius Lepidus, the latter a statesman descended from one of Rome's oldest and most distinguished families (indeed, according to family lore, from Numa Pompilius). The third was Caesar's hand-picked heir, his great-nephew Gaius Octavius (Octavian), then twenty years old and intent on avenging Caesar's death.

This new Gang of Three provided even less political stability than the first one had, more than a decade earlier. As the partnership fell prey to rivalry and the various parties jockeyed for position, Octavian outmanoeuvred Antony and Lepidus. Lepidus, depicted in the sources as weak and indecisive, was ousted from the triumvirate, while Octavian managed to portray Antony – who ruled the empire in the East with help from Cleopatra (by then his lover) – as a traitor to both Rome and his wife (who happened to be Octavian's sister). In the summer of 32 BCE Octavian declared war on Cleopatra, and a year later his forces defeated Antony in the Ionian Sea off Actium in northern Greece. Antony fled to Alexandria where, following another victory by Octavian, he committed suicide, skewering himself with his sword. Cleopatra, by then the mother of three of his children, likewise committed suicide – though probably not with a snake in the basket of figs but more likely, according to ancient sources such as Plutarch, by stabbing herself in the arm with a poisoned hairpin. Her son and co-ruler, the seventeen-year-old Caesarion, was murdered on Octavian's orders. Before leaving Egypt, Octavian busied himself with a bit of tourism: he asked to see the sarcophagus of Alexander the Great, whose embalmed remains he strewed with flowers, and whose skull he crowned.

He would then spend the rest of his life emulating Alexander's example.

A painted image from Herculaneum of an auburn-haired woman believed – on the basis of her royal diadem, long nose and full lips – to be Cleopatra.

Octavian returned to Rome as the conqueror of Egypt – the oldest and wealthiest kingdom in the Mediterranean – and the sole ruler of the Empire. Following decades of civil war, Rome finally had a chance for peace and political stability. Even so, Octavian must have seemed an unlikely bringer of peace and concord to the troubled Empire. Revoltingly cruel and vengeful during the ruthless struggle that brought him to power, he took to delivering his pitiless reprisals with the words: 'You must die.'[1] He once even gouged out the eyes of a rival with his own hands. And he had been the one behind the order to cut off Brutus's head and bring it back to Rome to be bounced in front of Caesar's statue. And yet Octavian was the one who ushered in what became known as the *Pax Romana* – the 'Roman Peace'.

Octavian was a boy from the country. He had been born in 63 BCE in the town of Velitrae (modern Velletri), about

40 kilometres southeast of Rome. His family supposedly came from modest origins. Mark Antony once taunted him that his paternal great-grandfather had been a freed slave turned rope-maker, and that his maternal great-grandfather, of African descent, ran a perfume shop. These gibes would have done little to trouble Octavian. He cultivated an image of modesty and simplicity by wearing homespun clothing and boasting that all the women in his family could spin wool.

Be that as it may, Octavian's mother, Atia, was Caesar's niece, and in September 45 BCE, after evidently impressing Caesar with his youthful pluck and prowess, Octavian became his adopted son. He inherited Caesar's fabulous wealth as well as his name, going after the dictator's death as Gaius Julius Caesar Octavianus. On 13 January 27 BCE, the Senate created a title for him, 'Augustus' (Revered One) – the name by which history remembers him. The title has its roots in the augur, the priest who (as we've seen) interpreted the will of the gods by observing omens. Octavian, as Augustus, was therefore the man of Providence – the fulfilment of the wishes of the gods.[2]

Augustus ended nearly a century of bloodshed and civil strife, ruling for forty years in relative tranquillity. This peace came at the price of political liberty, though it must be said that few people in Rome apart from the *optimates* (whose power Augustus shattered) had ever truly enjoyed its fruits. For, whatever lip-service was paid to concepts of 'liberty' and 'the people', the Roman Republic had always been an oligarchy. It had been ruled, at any given time, by a self-selecting group of some twenty or thirty men drawn from a dozen prominent families whose roots stretched back many centuries. But as Antony's sneering about rope-makers and perfumers made clear, Augustus was not originally from this wealthy and noble ruling elite.

Most of his advisers came, like him, from outside Rome and its oligarchic families. It's revealing that his right-hand man, Marcus Agrippa, was from a plebeian family so undistinguished that he ditched his surname, Vipsanius – completely unheard-of in the annals of Roman history – because it betrayed his obscure origins.* Even so, we should not regard Augustus's victory over the old nobility as the triumph of the *populares*: the struggle was less concerned with justice and equality than, as one historian has pointed out, 'the strife for power, wealth, and glory'.[3]

The secret of Augustus's success was, in part, his personal style of leadership. To avoid alienating the Romans by becoming an autocrat like Julius Caesar, he presented himself as a restorer of the social and political order following decades of civil war. Although his official title was *Imperator Caesar divi filius Augustus*, the term he chose to indicate his role was *princeps* (translatable as 'first citizen'). He kept intact, and treated with respect, venerable institutions such as the Senate and Rome's various magistracies. He was therefore able to maintain the façade of a republican government and endorse the fiction that he was merely first among equals. 'I excelled all in influence,' he claimed in a famous inscription, 'although I possessed no more official power than others who were my colleagues in the various magistracies.'

Augustus's political achievements in bringing stability to the Empire were mirrored by cultural achievements that made Augustan Rome one of history's greatest ages for art and architecture. A list he compiled of his numerous accomplishments, known as the *Res Gestae divi Augusti* (Achievements of the Divine

---

* The cognomen Agrippa appears to have come from the Latin *aegre partus* ('difficult birth'). Children born feet-first were known as *agrippae*.

Shown commanding his troops, Augustus wears a breastplate and is enfolded in the *paludamentum*, or 'cloth of command'. The inclusion of a tiny Cupid, Venus's son, indicates that Augustus, like Caesar, believed his family tree led back to the goddess.

Augustus), declared that he had found Rome a city of brick and left it one of marble. In fact, Rome during the Late Republic was hardly as dire a sight as his boast suggests. It did indeed have, in many districts, narrow and haphazard streets over which loomed slightly ramshackle buildings such as the jam-packed, high-rise *insulae* (whose height Augustus limited to 70 Roman feet, some 21 metres or five storeys). Nonetheless, the decades following the death of Sulla had witnessed the raising of impressive monuments, both public and private. Pompey built his magnificent theatre in 55 BCE, and by the time of Caesar's death the city featured a hundred palaces – the luxurious piles of wealthy senators, generals, men of business, civil servants and anyone else able to share in the seemingly boundless loot of the Empire. The most expensive residential neighbourhood was on the Palatine (from whose name we get the word 'palace'). Rome's wealthiest citizens, including Mark Antony and Augustus, owned homes there – though Augustus's home, characteristically, was modest rather than palatial.

Whatever Rome's grandeur before the start of his reign, Augustus did indeed adorn the city with wonderful new monuments, many built at his own expense using marble and granite taken from all corners of the Empire. He inaugurated a new forum, the Forum of Augustus, spectacularly presided over by a Temple of Mars Ultor (Mars the Avenger), which commemorated his vengeance against Caesar's assassins. He boasted that he built or restored more than eighty temples – all part of his plan to both beautify Rome and revive the veneration of the gods.

One of Augustus's finest buildings was the magnificent Theatre of Marcellus, constructed on the right bank of the Tiber and named in honour of his beloved nephew and intended heir, Marcus Claudius Marcellus, who died in 23 BCE at the age of nineteen. We can still admire the graceful crescent of pock-marked limestone arches, albeit stripped of the marble and stucco decorations and less than a third of the original building's imposing size. The theatre could seat 15,000 spectators. As a last resting-place for himself and other members of his family, Augustus built his Mausoleum, a circular structure almost 90 metres in diameter and 40 metres in height, no doubt inspired by ancient Etruscan tombs. It was clad in white marble, planted with evergreens and topped by his likeness in bronze. In a tribute to the craze for all things Egyptian following Rome's annexation of Egypt as province in 30 BCE, he brought two obelisks back from Heliopolis. He raised one, that of Ramesses II, in the Circus Maximus (it now soars some 20 metres above the Piazza del Popolo). The other was placed in the Campus Martius, where, according to one archaeologist, it functioned as a giant sundial, carefully positioned in such a way that on 23 September, Augustus's birthday, its shadow fell across the marble altar in the Ara Pacis – another peerless combination of impressive architectural design and unbridled self-promotion.[4]

The Theatre of Marcellus, inaugurated by Augustus in 12 BCE. It had a retractable roof, the *velario*, an awning that protected theatre-goers from the scorching Roman sun.

Augustus encouraged other wealthy Romans to follow his example in adorning the city with monuments. A magistrate named Gaius Cestius, likewise referencing the wonders of Egypt, obliged by building as his own last resting-place the marble-clad, 37-metre-high pyramid that can still be seen near the Piramide Metro station. But the most prolific enthusiast for beautifying Rome was Marcus Agrippa, whose naval command had been decisive at Actium. He built a new basilica to celebrate this victory (the Basilica of Neptune) and an immense voting hall that for many centuries possessed the widest span of any building in Rome. It featured beams of larch almost 30 metres long; one of them, surplus to requirements, was put on public display as a kind of tourist attraction.

Agrippa also founded Rome's first public bath, built a new bridge over the Tiber and raised a temple to all the gods known as the Pantheon (subsequently rebuilt in spectacular style more than a century later). One of his greatest achievements was restoring Rome's sewers and building two new aqueducts: the Aqua Julia, named for Augustus's daughter (and Agrippa's wife); and the Aqua Virgo, named for the young woman who, according to legend, first spotted the waters of the bubbling spring outside Rome. Together, these two new aqueducts provided the city with more than 150,000 cubic metres of water per day, enough to fill sixty Olympic-sized swimming pools. It was a vital resource for a population, during Augustus's reign, of more than a million people. A Greek visitor marvelled that 'almost every house has cisterns, and service-pipes, and copious fountains'.[5]

Indeed, Dionysius of Halicarnassus wrote that the three most magnificent works of Rome, 'in which the greatness of her empire is best seen', were the aqueducts, paved roads and sewers.[6] By the time of Augustus, builders and engineers had contributed as much as the Roman legions to the fame of the Empire. Augustus perceived the need for infrastructure spending in the Italian hinterlands – on roads, ports, bridges, walls and sewers – which had been devastated during decades of warfare. Italian unity and cohesion depended on the ease of travel and communication around the peninsula. Rome had long enjoyed an extensive road system, including Via Appia, the 'queen of roads', constructed in 312 BCE (largely to enable rapid troop movements during the wars against the Samnites) and running south from Rome to Brundisium. However, by the time of Augustus the roads, like so much else, were in dire need of repair. Augustus proudly took the title *curator viarum* (commissioner of roads), funding their repair and upkeep from his own coffers and encouraging his wealthy friends to follow suit – an ancient version of the American Adopt-a-Highway program.

Another important builder during Augustus's reign was his wife, Livia Drusilla (the granddaughter of Marcus Livius Drusus, the politician whose assassination kicked off the Social War). A forceful character, she became known as the *princeps femina*, or 'first lady', and even *genetrix orbis* ('mother of the world'). One of her grandsons, the future emperor Caligula, called her *Ulixem stolatum* – 'Ulysses in a dress'.[7] Enjoying great power, prestige and autonomy, she owned vast amounts of land, not only in Italy but also in Asia Minor, Gaul and Palestine. She used her abundant financial reserves for acts of philanthropy such as providing dowries for poor families and relief for victims of a fire in 16 CE. She contributed to Augustus's campaign of beautification by restoring various temples and constructing both a market (the Macellum Liviae, or 'Livia's Market') and the Portico of Livia, a spectacular covered walkway and garden through which Romans could stroll in their moments of leisure and recreation.[8]

Livia also owned an opulent villa at Prima Porta, 15 kilometres north of Rome. The Villa ad Gallinas Albas, or 'Villa of the White Hens', as it became known, was named for a famous omen that occurred around the time of her marriage to Octavian. According to ancient historians, while Livia was sitting outdoors an eagle dropped into her lap a hen of remarkable whiteness, carrying a sprig of laurel in its beak. The augurs advised preserving any chicks produced by the hen as well as planting the sprig of laurel in the ground. The brood of white chickens flourished and the laurel became an entire grove, from whose trees Augustus would carry a branch whenever he celebrated one of his numerous triumphs.

Livia Drusilla in the garb of a traditional Roman matron. Over her tunic she wears a *stola*, the sleeveless gown symbolic of married women. The *palla*, a rectangular cloak, is modestly draped over her shoulder and head.

The vast majority of the work on these construction projects was done – as was so much other labour – by slaves. By the time of Augustus, slaves accounted for perhaps as much as 35 per cent of the population of the Italian peninsula.[9] The last centuries of the Roman Republic saw wars of conquest resulting in the mass enslavement of Gauls, Celts, Carthaginians, Syrians, Thracians, Armenians and other 'barbarians'. To give one example, after they conquered Agrigentum (in Sicily) in 262 BCE, the Romans enslaved the entire population – some 25,000 people. Following the Social War, the Romans tended not to enslave their fellow Italians, although any Roman child abandoned by their parents (a lamentably common occurrence) could be used as a slave by whoever found him – or, more usually, her (for girls, we'll see, were more often discarded by their parents). Likewise, a large number of enslaved people were *vernae*, that is, children born to female slaves in the house (and often from the loins) of the master.

Slaves could be purchased from a market behind the Temple of Castor and Pollux in the Roman Forum as well as in a dedicated area of the Emporium, the river port. The slaves on display might wear labels proclaiming their place of origin and their name, usually an optimistic and reassuring one bestowed by the slave merchant: Celer (Speedy), Hilarus (Cheerful), Iucundus (Agreeable) or Suavis (Sweet).[10] Much poking, prodding and disrobing attended these sales. Seneca the Younger advised how, when buying a slave from the market, one should 'pull off the garments... so that no bodily flaws may escape your notice'. Crafty dealers countered these measures, making their slaves look healthier and more appealing by oiling their limbs with an ointment made from the resin of the terebinth tree.[11]

A copper tag that would have been riveted to the collar worn by an enslaved person, featuring the words: 'Hold me, lest I flee, and return me to my master Viventius on the estate of Callistus.'

A gaunt or sickly appearance was only to be expected: some of these unfortunates would have been captured by pirates (ever reliable suppliers) and sold to Roman dealers at the market on the Aegean island of Delos, where 10,000 slaves were traded each day.[12]

Slaves could be found in virtually every industry and sector of Roman society, both urban and rural. They were especially numerous on the *latifundia*, the large plantations, and in the many mines, where conditions were atrocious. A document detailing the jobs of slaves in the countryside listed thirty-five different occupations, including *aquarius* (water-carrier), *topiarius* (gardener), *scoparius* (sweeper) and *seppellecticarius* (furniture supervisor).[13] Many Roman households included a few slaves for cooking and laundry, and the wealthiest possessed dozens – if not hundreds. A list of the slaves owned by Livia encompassed fifty different occupations, from doctor, reader and secretary to clothes-folder, furniture-polisher, pearl-setter and *purpuris* – the slave in charge of her purple garments. Her tally fell far short of that of a rich landowner named Gaius Caecilius Isidorus, who, at his death in 8 BCE, owned more than 4,000 slaves.[14] Slaves could actually cost an employer more than waged labourers: if there was no work, a proprietor could simply dismiss a labourer, who then ceased to be his responsibility and needed to rely on the charity of the corn dole – hardly sufficient to raise a family. This precarious existence meant that freedmen sometimes sold themselves back into slavery.[15]

Slaves could be emancipated by their owners, often at the owner's death, when the newly manumitted slaves walked in the funeral procession as a visual testament to the generosity of the deceased. A few freed slaves went on to enjoy successful careers. The playwright Terence, for example, originally came to Rome in the 180s or 170s BCE as a slave from Carthage, serving a senator who, recognising his talent, soon set him free. Horace's father was a freed slave who became a tax collector affluent enough to send his son off to Rome (with a small team of slaves) 'to be taught those studies that any knight or senator would have his own offspring taught'.[16] Cicero manumitted the slave he called 'my dear Tiro', a man who served for many years as his scribe and secretary. 'Your services to me,' Cicero wrote to him, 'are beyond count – in my home and out of it, in Rome and abroad, in private affairs and public, in my studies and literary work.'[17]

Most slaves were not held in such high regard. Seneca the Younger wrote how the Romans treated their slaves 'as if they were beasts of burden'.[18] Other writers such as Juvenal, Petronius and Martial all make frequent references to masters and mistresses flogging their slaves, and we probably have little reason to doubt the accuracy of Petronius's description of a sign in a Roman house declaring: 'ANY SLAVE LEAVING THE HOUSE WITHOUT HIS MASTER'S PERMISSION WILL RECEIVE ONE HUNDRED LASHES.'[19] Moreover, both male and female slaves could be victims of the sexual demands of their masters (or mistresses). Seneca the Younger described one male slave who was forced to dress like a woman, pluck his body hair and submit to 'his master's drunkenness and his lust'.[20] The lives of many were beyond question hideous, especially those who worked in the mines and on the galleys, as chained workers on the *latifundia* or on large public works such as digging canals. Cities such as Pompeii featured graffiti that, rather like 'Wanted' posters, appealed for help in catching runaway slaves. A museum in Rome holds a sobering exhibit, a slave collar that consists of an iron neck-ring with a bronze label that reads: 'I have run away.

Hold on to me. When you have brought me back to my master Zoninus, you will receive a gold coin.'[21] So many slaves ran away that a special profession developed, that of the *fugitivarius*, or slave-catcher. The foreheads of the slaves they recaptured were branded or tattooed with 'FVG' (short for *fugitivus*). An even more unpleasant occupation to consider is that of the *manceps*, the public official whose job it was to torture slaves on behalf of their master, and, if necessary, to execute them.[22] Such sobering facts must remind us how the 'grandeur that was Rome' was (like many other societies, both ancient and more recent) created in part through human exploitation and suffering virtually unimaginable in scale.

*

From the *vernae*, the home-born slaves of Rome, we get the word 'vernacular', because presumably these second-generation slaves spoke a less refined version of Latin than the master and his better educated legitimate children. Good Latin was a matter of pride to many Romans, who would develop and then export not only their architecture and engineering but also their language, which would travel to, and take root in, distant countries and far-off centuries.

By the time of Augustus, Latin had superseded most other languages on the peninsula, including Oscan and Etruscan. Greek was another matter. Still read and spoken in southern Italy – in the former cities of Magna Graecia – it was the first language of many slaves and immigrants as well as a prestigious acquisition of the Roman intelligentsia. As a young man, Julius Caesar had gone to Rhodes, in a kind of gap-year immersion, to perfect his Greek. Augustus was probably one of the few high-ranking Romans not completely at ease in the language. According to Suetonius, he enjoyed Greek literature but never acquired fluency.

For centuries the Romans had believed their language to be inferior to that of the Greeks. Just as they had coveted Hellenistic art after seeing the plunder from the conquests of Greece and Sicily, so too they envied the Greek language as a vehicle for literary, oratorical and philosophical expression. Campaigns had been launched at least from the time of Cato the Censor – the opponent of the 'vile and unruly' Greeks – to put Latin on an equal intellectual and literary footing. Over the course of the first century BCE, Latin was polished and refined, becoming, in the hands of the best writers, a supple and elegant language. Today we know it as Classical Latin – one of the greatest creations of the human mind. Its foremost practitioner was the writer and statesman Cicero, an ally of Pompey the Great who, after a stellar career as an orator, lawyer and politician, was executed at the behest of Mark Antony in December 43 BCE. Cicero had wished to purify, perfect and promote Latin as a worthy vehicle for oratory, poetry and philosophy. The richness and elegance of his works, later adulated by writers of the Italian Renaissance and prominent in the curricula of English public schools, attest to his success.

Cicero asserted that Latin contributed more to the prestige of Rome than the legions storming fortresses. Augustus promoted beautiful Latin to enhance his own cultural stature and glorify his regime. He even tried his own hand at literature, composing poetry as well as a set of epigrams that, according to Suetonius, he wrote in the bath. Perhaps fortunately for his reputation, none has survived. It was as a patron rather than a poet that Augustus made his contribution to letters. He encouraged

Virgil to compose *The Aeneid*, which the poet read aloud to him and his sister Octavia (who fainted at the mention of her dead son Marcellus in Book 6).

Most of the credit for the lustre of Augustan literature must go, however, to Augustus's wealthy friend and trusted adviser Gaius Maecenas. He served as an unofficial minister of culture, ultimately giving his name, thanks to his generous support for Latin poets, to munificent patrons of the arts everywhere. Maecenas was a curious and conspicuous figure. Claiming to be descended from Etruscan royalty, he strolled about Rome attended by two eunuchs ('both of them more men than himself').[23] Unlike the abstemious and puritanical Augustus, who contented himself with common fare, including coarse bread and whitebait, Maecenas enjoyed tucking into such delicacies as roasted foal of donkey. He possessed impeccable literary tastes, patronising and promoting poets who became the finest of the age, including Virgil, Horace and Sextus Propertius. Horace (as we've seen, the son of a freed slave) had been working as a clerk before he gained the support of Maecenas, who invited him to literary dinners, gave him an estate with farms outside Rome, and (as the poet himself wrote) 'made me rich'.[24] Maecenas saved Virgil from a spot of bother when the poet's lands were confiscated and (in an example of how land reform worked) given to a war veteran – a situation that Virgil bitterly deplores in the *Georgics* ('Is a godless soldier to hold these well-tilled fallows? a barbarian these crops?').[25] The result of Maecenas's munificence was that Horace and Virgil, along with many others, had the leisure time to write the works that would give Rome a language and literature fit for its magnificent empire. Maecenas's death in 8 BCE was deeply mourned by Rome's poets.

# The Julio - Claudians

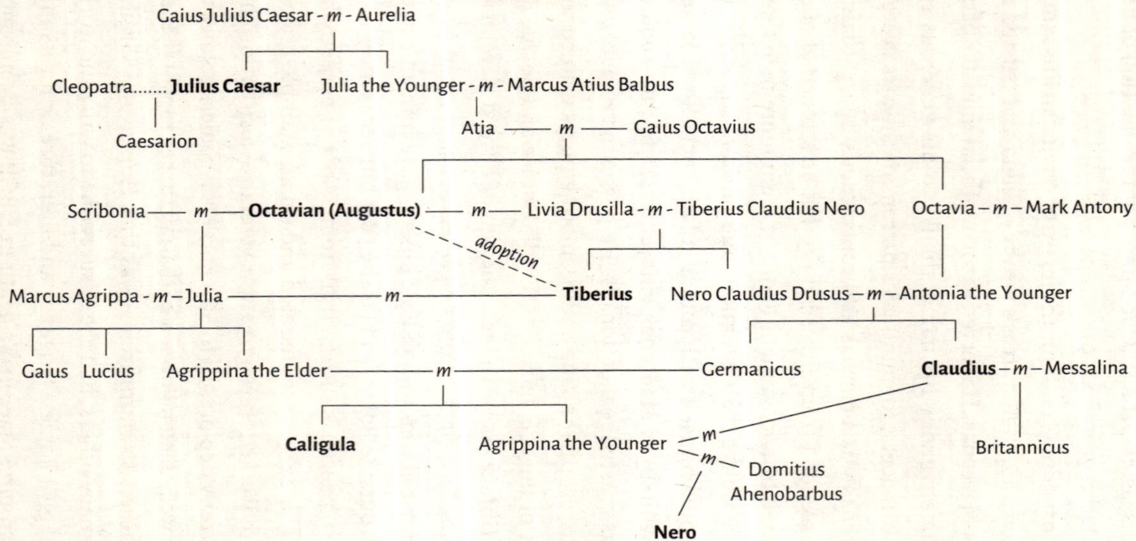

*

Despite his three marriages, Augustus failed to produce a son and heir. The search for a successor therefore led to a series of tangled and often unhappy alliances within the Roman imperial family. At its heart lay a dynamic between Augustus, his daughter Julia and his stepson Tiberius, the son of Augustus's third wife, Livia Drusilla – another prominent player in the drama.

Julia's dizzying marital journey epitomised the complexities of unions within the imperial family. She was born to Augustus's second wife, Scribonia, in 39 BCE, on the same day that Augustus divorced Scribonia to marry Livia. The historian Cornelius Tacitus, writing more than a century later, referred to Augustus's marriage to Livia as an 'abduction' – because Augustus compelled her to divorce her husband, Tiberius Claudius Nero, the father of her son, the future emperor Tiberius (b. 42 BCE). Tacitus therefore linked the founding of Augustus's reign with what has been called the 'Lucretia story' – the rape or abduction of a woman (such as Lucretia or Verginia) as the catalyst for political change.[26]

Although Tiberius Claudius Nero was elbowed aside by Augustus, his name – and that of his ancient and distinguished family, the Claudii – would endure because the four emperors who succeeded Augustus became known as the 'Julio-Claudians', a reference to the blending of the Julii and Claudii lineages. The fate of the Roman Empire would ultimately hinge on a turbulent family drama, depending on a series of toxic and often incestuous personal relationships: of marriages between cousins, and between uncles and nieces; of divorces, rivalries, adoptions, exiles, poisonings and executions; of uncles killing their nephews, nephews their uncles, husbands their wives,

wives their husbands, and sons their mothers. These gruesome feats have led historians and medical professionals to diagnose neurological disorders in the various family members, including epilepsy, dystonia, dementia, depression, encephalitis and neurosyphilis. Given the many consanguineous marriages, some of these conditions may well have had a genetic component.

Julia's first marriage had been to her cousin Marcellus, the son of Augustus's sister Octavia. Augustus's plans for succession had rested on Marcellus until his untimely (and possibly suspicious) death at the age of nineteen in 23 BCE. Julia was then married off to her father's trusted friend, the great general Marcus Agrippa. This marriage (which required Agrippa to divorce his wife, Marcella) produced a pair of grandsons for Augustus: Gaius (b. 20 BCE) and Lucius (b. 17 BCE), the latest candidates in his dynastic designs.

Following Agrippa's death in 12 BCE, Julia was coerced by her father into marrying Tiberius. This union was far from blissful. Not only had Tiberius been obliged to divorce his beloved wife Vipsania, the daughter of Agrippa, but Julia soon became notorious for multiple adulteries, including an affair with one of Mark Antony's sons (who was married to Julia's cousin Marcella – the wife earlier dumped by Agrippa). So freely did Julia share her charms that her father was pleasantly surprised when her children looked like Agrippa.

Julia's conduct proved distinctly awkward for Augustus. He himself certainly conducted affairs, though these were motivated not so much by lust as by the desire to learn, through pillow talk, the secrets of his colleagues. He maintained conservative political and moral values, including the old Roman attitude of duty and respect towards parents, the gods and the fatherland. Despite his own philandering and lack of children (his only child with Livia was stillborn), in 18 BCE he had enacted a law aimed at boosting the birth rate and stabilising family life while penalising promiscuity and adultery. Adulterers could be deprived of their property, deported and even, in some cases, killed. Augustus's target was the selfish, profligate and licentious nobles whose behaviour, he believed, had led to the destruction of the Republic. But old habits die hard, and there was such resistance to these reforms that Augustus felt the need to wear armour beneath his toga to foil would-be assassins.

So furious was Augustus with Julia's scandalous behaviour that, according to Suetonius, he toyed with the idea of putting her to death. Instead, in 2 BCE he took the less drastic action of banishing her from Rome to Ventotene, a volcanic island some 80 kilometres from Naples where – in a cruel blow to her party-girl lifestyle – she was allowed neither wine nor male company. By that time, Tiberius had retreated to voluntary exile on Rhodes, in part because of disgust at Julia but also to leave the way clear for one of her children with Agrippa, either Gaius or Lucius, to succeed Augustus. Fate had other plans in store, as both young men died prematurely: Gaius at the age of twenty-three from wounds suffered while suppressing a revolt in Armenia, Lucius at nineteen from an illness while on his way to Spain. The historian Tacitus saw at work (probably unfairly) the hand of their stepmother, Livia, who he claimed had them eliminated to ensure the succession of her son Tiberius.

Whatever the case, Tiberius was last man standing among the potential heirs. After returning to Rome, he was grudgingly adopted by Augustus, in 4 CE, as his son and heir. Relations between stepfather and stepson had never been close or affectionate, and over the next few years there were rumours that Augustus had begun mulling over other candidates, speaking openly about the respective qualities of various allies and distant relations. This canvassing abruptly ceased following a series of alarming omens in 14 CE: a thunderbolt struck Augustus's statue on the Capitoline Hill, blood-red comets streaked across the sky, and an owl hooted on the roof of the Senate. Sure enough, Augustus died shortly afterwards at what had been his father's house in Nola, near Pompeii, at the age of seventy-six. Suspicions over his death fell on Livia, who, eager for Tiberius to succeed, supposedly served her husband a dish of poisoned figs.

As with the deaths of Marcellus, Gaius and Lucius, this case against Livia stands on uncertain foundations. Tacitus regarded her as a treacherous intriguer and multiple murderer: 'a curse to the realm'.[27] However, her true crime, in the eyes of historians such as Tacitus and Cassius Dio, was not serving poisoned figs so much as filling a prominent public role and wielding considerable power – something unheard-of in a woman. 'She occupied a very exalted station,' Cassius Dio reported disapprovingly, 'far above all women of former days.' He claimed she received senators in her house and 'possessed the greatest influence'. Following the death of Augustus, she 'undertook to manage everything as if she were sole ruler', attempting to take precedence over Tiberius, the credit for whose succession she was happy to claim.[28]

Whatever Livia's role, if any, in the deaths of Augustus and his heirs, there can be no doubting either her dedication to securing her son's position or her acumen and dexterity in navigating the political landscape to achieve it. Aware that a smooth transition was essential to avoiding the chaos and violence of the civil wars of the previous century, the Senate quickly granted Tiberius all the powers formerly held by Augustus. The Empire, for the first time in four decades, had a new ruler.

# 5

# THE 'BAD EMPERORS': TIBERIUS, CALIGULA, CLAUDIUS

TIBERIUS WAS FIFTY-FIVE YEARS OLD: tall, slim, blue-eyed, short-sighted and bald, with an inscrutable, pockmarked face and solitary habits. Taking power after Augustus's successful forty-year reign must have been an immensely daunting task, for which Tiberius displayed little appetite – or, indeed, ability. One senator voiced the opinion that Augustus, knowing Tiberius's many deficiencies and vices, selected him as heir 'to heighten his own glory by the vilest of contrasts'.[1] If so, he was to get his wish.

Tiberius's misgivings about the job would have been confirmed when the will of Augustus was read aloud in the Senate: the preamble asserted that Tiberius was his heir only because 'a cruel fate has bereft me of my sons Gaius and Lucius'.[2] Tiberius called the role of *princeps* 'a wretched and burdensome slavery', agreeing to serve as ruler only until, as he told the Senate, 'it may seem right to you to grant an old man some repose'.[3] His reign set a pattern to be followed with dismaying regularity by many ensuing emperors: an encouraging start followed by a rapid and disastrous decline.

The first dozen years did go remarkably well. Tiberius preserved the dignity of the Senate and the consuls, awarded promotions based on merit, enforced the laws, respected property rights and declined to impose new taxes either at home or in the provinces. When in 17 CE a devastating earthquake struck the cities of Smyrna, Magnesia and Philadelphia (in western Turkey), he exempted them from taxes and sent massive amounts of aid. Such was his modesty that he refused to allow the month of September to be renamed in his honour. He also lived a humble lifestyle, becoming known for such frugal measures as serving leftovers at formal banquets (no doubt disappointing the incredulous invitees).

Things began to go wrong with the deaths of his two possible successors. First to go, in 19 CE, was Tiberius's 34-year-old nephew Germanicus, a handsome, brilliant and extravagantly popular general whose appearances in Rome brought adulating mobs into the streets. According to Suetonius, Germanicus 'possessed all the highest qualities of body and mind, to a degree never equalled by anyone'. He was both a scholar and a valiant soldier, a man gifted with 'unexampled kindliness and a remarkable desire and capacity for winning men's regard and inspiring their affection'.[4] Comparisons with Alexander the Great were bandied about. Such a paragon could hardly be tolerated by Tiberius, who dispatched him on a mission to Syria, where he died under circumstances as mysterious as they were suspicious. A forensic examination of Germanicus's chamber in Antioch revealed 'implements of witchcraft': spells, curses, charred human remains and lead tablets inscribed with Germanicus's name. Rather than hocus-pocus, however, Tacitus reported that Germanicus believed the 'cruel virulence' of his illness was the result of poison administered on orders of Gnaeus Calpurnius

Piso, the governor of Syria, who was acting, in turn, on orders from Tiberius.[5]

The way was then clear for Tiberius's son Drusus (his son by his beloved Vipsania) to succeed his father. But Drusus died suddenly at the age of thirty-six – poisoned by his wife (and first cousin) Livilla, Germanicus's sister. The plot had been hatched by Tiberius's friend and adviser Aelius Sejanus, a cunning and unscrupulous nobleman who hoped to claim the imperial crown for himself. Sejanus seduced Livilla, tickling her fancy with a 'dream of marriage, a partnership in the empire, and the murder of her husband'.[6] A eunuch administered a slow-acting poison that caused Drusus to fall ill and, in September 23 CE, die. At this point the grief-stricken Tiberius knew nothing of Sejanus's nefarious plans. He suspected nothing even when Sejanus encouraged him to retire from the drudgery of Rome to the island of Capreae (Capri). Here, in his complex of luxurious villas, accompanied by a dissolute entourage, the ageing emperor neglected state business and gave himself over to what Tacitus called *malum otium* – 'evil leisure'.[7] Rumour had it that he indulged such delights as watching the inventive copulations of a troop of sexual acrobats. One villa helpfully featured a library of erotic papyri in case any of the performers required visual guidelines.

Meanwhile, the deaths of potential heirs and rivals continued as, egged on by Sejanus, Tiberius vigorously pruned the family tree. He banished one nephew, Germanicus's eldest son, to the island of Pontia, where, in 31 CE, he was put to death. Another nephew, Germanicus's second son, Drusus, he starved to death in prison. Their mother, Agrippina, was banished to Ventotene, scene of her mother Julia's exile; she, too, was starved to death. When Sejanus's machinations finally came to light,

Tiberius had him strangled and then embarked on a further spree of murderous reprisals. 'It is a long story to run through his acts of cruelty in detail,' sighed Suetonius, noting that 'there was no one whom Tiberius spared from torment and death', and that he took pleasure in devising 'long and exquisite tortures' for his victims.[8] It must have seemed as if the dark days of Sulla's rule had returned.

This reign of terror finally came to an end in 37 CE, when Tiberius fell ill. He felt no need to consult physicians because his personal fortune-teller assured him he would live another ten years. He didn't even take fright at such events as the Tiber flooding, a fire raging on the Aventine, or a phoenix appearing in the Egypt desert – all taken by others as undeniable portents of his death. It turned out that the omens were right. He was suffocated under a load of blankets placed on his bed – on the pretence of keeping him warm – by the sole surviving son of Germanicus, a 24-year-old whom Tiberius had taken with him, virtually as a prisoner, to Capreae. This young man bore the name Gaius Caesar Augustus Germanicus. However, because of the hobnailed sandals (*caligae*) he had worn as a toddler when accompanying his father on military campaigns, he came to be known as Caligula ('Little Boots').

*

Caligula proved a popular choice as emperor, both in Rome and in the provinces. He was not only the son of Germanicus but also the grandson, on his mother's side, of Marcus Agrippa, and the great-grandson of both Augustus and Mark Antony. Although without meaningful military experience, he was popular with the Roman troops: many fondly remembered the pint-sized, uniformed child who, from the age of two, had served as a mascot on his father's campaigns against the Germans.

Caligula was adored by the people of Rome, too, in part because of their love for Germanicus but also out of sympathy for the terrible persecutions suffered by his family: Tiberius had murdered Caligula's mother, his father, his two brothers and his aunt, Livilla. As he made his way north from Capreae to Rome, escorting the corpse of the dead emperor, he was accompanied by a 'dense and joyful throng' who hailed him affectionately as their 'star' (*sidus*) and their 'chick' (*pullum*).[9] In March 37 he was quickly proclaimed the new *princeps* (the title that Tiberius, following Augustus, had also used). Such was the joy at his accession that in the space of a few weeks 160,000 birds and animals were sacrificed in thanks to the gods for granting them such a fine leader.

Caligula in his military finery, including a breastplate with the scowling face of Medusa and the *corona civica*, a crown of oak leaves bound with a ribbon that trails onto his shoulders.

Caligula quickly began repaying the love of the people and the faith of the Senate. He showed great deference to the senators, pledging to share power with them. He allowed them to sit on cushions rather than, as before, on bare benches, and to wear broad-brimmed straw hats in the hot weather. He lowered taxes on sales at auction, allowed the circulation of books banned by Tiberius, recalled those whom Tiberius had exiled, and banished the sexual contortionists whose antics had catered to the old emperor's depraved fancies. (He was narrowly dissuaded from throwing them into the sea.) Whereas Tiberius gave no public shows at all, Caligula staged plays and gladiatorial combats as well as chariot races in the intermissions – for which he introduced such exciting new attractions as panther-baiting. He added an extra day to the Saturnalia, the popular festival during which gifts were exchanged and days on end were spent eating and drinking. He renamed the month of September as Germanicus, in honour of his beloved father. He completed large public works, such as rebuilding the port at Rhegium, refurbishing the Theatre of Pompey (badly damaged in a recent fire) and bringing a 25-metre-high obelisk (the one now pointing heavenward in St Peter's Square) from Egypt. Construction also started on a new aqueduct and another amphitheatre.

Some of Caligula's antics, however, caused some concern. Dressing in women's clothes, donning the armour and weapons of a gladiator, carrying around a thunderbolt or trident as a prop, or insisting that he held conversations with the moon: such caprices may have seemed harmless or amusing eccentricities. So too, perhaps, his habit of urgently convening the Senate in the middle of the night only to – once the great men had assembled, expecting to discuss weighty matters – treat them to a performance of his latest dance moves. But other behaviour was more disquieting, such as removing from office two consuls who forgot to send him birthday wishes, or forcing his grandmother (the daughter of Mark Antony and Octavia) to commit suicide 'because she had rebuked him for something'.[10]

These were the first indications that the new *princeps* was – if we accept the lurid testimony of the sources – severely and hopelessly deranged. Most of what we know of Caligula's life and reign comes from six ancient writers: Seneca the Younger and Philo of Alexandria, both of whom knew him personally; Tacitus and Josephus, who knew people who had known Caligula; and finally, Suetonius and Cassius Dio, whose works were not written until, respectively, some eighty and 190 years following Caligula's reign. Almost all the material on Caligula from the best historian on the Julio-Claudian period, Tacitus, has been lost, and it's unclear if the sources available to Suetonius and Cassius were entirely reliable. At the start of his *Annals*, which appeared in 116 CE, Tacitus observed (quite accurately) that the histories of emperors like Tiberius and Caligula were 'falsified through cowardice while they flourished, and composed, when they fell, under the influence of still rankling hatreds'.[11] We do not have, in other words, unbiased accounts of their lives and reigns. We must therefore be wary of accepting much of the evidence – especially the more shocking and sensationalised stories – at face value. This same problem, we shall see, likewise complicates our understanding of many later emperors.

Caligula certainly seemed to give plenty of cause for hatred to rankle. It's unclear what exactly might have led to his monstrous exploits. Medical sleuths have diagnosed him with everything from alcoholism and a thyroid disorder to encephalitis, temporal lobe epilepsy, lead poisoning, schizophrenia and neurosyphilis.[12] Suetonius reported that he was driven mad by an aphrodisiac administered by his wife (though his libido, if we trust the sources, was scarcely in need of encouragement). Yet it's difficult to imagine how any of these agents or ailments could have been responsible for his gratuitous and sadistic violence – for what Cassius Dio called his 'insatiable desire for the sight of blood'.[13] He seems to have earnestly believed what he once told his grandmother: 'Remember that I have the right to do anything to anybody.' And so he did: no one, it appears, was safe from his psychopathic whims. 'Off comes this beautiful head whenever I give the word,' he would tenderly whisper to his wives and mistresses.[14] When the two consuls sitting beside him at a sumptuous feast asked why he was chuckling, he explained the cause of his mirth was that at a single nod he could have their throats slit.

At least his wives and the consuls were spared. Hundreds or even thousands of others were not. Cassius Dio recorded the disturbing story that when there was a shortage of condemned criminals to be fed to the lions, Caligula ordered a random group of spectators – 'some of the mob standing near the benches' – to be seized and thrown to them. 'To prevent the possibility of their making an outcry or any reproaches,' Cassius claimed, 'he first caused their tongues to be cut out.'[15] Other of his bloody acts were aimed at eliminating rivals, such as his eighteen-year-old cousin Tiberius Gemellus, the son of Drusus and Livilla: he was forced to commit suicide. Another victim was a distinguished visiting guest, important ally and distant relative, King Ptolemy of Mauretania. Legend had it that King Ptolemy was murdered because Caligula grew jealous of the ardent admiration sparked by his magnificent purple robe. More probably, Caligula disposed of him because Ptolemy, as the grandson of Cleopatra and

Mark Antony, represented a threat to his power.

Caligula's murders had an economic as well as a political motive. In the first two years of his reign, his wild extravagances virtually exhausted the treasury. Desperately in need of funds, he took to confiscating the assets of his victims, who were denounced on trumped-up charges and then executed merely so he could get his hands on their money. 'No one who possessed anything', reported Cassius Dio, 'got off unscathed.'[16]

Pompey the Great and Julius Caesar had raised vast sums through their wars of conquest, and so Caligula, hoping to emulate their example, embarked on several military expeditions. He first went to Gaul, but his invasion force of actors, gladiators and women, all equipped with the 'trappings of luxury', failed to inflict any damage.[17] He soon returned to Rome. A campaign in Britain fared no better: he reached the English Channel but instead of crossing the waves, like Julius Caesar, and engaging the inhabitants, he perched on a lofty platform on a French beach and, after much tooting of trumpets and other warlike preparations, simply ordered the soldiers to gather seashells. The bizarre episode no doubt puzzled his soldiers as much as it does modern historians.

Caligula is probably most famous today for his plan to make his horse Incitatus ('Speedy') a consul. Although he never took office, Incitatus did enjoy a marble stall decked out with an ivory manger and purple blankets, and his meals of gilded barley arrived at the table in a golden cup. A team of slaves catered to his every need, and besides his stable he had at his service a well-furnished house to which guests were invited in his name for elegant entertainments – surely one of history's stranger dinner invitations.

Caligula has become equally infamous for his sexual

appetites (relishingly depicted in the 1979 erotic drama *Caligula*). Both Suetonius and Cassius Dio claimed Caligula committed incest with his three sisters, though it's probably worth questioning the veracity of these accusations – and, in any case, he soon sent two of them into exile. He was, however, obsessed with his sister Julia Drusilla, four years his junior. Following her death in 38 CE at the age of twenty-one, he had the Senate declare her a goddess, Diva Drusilla. He announced an official period of mourning, when it was a capital offence to laugh or take a bath.

Caligula took male lovers, including his brother-in-law Marcus Aemilius Lepidus. He married four times, and each of his first three marriages lasted a year or less. One of his wives he carted off as her nuptials to another man were being celebrated (yet another Roman abduction). The union lasted two months. Relations with another of his brides no doubt turned awkward after he slit her father's throat. He was passionately devoted to his fourth wife, Caesonia, 'a woman of reckless extravagance and wantonness' whom he proudly displayed in the nude to his friends.[18] He was tempted to torture her, he claimed, to discover the secret of why he found her so appealing. When she gave birth to a child, Julia Drusilla – named for his beloved sister – Caligula took as proof of her paternity the girl's habit of trying to scratch out the eyes of her little playmates.

Of greatest concern to the wiser heads in the Senate was Caligula's rapid lurch towards absolute monarchy. He even began to think of himself as a god. Julius Caesar and Augustus had both been deified after their deaths, but Caligula wished to be worshipped in his own lifetime. He began encouraging people to hail him as Jupiter. He sent to Athens for famous statues of Greek gods, then replaced their heads with marble replicas of his own. He built a temple to himself, complete with a team of priests and a life-sized statue of himself in gold. This resplendent mannequin was carefully dressed each day in clothes matching those donned by Caligula – which must have made for arresting sights on the days when he masqueraded as Diana or Venus.

Such lunacy guaranteed a brief tenure, and Caligula's end came soon enough. After a soothsayer told him to beware someone named Cassius, he took the precaution of having an official named Cassius Longinus murdered – forgetting there was another Cassius more intimately in his midst: Cassius Chaerea, a member of the Praetorian Guard, the elite troops who protected the emperor and his family. Ever cruel and mocking, Caligula had alienated Chaerea by taunting him for his effeminacy and love of luxury (an odd line of attack from someone who dressed in women's clothes and drank pearls dissolved in vinegar). Chaerea struck in a corridor in his palace in Rome, coming at Caligula from behind and splitting his jawbone with his sword. Other members of the Praetorian Guard who had joined the conspiracy quickly fell on Caligula, dispatching him with thirty wounds, 'and some even tasted of his flesh'. His wife, Caesonia, was then killed too, along with little Julia Drusilla, whose head was dashed against a wall. So ended, after three years, ten months and eight days, the reign of Gaius Caligula, who, as Cassius Dio gleefully put it, 'learned by actual experience that he was not a god'.[19]

*

Upon Caligula's death, the senators hastily convened on the Capitol to debate the merits of restoring the Republic or appointing one of their own as the new ruler. Their bickering and dithering were soon overtaken by events. Soldiers who entered the imperial palace looking for easy plunder discovered, cowering behind a curtain, a member of the imperial family, convinced he was to be their next victim. Tiberius Claudius Nero Germanicus – Claudius for short – was the fifty-year-old nephew of Tiberius, the younger brother of Germanicus and the uncle of Caligula. The Praetorian Guard immediately entrusted supreme power to him, according to Cassius Dio, 'inasmuch as he was of the imperial family and was regarded as suitable'.[20] They were further swayed by Claudius's offer of 3,750 denarii per man: the equivalent of more than five years' salary. Claudius therefore became, as Suetonius grimly noted, 'the first of the Caesars who resorted to bribery to secure the fidelity of the troops'.[21] It was a precedent that would come back to haunt his successors.

The Praetorian Guard may have regarded Claudius as suitable, but few others can have done. No one in the imperial family had ever contemplated Claudius – widely regarded as an imbecile – ascending to the throne. Augustus had considered him an embarrassment, deficient in both body and mind. His grandmother, Livia, treated him with scorn and brutal discipline. His mother, Antonia, called him 'a monster of a man, not finished but merely begun'.[22] For a tutor he was given a former muleteer who treated him much as he had his mules. Dominated and cuckolded by his various wives, he served as the butt of Caligula's humiliating jokes and as a victim of pranks at state banquets where, a glutton and drunkard, he invariably fell asleep at the table. One favourite trick was to stick a feather down his throat (his mouth would be gaping open as he snored) to make him vomit. Later, Claudius claimed that to stop Caligula from killing him he had feigned imbecility (or what Cassius Dio tartly called 'a stupidity greater than was really the case').[23] If so, he played his part remarkably well, at one point advocating for an edict to allow the privilege of farting ('quietly or noisily') at banquets.[24] Another of his hobbyhorses was introducing three new letters into the Latin alphabet, one of which was an upside-down F.

A 'monster of a man': the clumsy and infirm Claudius was the butt of jokes, but his feeble body belied an inquiring if eccentric mind.

In fairness to Claudius, he was feeble of body but not of mind. He had a speech impediment and a tremor, and he walked with difficulty, dragging his right foot behind him. However, he had an acute and curious (if eccentric) mind. He spent his time out of the spotlight not only drinking, eating and gambling but also reading and writing. A devoted student of history, he composed a book on Rome during the civil wars and a bulky treatise on the reign of Augustus. He also wrote, in Greek, histories of both the Carthaginians and the Etruscans. He was one of the few people left in the first century CE who could read Etruscan.

For such an unprepossessing candidate, Claudius certainly began well. One of his first acts was to destroy the huge cache of poisons found in Caligula's palace. He also dismantled the oppressive taxation policies imposed by his predecessor to fund his lavish lifestyle, restored confiscated properties and showed clemency by releasing political prisoners and granting amnesty to exiles. He built a harbour at the mouth of the Tiber to safeguard the import of grain, and completed the construction of various of Caligula's infrastructure projects. Prominent among them was the aqueduct known as the Aqua Claudia, which brought 190,000 cubic metres of water into Rome each day – enough to fill seventy-five Olympic-sized swimming pools.

One of Claudius's greatest legacies was a new Roman province. In 43 CE his armies crossed the English Channel and conquered the Catuvellauni in southeast England, thereby adding to the Roman Empire the province of Britannia, which (as Cassius Dio remarked) lay 'outside the limits of the known world'.[25] Claudius even made the voyage to join his legions in Britain, crossing the Thames with his troops. The longstanding myth (based on a short passage in Cassius Dio) that Claudius took a battalion of war elephants with him to subdue the fractious locals, and even rode one of the beasts in triumph through the streets, was unfortunately just that – a myth.[26]

Another legacy was Claudius's enlightened policy regarding eligibility for public office. Recognising the historical significance of Rome's assimilation of diverse ethnic groups – the contribution of Sabines, Etruscans and Samnites – he embarked on a bold initiative to broaden representation in the Senate. This process had begun tentatively under Julius Caesar and then Augustus, both of whom admitted into the Senate men from up and down the peninsula. Much resistance came from the old Roman families, who dreaded the thought of the Senate and important public offices filling up with people whose blood was not (as they claimed in a debate in the Senate) 'akin to their own'. However, Claudius argued passionately for senators who could represent the entire peninsula, including men from the Gallic tribes. In response to those who wanted to block senatorial privileges to people whose ancestors had fought against the Romans, he gave a stirring speech pointing out that many Greek cities, including Athens, had declined precisely because they refused to grant citizenship to the people they conquered. 'But the sagacity of our own founder Romulus was such', he argued, 'that several times he fought and naturalised a people in the course of the same day.' He won the debate, and the doors of the Senate swung open to Gauls and other men whom Claudius called 'the stoutest of the provincials'.[27]

Much of the responsibility for Claudius's downfall was pinned by Suetonius and Tacitus on the scandalous deeds and murderous schemes involving the final two of his four wives. He had a patchy marital record to say the least, having divorced his first wife, a woman named Plautia Urgulanilla, for 'scandalous lewdness and the suspicion of murder'.[28] Wives three and four were, if anything, even worse. In keeping with the heedless endogamy of the Julio-Claudians, each was closely related to him. When Claudius became emperor he was married to his third wife, his cousin Messalina ('the most abandoned and lustful of women', or so claimed Cassius Dio).[29] Her two grandmothers were half-sisters, while her grandmother and Claudius's grandmother were sisters, the daughters of Octavia and Mark Antony.

The union between Claudius and Messalina was anything but joyous. If the ancient historians and the satirist Juvenal can be believed, Messalina's behaviour – her exploration of what Tacitus called 'untried debaucheries'[30] – was stupefying even by the standards of first-century Rome. In his *Satires*, Juvenal offered a picture of the 'whore-empress' donning a blonde wig and, once Claudius lapsed into a drunken sleep, slipping out of the palace and making her way to a brothel. She then offered herself 'naked and for sale, with her nipples gilded, under the trade name of "She-Wolf"'.[31] This portrait is highly dubious, catering to the propaganda of the day as well as to the misogyny and salacious appetites of posterity. Even so, Messalina certainly seems to have been a zealous lover and, in fact, a bigamist. In 48, with Claudius away from Rome, she celebrated an expensive and licentious marriage ceremony with one of her paramours, an ambitious politician named Gaius Silius on whom she lavished a sumptuous villa filled with Claudius's most precious heirlooms. Getting wind of these events, Claudius hurried back to Rome and put the pair to death.

Claudius's eldest son, Drusus (from Plautia Urgulanilla), had died prematurely a few years earlier after throwing a pear into the air, catching it in his mouth and then choking to death on it (a clumsy antic that suggests poor Drusus was cut from the same cloth as his father). But Claudius also had another son, Claudius Tiberius Germanicus, born to Messalina in 41 CE and proudly nicknamed Britannicus after Rome's new province. With this young heir in place, Claudius vowed not to remarry, even asking the Praetorian Guard to strike him dead should he ever contemplate such an act. However, he reconsidered his plans after falling under the spell of his niece, Agrippina, the daughter of his brother Germanicus and the younger sister of Caligula. She was beautiful, ambitious and (in the account of Cassius Dio) rather more affectionate and solicitous in her conduct than strictly became a niece. Although Claudius claimed this union was conducive to the public interest, Suetonius and Cassius Dio depicted him as a foolish older man in thrall to a mercilessly scheming younger woman who quickly gained complete control over him.

Agrippina's elegant curls could have been produced with the *calamistrum*, a hollow metal rod heated in hot coals or wood ashes.

Agrippina had formerly been married to a prominent Roman aristocrat, a grandson of Mark Antony and nephew of Augustus named Gnaeus Domitius Ahenobarbus, known for his ruthless nature. The pair had a child, Lucius Domitius Ahenobarbus, born in 37 CE. Following his marriage to Agrippina, Claudius adopted the boy – who then changed his name to Nero – and married him to Octavia, his daughter from Messalina. Nero was three years older than Britannicus and therefore took precedence over him. Even so, Agrippina was taking no chances with the succession and, in October 54, arranged for the gluttonous Claudius to be served one of his favourite treats, a bowl of mushrooms. ('Tell me,' Claudius once asked, 'who can live without a snack?')[32] Despite a recent series of worrying omens – a comet, a shower of blood, a swarm of bees in the camp of the Praetorians – Claudius cheerily tucked in. However, the mushrooms had been poisoned by an expert in such matters, a woman named Locusta, and presented to him, treacherously, by his food-taster, a eunuch named Halotus. According to one report, he vomited the mushrooms but was quickly served a gruel to settle his stomach. It too had been poisoned, and he died soon afterwards. Nero wittily retorted that, given how Claudius was deified following his death, mushrooms were the food of the gods. Seneca the Younger wrote a play mocking the late emperor's deification, which he called an *Apocolocyntosis*, or 'Pumpkinification'. Even in death, Claudius got little respect.

# 6

# 'LET THE EARTH BE CONSUMED BY FIRE': THE AGE OF NERO

CERTAIN OMENS HAD SUGGESTED A GREAT – if troubled – future for Nero. When he was a child a soothsayer offered two predictions: first, that he would become emperor, and second, that he would murder his mother. 'Let him kill me,' retorted Agrippina, 'only let him rule.' She would come to regret this sharp-elbowed ambition. Nero's father made his own dire forecast: 'It is impossible for any good man to be sprung from me and this woman.'[1]

It was a rare moment of self-knowledge for a man – the aforementioned Gnaeus Domitius Ahenobarbus – who otherwise proved himself a vicious and intemperate brute. Once, in a drunken rage, he killed one of his servants; the act appalled even his boon companion, Caligula. Another time, driving his chariot through a village outside Rome, he purposely ran over and killed a child playing in the street. In the Roman Forum, he gouged out the eyes of a man who chastised him. He was accused of treason against Tiberius and of incest with his sister, Lepida. He escaped retribution for the first charge when Tiberius died, and for the second when, at the age of thirty-eight, he dropped dead.

Nero was only three years old at the time of his father's death in 41 CE. His first years were troubled: Caligula exiled Agrippina and confiscated Nero's inheritance, so he was raised in the house of his paternal aunt, Lepida, with a dancer and a barber serving as his tutors. Earlier, during Claudius's reign, he narrowly escaped death when Messalina sent stranglers to throttle him in his bedroom during his afternoon nap. The would-be assassins were frightened off by a snake that, according to legend, darted out from under his pillow. A grateful Agrippina fashioned the snake's sloughed-off skin, later found in the corner of the room, into a bracelet for her son.

The name Nero, coming from an Oscan word, meant 'strong and valiant'. But Nero did not share the heroic military aspirations or background of so many of his strong and valiant forebears. Blue-eyed, with freckles and curly blond hair, he had a passion for art – painting, singing, playing musical instruments – rather than warfare. Agrippina appointed as his tutor, when he was about twelve, the philosopher Lucius Annaeus Seneca, known as Seneca the Younger, who schooled him in rhetoric, philosophy and literature, aiming to inculcate in him the Stoic principles of wisdom, justice and self-control. Despite his youth and inexperience, Nero, like so many of his ill-fated predecessors, made a decent start to his reign – so impressive, apparently, that a later emperor, Trajan, claimed Nero's first five years in power had been more successful than those of any other emperor.

Nero secured his position, like Claudius, by paying 3,750 denarii each to the men in the Praetorian Guard, and then at first left much of the government in the hands of Seneca, whose writings included *On Clemency* and *On the Tranquillity of the Mind*. Nero made the usual friendly overtures to the Senate while issuing coins featuring an oak tree, the symbol of liberty. He ate and drank in modest quantities. Hopes in Rome rose high. The poet Calpurnius Siculus fawned over this young god 'sent from heaven itself' to usher in a new Golden Age.[2]

However, Nero's artistic passions and ambitions soon began to sour with elite Romans. For Nero was attempting a kind of cultural revolution. As a lover of art, music and Greek athletics, he wished to wean Romans from their bloody and violent pastimes by offering more enlightened and sophisticated amusements. Although he built a new circus in Rome and sponsored gladiatorial battles, he also provided Romans with gymnasiums, public baths and a large wooden amphitheatre for staging plays and musical entertainments. He instituted festivals such as the Juvenalia and the Neronia, featuring theatrical performances as well as wholesome athletics contests along the lines of the Olympic Games. He even provided competitors with free body oil for their massages.

Many conservative Romans viewed these cultural developments with suspicion, fearing that the martial values and military training of rustic Latium were being supplanted by the more languorous pursuits of the decadent Greeks. Even worse, in their eyes, was the fact that Nero himself participated in these entertainments. His public performances, where he played the harp, acted in plays or raced chariots, were widely considered beneath the dignity of an emperor – since it was the lower classes who were meant to entertain their betters, not vice versa. Actors, gladiators and other performers were deemed *infames* (from which we get 'infamous'): people whose occupations disqualified them from the right to hold office or even to vote. Members of Rome's ruling class regarded appearing on stage or in the arena so shameful that when Nero forced noblemen and public officials to take singing lessons and then participate in these performances, many covered their faces with masks while others 'regarded the dead as fortunate'.[3] He forbade anyone to leave the theatre when he was performing – an edict so strictly enforced that women gave birth in their seats and men faked death so they could be carried away.

Nero's sexual behaviour was apparently on a par with that of his uncle. Indeed, he became determined to surpass Caligula, 'for he held it to be one of the obligations of the imperial power not to fall behind anybody else even in the basest deeds'.[4] He took numerous lovers, including married women. He forced himself on a Vestal Virgin, one of the priestesses dedicated to Vesta, the goddess of the hearth, home and family. The rape was scandalous since the Vestals, who played a crucial role in maintaining the sacred fire of Vesta – thought to be vital for the security and longevity of Rome – took vows of chastity. The punishment for a Vestal who broke her vow was harsh: she was stripped of her sacred garb and buried alive.

Other of Nero's relationships were more unusual. He castrated a boy named Sporus whom, according to Suetonius, he dressed in women's clothes, kissed tenderly in public and then married with the usual legal and religious ceremonies. Prayers were said 'that legitimate children might be born to them', though the gods proved indifferent to these entreaties.[5]

Nero was not alone in making this kind of union, for marriages between men – complete with public rituals and legal contracts – were not uncommon in Rome. A passage in Cicero's writings suggests that same-sex unions were both socially acceptable and sanctioned by law. Cicero (one of Rome's great legal minds) urged a friend, Curio the Elder, to honour the debts his son had incurred on behalf of one Antoninus because Antoninus was united with Curio's son in 'a stable and permanent marriage, just as if he had given him a matron's gown'.[6] Not everyone was so tolerant. More than a century after Cicero, the satirist Juvenal saw such unions as symptomatic of a decay of Roman spirit. 'The marriage contract has been witnessed, felicitations offered, a huge company invited to the feast,' he wrote bitterly about the marriage between a man named Gracchus and a male musician. Juvenal (and perhaps many others) found it an 'appalling outrage' that 'a man illustrious in family and fortune' should be 'handed over in marriage to another man'.[7] As we've seen, opprobrium in such relations was attached to the passive partner. The critics would have been mortified by Nero's other same-sex union, when he married another man but this time (at least, according to Suetonius) took the part of the bride and, on his wedding night, went so far as to 'imitate the cries and lamentations of a maiden being deflowered'.[8]

As for his wife Octavia, Claudius's daughter, Nero bitterly hated her and later put her to death. He married a woman from Pompeii named Poppaea Sabina but took as his favourite mistress a former slave from Asia Minor, Claudia Acte. The latter union caused a breach with his mother, who resented this low-born woman she tactlessly called 'my daughter-in-law the waiting-maid'.[9] And so began yet another of the homicidal family dramas in which the Julio-Claudians specialised.

Agrippina had probably murdered Claudius so that Nero could become emperor when he was still young enough for her to control. At first mother and son ruled together, with Agrippina taking such a prominent role that her head appeared on coins. Nero was happy to play along, adopting as a watchword for his Praetorian Guard the loving phrase *optimam matrem* ('the best of mothers'). The bond between mother and son was so close that Suetonius documented rumours that, when the pair travelled together in a chariot, Nero's attire, as he disembarked, revealed traces of their affectionate intimacy.

If Agrippina resented Claudia Acte, Nero soon took offence at his mother's criticisms and her attempts to control and dominate him. As the breach widened, Agrippina began courting the adolescent Britannicus, whom she called 'the genuine and deserving stock to succeed to his father's power'.[10] Nero promptly sent for Locusta, and as Britannicus sat down to a banquet one day in February 55 he could not have known that his funeral pyre had already been prepared. Indeed, he was cremated that very evening after Locusta's fast-acting poison carried him off between courses. Meanwhile, after a brief pause for Britannicus's paroxysms, the feasting continued.

Nero next began plotting Agrippina's death. Three attempts with poison failed because, like King Mithridates, she had made herself immune by ingesting small doses of toxins. Nero therefore tampered with the ceiling of her bedroom such that it would collapse and kill her while she slept. When she got wind of the plot, he came up with an even more harebrained scheme after witnessing a play in which a ship on the stage parted to allow beasts to exit, then came together again. He had just such a ship constructed for Agrippina – one that would split apart and sink as it transported her across the Bay of Naples. However, she survived the wreck despite the sailors on board bludgeoning her with their oars when she fell into the water. She paddled safely ashore and retreated to her villa where, hours later, one of Nero's assassins, Anicetus, came for her. He ran his sword – as she requested – through her womb. 'Strike here, Anicetus,' she had urged him, 'strike here, for this bore Nero.'[11]

Nero arrived to view the corpse for himself a short while later. He had her stripped and exposed before him, minutely inspected her nude, lifeless body, and then uttered: 'I did not know I had so beautiful a mother.'[12]

*

Agrippina belonged to what a historian in the 1960s called 'that small group of ferocious and licentious royal females'.[13] Ancient sources all too often depicted Roman women like Livia and Agrippina as scheming, power-mad killers, or otherwise (as we've seen) as tragic victims (Lucretia, Verginia) and insatiable sex maniacs (Messalina). The reality of women's lives was naturally far more complex, nuanced and less salacious and sensational. The 'ferocious and licentious females' were both few and far between and, we must suspect, largely the construction of disapproving male writers. However, assessing their lives is difficult because virtually everything we know about Roman women comes from male sources, many of whom, such as the satirist Juvenal – author of a long and bitter diatribe on the supposed failings of Roman women – were heavily biased against them.

Women in Ancient Rome lacked most political and many legal rights: they were unable to vote, hold office or speak at political assemblies. The fear with which many Roman men regarded female participation in the public sphere was revealed in a famous episode in 195 BCE when women took to the streets to demand the repeal of a controversial law that prevented them from appearing in public in richly decorated clothing. Their outrage was such, according to Livy, that they 'could be kept indoors by no authority, no feelings of modesty, and no command from their husbands'. The demonstrations grew as women from outside of Rome began pouring into the city and blocking the streets. Cato the Censor fought his way through the protesters mobbing the Forum and took to the rostrum to denounce this 'female indiscipline'. Repeal of the law was only, he believed, the thin edge of the wedge: 'What they want is freedom – no, complete licence, if we are willing to speak the truth – in everything. If they win on this point, what then will they not try?' He had a grim warning for Roman men: 'As soon as they begin to be your equals they will immediately be your superiors.'[14] These doom-laden entreaties failed and the law was repealed. The episode reveals how Roman women, despite the rigid strictures placed on them, could become effective political agents. However, Cato's nightmare of gender equality certainly did not come true.

For Cato and many others, a woman was meant to occupy the home as a dutiful wife and devoted mother. Her married life could begin as early as twelve, the age that Augustus (who had married his first wife, Claudia, when she was only ten) eventually set as the minimum. The girl's betrothal to her husband, usually a decade older, was sealed with a ring she wore on the fourth finger of her left hand: the *vena amoris* (vein of love) was believed to connect this finger directly with the heart. No such vein exists, but the practice indicates how at least some matches were expected to harbour a sentimental element. Indeed, although most marriages were arranged by the parents, some of them no doubt were, or at least became, love matches. However, Cato the Elder claimed the custom of husbands kissing their wives on the lips originated not from any feelings of passion but because the men wished to detect the smell or taste of wine – forbidden to women – on their spouses' lips. Cato also wrote that if a man caught his wife in adultery, he could put her to death 'without a trial and with impunity'. If, on the other hand, the wife caught her husband, 'she should not dare to lay a finger on you'.[15]

Marriage ceremonies were governed by numerous rituals. On the day of her nuptials the bride's hair was parted – not with a comb but, rather, a spear – into six sections, each of which was braided. Her betrothed then broke into the house and staged her kidnapping. This ritual was intended to dupe the household gods into thinking she was leaving the family home unwillingly. It also recalled the mass abduction of the Sabine women. References to Rome's origins in bridenapping did not end there: when the girl reached the groom's home, she was carried over the threshold.

A wife's main task was to bear and raise children, preferably boys. Dionysius of Halicarnassus, writing during the time of Augustus, cited a law implemented by Romulus, and still apparently in place, whereby parents were obliged to bring up all of their male children except for those 'maimed or monstrous from their very birth' (a deformity to which no fewer than five neighbours needed to testify). As for girls, only the firstborn needed to be raised; any others could be abandoned – ironically, as Romulus himself had been. The high mortality among infants took a heavy toll on both sexes, with as many as 30 per cent of babies dying within the first month of life.[16] The death of young wives in childbirth was lamentably common too.

Many girls did receive an education. Well-born Roman daughters were often educated by private tutors or else in private, fee-paying schools. Girls might attend these schools for several years before their education was interrupted by their weddings. Plutarch thought it the duty thereafter of a husband to be the 'guide, philosopher and teacher' to his wife – because a woman studying geometry or the works of Plato would not, he believed, go in for dancing and superstition.[17] Even so, he objected to the 'unpleasant officiousness which such accomplishments are apt to impart to young women', and Juvenal abhorred 'excessively clever and eloquent' women who could discuss Virgil's *Aeneid*, correct their husbands' grammar and 'quote lines I've never heard'.[18] However exaggerated for the purposes of satire, Juvenal's diatribe suggests that such learned and eloquent women did exist. We have vanishingly little written by Roman women, one striking exception being a series of short poems composed during the reign of Augustus by a woman named Sulpicia (about whom almost nothing is known). Another female poet, also confusingly named Sulpicia – and about whom even less is known – wrote several decades later; only a single fragment of her work survives, an erotic poem about her love for her husband.

Found in Pompeii, this fresco shows a woman holding a stylus and tablets of waxed wooden boards. She is often identified with Sappho, the Greek poet from Lesbos, but the Romans produced female poets of their own.

Roman women, or at least the more elite among them, enjoyed certain liberties. A contemporary and friend of Cicero boasted that while women in Greece were shut away in their houses, forbidden to dine with anyone but relatives, Roman women could show themselves in public and go to mixed-sex dinner parties.[19] They were allowed to leave the house to attend banquets, festivals, the theatre and entertainments in the Circus Maximus – indeed, Juvenal griped about them 'brazenly racing all over Rome'.[20] According to a law passed under Augustus (who wished to boost the birth rate) a woman who gave birth to three children earned the reward of financial independence from her husband. Subsequently the names and deeds of many women were inscribed on the temples and other buildings they charitably endowed. One inscription records how Publicia, wife of Gnaeus Cornelius, built and adorned a temple of Hercules. 'All these things she did,' the tablet declared, 'with her own and with her husband's money. She oversaw that it was done.' A woman named Octavia took care of refurbishments at a temple to Bona Dea, adorning the portico, setting up benches and roofing the kitchen.[21]

It was fitting that a woman should have repaired a temple dedicated to Bona Dea ('Good Goddess'). Bona Dea was a deity worshipped exclusively by women at secretive nocturnal festivals in Rome and the surrounding countryside. The rites have remained largely a mystery, as has the name of the goddess herself (known only by her generic title), because no men were allowed at the festival and women were prohibited from ever uttering her name in the presence of men. Even male animals were evicted from the premises before the festivities commenced. The temple was festooned with myrtle branches, snakes were turned loose and wine (ordinarily forbidden to women) was made freely available – albeit called 'milk' and served in a *mellarium* ('honey-pot'). The festival seems to have its origins in the myth of the chaste and innocent daughter of

Faunus, a Pan-like god of the forest who kept the girl a virtual prisoner in their house, unseen by all other men. One day, after plying her with wine, Faunus tried to take advantage of her and, when she resisted, thrashed her with myrtles until both of them turned into snakes (hence the ritualistic presence of myrtles and snakes). In another version, the daughter (always nameless) got drunk after downing a bottle of wine, causing an enraged Faunus to beat her to death with myrtle branches and then, filled with regret, turn her into a goddess.

Juvenal claimed that, despite the secrecy, 'everyone' knew what went on during this festival. He described how wine flowed, music played and the women worked themselves into an orgiastic frenzy, squealing and flinging themselves about, 'all on fire to get laid'.[22] We must be suspicious of much that this notorious misogynist wrote about women. Yet it is pleasant to contemplate how, if his description is true, Roman women turned a legend of a young woman's isolation, privation and abuse into a boozily hedonistic, girl's-only celebration of a female deity.

*

Nero's legacy has become intertwined with one of the darkest chapters in Rome's history. The city had twice been devastated by large fires, once in 37 CE (when the Circus Maximus and many buildings on the Aventine burned) and again in 53 CE. But the conflagration that began in the early hours of 19 July 64 CE, among the slums and shops on the eastern end of the Circus Maximus, was on a different scale: large parts of the city, including many temples and other hallowed monuments, were devoured by flames that burned for more than a week. The earliest surviving sources, such as Pliny the Elder, Suetonius and

Cassius Dio, blamed Nero, to whom Suetonius, for example, attributed a crazed and apocalyptic desire to burn the city to the ground – in effect, to bring the world to an end. He claimed that someone once quoted a line from a play by Euripides ('When I am dead, let the earth be consumed by fire'), to which Nero eagerly replied: 'Nay, rather while I live.'[23] Both Suetonius and Cassius Dio described Nero, dressed in his stage costume, enjoying the spectacle of the conflagration from the tower of the palace (that built by Maecenas) on the Esquiline Hill. From this vantage point, plucking at a lyre, he regaled the distressed and fleeing Romans with snatches of song from 'The Sack of Ilium', an epic he had composed on the fall of Troy.

Nero's self-indulgence at a moment of extreme crisis has come to typify the actions of heedless and hedonistic tyrants.

The accounts of this tower-top performance strain credulity. According to another historian, Tacitus, Nero was actually away from Rome, at Antium (Anzio), when the fire broke out. On learning of the fire, he promptly returned to Rome, took charge of the firefighting operations and offered assistance by opening his gardens to the displaced populace and distributing grain supplies. Whether the fires were instigated on his command remains a matter of debate. Tacitus claimed the fire broke out in shops packed with inflammable goods and then, impelled by the wind, swept through the city – although he, too, reported that men were seen setting the fires, and that Nero wished to burn down Rome in order to replace it with a city called Neropolis (the month of April had already been renamed Neroneus).

Tacitus actually described the conflagration as two separate fires, one following the extinguishing of the other. It's possible that the first fire was accidental but that Nero then instigated the second – which broke out after his return to Rome – when, seeing the destruction of the chaotic older buildings, he began contemplating the prospect of a more thoroughgoing urban redevelopment. Nero certainly benefited from the fire, claiming for himself a large area between the Esquiline and Caelian hills, where he built his Golden House (Domus Aurea). This vast complex included a villa, landscaped parkland, artificial lake, large octagonal dome and what would become one of Rome's most dominant and conspicuous monuments: a 30-metre bronze statue of Nero in the guise of the Greek sun-god, Helios, which became known as the Colossus of Nero.

Nero oversaw the swift reconstruction of Rome and implemented a set of regulations to enhance building safety and prevent future fires. He also performed rituals to mollify the angered gods. Still, suspicions lingered regarding his involvement in the fire. According to Tacitus, to dispel rumours and shift blame away from himself, he cast about for a scapegoat, which he quickly identified. 'Nero substituted as culprits,' wrote Tacitus, 'and punished with the utmost refinements of cruelty, a class of men, loathed for their vices, whom the crowd styled Christians.'[24]

Instances of religious persecution were relatively uncommon in the Roman Empire, whose pragmatic approach to religion was characterised by acceptance and assimilation. Rome possessed a polytheistic and eclectic religious landscape that reflected the empire's diverse and cosmopolitan nature. The Romans tended to treat foreign gods much as they treated foreigners themselves (including their former enemies): they absorbed them into their own culture. Alongside the official Roman cults, which had their own priests, temples, festivals and gods – many derived from the Greeks – various religions from far-flung lands were introduced to Rome. Immigrants and soldiers returning from foreign wars were responsible for these cultural exchanges. For example, following the campaign against Mithridates, soldiers of the Roman general Sulla brought back from Cappadocia the cult of the warrior goddess Ma. Similarly, the goddess Isis – revered as a protector of women, marriage and newborn babies – was imported from Egypt.

One of the religious groups to suffer periodic repression was the Jews, who had arrived in Italy by the second century BCE. By Nero's time, they accounted for between 5 and 10 per cent of the population of the Roman Empire and, in Rome itself, could boast a dozen synagogues and a population of 50,000 (in a city whose population was approaching a million). Although generally well tolerated, they had been temporarily expelled from Rome on several occasions. In 139 BCE, the community was evicted for apparently 'trying to transmit their sacred rites to the Romans'.[25] A second crisis came during the reign of Tiberius in 19 CE, when they were expelled for reasons about which the sources give conflicting accounts. One of them, the historian

Josephus, claimed a Jewish immigrant, 'a complete scoundrel', enlisted some accomplices to swindle an aristocratic convert named Fulvia.[26] The expulsion must have been temporary, because they were banished yet again, a generation later, during the reign of Claudius, around 49 CE. The reason this time was owing to an uproar in the synagogues caused by the followers of a troublemaker whom Suetonius called 'Chresto'.

These troubles were no doubt between the Jews and a break-away sect that had recently arrived from the East. The leader of the small sect, Jesus of Nazareth, had been executed by means of crucifixion – a punishment reserved by the Romans for slaves and people of low status – outside the walls of Jerusalem around 30 CE, during the reign of Tiberius. Decades later, his devotees could be found on the Italian peninsula in Rome, Puteoli and possibly Pompeii, where a graffito, scrawled in charcoal, recorded the name conferred on them in Antioch in about 44 CE: Christians.[27] The name derived from the Greek *christos*, meaning 'anointed one' – a reference to the fact that the followers of Jesus believed him to have been the Messiah.

A small Christian community took root in Rome in the 40s CE, no doubt thanks to the links between Rome and cities such as Jerusalem (in the Roman province of Judea) and Antioch (in the Roman province of Syria). In the 50s CE, Paul of Tarsus (the future St Paul) wrote to the Christians in Rome that he longed to visit them, and that their faith was 'reported all over the world' (Acts 1:8). In another letter he fondly hailed twenty-six Christians living in the city (Romans 16:1–16). Their mixture of Greek, Roman and Hebrew names indicates how the cosmopolitan character of the little Christian community reflected that of Rome itself, and how the expanding Roman Empire offered a relatively stable and unified world through which Christians could travel and spread their faith. It is significant that Paul extended greetings to many women, such as Phoebe, Priscilla, Tryphena and Tryphosa – 'those women who work hard in the Lord'. These greetings are one of our first glimpses of how Christianity appealed to women, who were to become (as we shall see) disproportionately represented among Christian converts.

The 'Chresto' conflict was no doubt similar to that caused a decade or so later in Jerusalem when Paul was arrested as a troublemaker for 'stirring up riots among the Jews all over the world' (Acts 24:5). Thanks to this arrest, Paul got his wish to visit Rome. As a Roman citizen (Tarsus was in the Roman province of Cilicia, in present-day southern Turkey) he exercised his right to appeal to the authority of Nero. Guarded by a centurion named Julius and accompanied by Luke the Evangelist (later to write up Paul's adventures in the Acts of the Apostles) he boarded a ship bound for Italy. After a shipwreck on Malta and stops in Syracuse and Rhegium, he disembarked at Puteoli, near Naples.

Bound in chains, Paul arrives in Rome after long and arduous travels.

Such was his fame that, as he made his way north, Christians from Rome turned out to meet him at a rest-stop on Via Appia some 65 kilometres southeast of Rome known as the Tres Tabernae, or Three Taverns.

Paul spent the following two years under house arrest in Rome, albeit teaching 'with all boldness and without hindrance' (Acts 28:31). It's possible he was acquitted of the charges – the punishment for which would have been death – because, according to tradition, he sailed for Spain in about 62. By the time he returned to Rome a few years later, the situation for the small but burgeoning Christian community had changed drastically.

Tacitus claimed the Roman people detested the 'pernicious superstition' of the Christians – hence their appeal for Nero as scapegoats. But Tacitus was writing some fifty years later, and it's debatable how much the average Roman in the 60s CE actually knew about the beliefs and practices of this religious minority (whom they would have been hard-pressed to distinguish from the Jews). After all, Christians numbered only in their hundreds. Whatever the case, the leaders of the community were arrested, convicted and executed. Tacitus reported that, as a gruesome spectator sport, they were covered with the skins of wild animals and torn to pieces by dogs. Nero crucified many of them in the gardens of his palace and then, when darkness fell, burned them alive 'to serve as lamps by night'. The strategy ultimately backfired: the savagery of these reprisals touched the hearts of a Roman mob generally inured to extreme scenes of gore and violence. There arose, Tacitus claimed, 'a sentiment of pity, due to the impression that they were being sacrificed not for the welfare of the state but to the ferocity of a single man'.[28]

Tacitus remains the only surviving source for the claim that Nero persecuted Christians specifically because of the Great

Fire. However, whether this scapegoating actually occurred has been much debated.[29] Cassius Dio described the fire in detail but said nothing of Christians being blamed for starting it. Suetonius, writing around the same time as Tacitus, described the fire and spoke of Nero inflicting punishments on Christians. However, he mentioned these punishments not in the context of the Great Fire, but as part of Nero's law-and-order crackdowns that included such measures as banishing rowdy actors from Rome, stopping charioteers from racing through the city's narrow streets and banning taverns from serving any hot food except bean soup and boiled vegetables.

There is no doubt, however, that Nero did persecute and execute Christians during the 60s CE. An ancient tradition links two famous martyrdoms with his persecutions. St Paul appears to have been beheaded (his privilege as a Roman citizen) along Via Ostiensis outside the walls of Rome. It's possible he was actually executed a year or two before the fire, not for being a Christian but after a guilty verdict on the charge that brought him to Rome in the first place – stirring up sedition in Judea.

Another Christian executed around the same time was a fisherman from the Sea of Galilee named Shim'on, better known as Peter the Apostle. St Jerome, more than three centuries later, wrote that Peter lived in Rome for twenty-five years, having arrived during the reign of Claudius. Biblical evidence for Peter's time in Rome is, however, scanty: a single reference, in 1 Peter 5:13, to him writing from 'Babylon'. The literal Babylon, on the Euphrates, lay in ruins by this time, and so Peter must have been speaking metaphorically – and Babylon was perhaps an apt name for the Rome of the Julio-Claudians. Some scholars assert that no reliable evidence supports the idea that Peter ever set foot in Rome, and that on the balance of probability he died not as a martyr in Rome but, rather, 'peacefully in bed, in Judea'.[30] There is no doubting, however, the importance of Peter's mission or his significance for Christianity in general and the city of Rome in particular.

In the decades and then the centuries that followed the Neronian persecutions, the question of where the Church should be headquartered – in Jerusalem, Antioch, Alexandria or Rome – became urgent. Rome's claim for authority and pre-eminence was based on the ministries of Peter and Paul in Rome, as well as their martyrdoms and burials in or near the city. Legends were therefore assiduously produced and embellished to buttress the claim. A robust legend has Peter sailing for Italy and, following a storm, disembarking at the port of Gradus Arnenses (Grado) near Pisa on the Tuscan coast, from where he went to Rome and later became one of Nero's victims.

One version of his martyrdom is given in the apocryphal *Acts of Peter*, composed at least a century after his death (probably in the decades around 200 CE). Here, not fire but sex is the reason for his persecution – or, rather, the lack of sex. Peter's preachings about chastity persuaded the wives and concubines of Roman citizens to withhold their favours from their men. With resentment of the sex-starved Romans mounting against him, Peter took flight along Via Appia until he encountered Christ walking determinedly in the opposite direction, carrying his cross. Peter then put his famous question to him: *Domine, quo vadis?* ('Lord, where are you going?'). When Christ replied that he was going to Rome to be crucified, Peter, suitably chastened, returned to the city to be crucified upside-down (as artists such as Masaccio and Michelangelo would later show). When he learned of Peter's death, Nero grew furious because (as if crucifixion were not agonising enough) he wanted 'to punish him more sorely and with greater torment' – for he, too, had been suffering from his concubines' newfound enthusiasm for chastity.[31]

The Florentine artist Masaccio's 1426 representation of Peter's execution. According to the *Acts of Peter*, he requested the inverted crucifixion because he felt unworthy to die in the same manner as Jesus Christ.

The most ancient sources agreed that the pair were interred together in a pagan graveyard along Via Appia. The remains were, however, eventually removed from their resting-places. In the sixth century, the *Liber Pontificalis* ('Book of Popes') reported how in about 250 CE, in a secretive nocturnal raid, a woman named Lucina had the remains of the two apostles dug up and then interred close to the sites of their respective executions: Paul's in her own garden on Via Ostiensis, Peter's in a cemetery on the west bank of the Tiber, near to where Nero had built a track for chariot racing. 'I tell you that you are Peter,' Christ had informed his apostle, 'and upon this rock I will build my church' (Matthew 16:18). And it was on the site of Peter's burial that the

Church would, quite literally, rise. This cemetery was situated in a marshy valley beneath the gentle slope of one of Rome's many hills, the Mons Vaticanus, or Vatican Hill. Through the ages this location had gained significance as a place of pagan reverence and spiritual insight. Its name resounded with prophesy and ritual: 'Vaticanus' traces back to *vates*, signifying a prophet or soothsayer, while *cano* means to sing. (In Italian, *vaticinare* means 'to prophesy'.) Here, wrapped in purple and gold cloth, Peter's bones were placed in a grave, beside which someone scrawled emphatically in Greek: Πέτρος ενι ('Peter is here'). With the arrival of these relics, this sacred ground was imbued with renewed sanctity and this humble burial ground beside a racetrack evolved into the epicentre of the Catholic Church, radiating spiritual influence across the globe.

*

Nero's reign lasted almost fourteen years. After an assassination plot was uncovered in 65 CE, he took savage reprisals. Tacitus painted a grim picture of columns of manacled men winding through the streets, of men and women broken under torture, and of the air thick with smoke from funeral pyres. Victims included Seneca, Nero's old adviser, suspected of taking part in the plot. In *On Clemency* the philosopher had written eloquently about the virtue of mercy. When Nero showed him none, Seneca was forced to commit suicide. As befitted a Stoic, he did so calmly and implacably: he dictated the final lines of his last work, then opened his veins before climbing into a warm bath. To hasten the end, he quaffed a cup of hemlock provided by his doctor. Other bright literary stars were also snuffed out by Nero's frenzied revenge. One of them was Seneca's 25-year-old nephew,

Lucan, a brilliant poet of whose talents Nero was so jealous that at one point he banned him from writing poetry. The other writer who fell foul of Nero was Petronius, author of the racy *Satyricon*, with its animated scenes of orgies and lower-class life. He committed suicide by slitting his wrists while reclining at dinner and listening to his friends sing frivolous songs.

A woodcut from the 1493 *Nuremburg Chronicle* vividly imagines Seneca's suicide. Ever the Stoic, he remains remarkably composed as the arterial blood spurts from his arms.

Yet another victim was Nero's pregnant wife Poppaea Sabina, a wildly ostentatious woman who bathed in ass's milk and demanded gilded shoes for her horses. Nero kicked her to death in a rage after she chastised him for coming home late from the chariot races. He deeply regretted her death, and whenever he learned of someone who looked like her, he would immediately make her his mistress.

Nero eventually lost the support of several of his provincial governors and their legions. Rebellion broke out, first in Gallia Lugdunensis (in what is now northern France) and then in

Hispania Tarraconensis (the largest province in Spain). The governor of the latter, Servius Sulpicius Galba, was proclaimed by his legions as the new representative of the Senate and people of Rome – in effect, the new emperor. As Tacitus later wrote, 'The secret of empire was now revealed, that an emperor could be made elsewhere than at Rome.'[32] In other words, an emperor could be created by heavily armed legions rather than by the Senate and the people of Rome. Over the following centuries this practice would cause almost unimaginable chaos and bloodshed.

Nero learned of the rebellion in Gaul soon after his return from Greece, where he had gone in 66 CE to take part in the Olympic Games. (Thanks to threats, bribes and Greek sycophancy, he won 1,808 individual gold medals.) His preparations for battle against the rebels proved characteristically eccentric: his greatest priority was to find wagons to transport his costumes and musical instruments to the front. He also arranged for his mistresses to join him on the campaign, dressed like Amazons and with their hair shorn. Other tactics included composing lewd songs that ridiculed the leaders of the revolt. He also toyed with the idea of murdering all the senators, burning down Rome and retiring to Egypt, where he believed he could make a living as a lyre-player. 'Even though we be driven from our empire,' he reasoned, 'yet this little talent shall support us there.'[33]

Such curious antics inspired little confidence in Nero's soldiers, who soon defected to the rebels. Realising the cause was lost, he called for Locusta, who obliged him with a fatal concoction, only for his servants to make off with the vial along with most of his other possessions as they looted the palace. Two further suicide attempts miscarried before his end came at a villa a few kilometres outside Rome, to which he fled in a shabby disguise with a few loyalists, including Sporus, his beloved castrato. 'What an artist the world is losing!' he wept as he watched them gather the firewood for his cremation.[34] As Galba's soldiers came for him, he quoted a line from *The Iliad* – 'Hark, now strikes on my ear the trampling of swift-footed coursers!' – and thrust a dagger into his throat. He managed to fluff this final dramatic performance, however, and as he writhed in agony one of the 'swift-footed coursers' arrived to deliver the *coup de grâce*.

*

Ancient Roman historians and early Christian theologians took a dim view of Nero. In one Christian tradition he was equated with the Antichrist. Yet Nero was evidently wildly popular with a great many Roman people during his lifetime, and even more so following his death. Suetonius reported that each spring and summer his tomb was strewn with flowers, and that many people, not only in Rome but also in the East, believed he 'would shortly return and deal destruction to his enemies'.[35] More than 300 years later, St Augustine reported how this legend was alive and well, with people believing that Nero, still youthful and vigorous, was about to reveal himself and return to power. It is ironic that the persecutor of the Christians should himself have become, for some, a Christ-like figure whose followers eagerly awaited his second coming.

It is all too easy to abhor and denigrate the Julio-Claudians, especially if we choose to credit even half of what ancient historians wrote about them. In their favour, the Julio-Claudians were great builders who, like the first of their line, Augustus, oversaw the transformation of Rome into a massive city with an infrastructure allowing hundreds of thousands of people to be fed and watered, educated and entertained. The wealth and splendour of first-century Rome was summed up by the British chieftain Caratacus after he was brought to Rome as a captive following the defeat of the Catuvellauni: 'And can you, then, who have got such possessions and so many of them, covet our poor tents?'[36] (The point Caratacus evidently missed was that Rome's wealth was built on the conquests of people in their 'poor tents'.)

To meet the physical, social and intellectual needs of the population, the Julio-Claudian rulers erected or restored dozens of buildings and launched ambitious engineering projects. In the fifty-four years that separated the deaths of Augustus and Nero, Rome gained a dozen new temples, a new circus and two new aqueducts, the Aqua Claudia and the Aqua Anio Novus. Built during the reigns of Caligula and Claudius, these two aqueducts more than doubled Rome's water supply.[37] The Anio Novus was one of the biggest building projects of the century in terms of manpower, requiring tunnelling and mining skills as well as knowledge of hydraulic engineering.

Another great project, that of Claudius, was the draining of the mosquito-infested Fucine Lake to increase the food supply and mitigate against malaria. A massive feat of hydraulic engineering and manpower management, it provided 150,000 acres of fertile land some 85 kilometres from Rome, ensuring that Romans could be fed. The project, carried out between 46 and 53 CE, coincided with Claudius's even more colossal undertaking: the construction of the seaport of Portus, downstream on the Tiber from Rome (near the site of what is today Fiumicino Airport). It entailed the excavation of 500 acres of coastal dunes and the construction of breakwaters, dry docks, canals (one of which was almost 100 metres wide) and gigantic warehouses for holding grain. A Greek writer would later marvel at the achievement:

'Here is brought, from every land and sea, all the crops of the seasons and the produce of each land ... Whatever one does not see here it is not a thing which has existed or exists.'[38]

As for Nero, the Octagonal Room in his Golden House was a masterpiece of architecture and engineering: a soaring eight-side dome, made from concrete, that was almost 15 metres in span, with an eye at the top open to the sky. Tacitus wrote that Nero's architects and engineers possessed 'the ingenuity and the courage to try the force of art even against the veto of nature'.[39] This monument to Nero was sealed with a mound of earth following the *damnatio memoriae* (condemnation of memory) that followed his death, and the magnificent structure was lost to history for more than a thousand years. But after parts of the Golden House were rediscovered in the 1480s, the painted decorations in the vast complex excited the imaginations of Italian artists, including Michelangelo and Raphael. They and others lowered themselves into the cavernous spaces on a rope to see, and then to imitate, the delicate fantasies painted almost a millennium and a half earlier.

This combination of gross character deficiency with artistic innovation and undeniably capable infrastructure management was summed up by the poet Martial: 'What was worse than Nero?' he asked. 'What is better than Nero's baths?'[40]

# 7

# 'SAVAGE VICTORS': THE HEIGHT OF EMPIRE

AROUND THE TIME OF NERO'S DEATH in June 68 CE, the white chickens at Livia's villa in Prima Porta all perished, as did the grove of laurel trees. These omens indicated what was obvious to everyone: the Julio-Claudian line of emperors had been extinguished. The crucial question of who would assume control of the Empire therefore became urgent. It soon became apparent that the succession would not be determined by formal discussions in the Senate, auspicious signs or the enthusiastic approval of the Roman populace. Instead, the ascent of the new emperor would be decided by brutality and bloodshed. The period following Nero's demise is referred to as the 'Year of the Four Emperors', highlighting the swift and violent succession of rulers. The terror of the previous century's civil wars briefly returned in what Tacitus called 'a period rich in disasters, terrible with battles, torn by civil struggles, horrible even in peace'.[1]

Nero was succeeded by the 65-year-old Galba, but when he reneged on his promise to pay the Praetorian Guard for their support – as all emperors since Claudius had done before him – they extracted their own brutal remittance: on 15 January 69 they attacked and killed him in the Forum, then presented his severed head to the man they favoured as his successor, Marcus Salvius Otho. A former governor of Hispania Lusitania (in present-day Portugal), Otho lasted three months before committing suicide following the defeat of his legions in northern Italy by those of a rival, Vitellius, the cruel and gluttonous governor of Lower Germany. Vitellius's short stint ended when his legions were trounced by those loyal to Vespasian, a battle-hardened commander who had quelled rebellions in both Britannia and Judea. Caught by Vespasian's troops hiding in a doorkeeper's lodge outside the palace, Vitellius was dragged half-naked through the streets of Rome with a noose round his neck. After being insulted by the mob and pelted with dung, he was stabbed to death and his body thrown into the Tiber. These violent and undignified ends revealed how far the emperors had come since the glory days of Augustus.

The job of Roman emperor was certainly proving one of the world's most dangerous. Not only did four successive emperors fall by the sword between June 68 (Nero) and December 69 (Vitellius), but Tiberius, Caligula and Claudius had all been murdered too, and Tacitus claimed (as we have seen) that even Augustus had been poisoned – eliminated by Livia to make way for her son Tiberius. The new emperor, Titus Flavius Vespasianus, would buck this trend. A rugged sixty-year-old with a brusque and unpretentious manner, he would reign for the next decade, dying of natural causes in June 79 after quipping: '*Vae, puto deus fio*' (Dear me, I think I'm becoming a god).[2] He was indeed deified by Titus, his son and successor – whose reign, depending on which source we believe, saw the return of the brutal trend: the philosopher and historian Philostratus, writing more than a century later, claimed Titus was poisoned by Domitian, his younger brother and successor. Together, the father and two sons from the Flavii family made up the three emperors of the Flavian Dynasty, which ruled from 69 to 96.

Following on the heels of the spendthrift Nero, Vespasian was forced to put Rome's finances in order. He doubled some taxes, introduced new ones and raised funds through such dubious practices as selling public offices to the highest bidder and accepting money from criminals in return for their freedom. He became famous for a tax imposed on the entrepreneurs who collected urine from public latrines for use in industries such as tanning and laundering (the ammonia in urine gave the toga its pristine whiteness). After Titus objected to his father's new tax, Vespasian held a coin to his son's nose and inquired if its odour was offensive. When Titus said no, the affable emperor replied: 'Yet it comes from urine' – the origin of the saying *pecunia non olet* (money doesn't stink).[3] Although such fiscal measures did little for Vespasian's popularity, they allowed him to restore both the Theatre of Marcellus and the buildings on the Capitol burned during the recent turmoil.

The Flavians left an enduring mark on Rome with their most renowned monument, the gigantic, oval-shaped sports arena known as the Flavian Amphitheatre. Although gladiatorial battles had been fought in Rome since 264 BCE, for centuries thereafter the city did not feature a large or impressive arena, only temporary wooden structures that were disassembled following the games. Rome's first stone amphitheatre was constructed as late as 29 BCE, financed by a wealthy senator and friend of Augustus named Statilius Taurus. But it was unassuming enough that in 54 CE Nero constructed a second, larger one, albeit of wood. Both venues were destroyed in the Great Fire.

The new amphitheatre was of a completely different order.

Initiated by Vespasian around 72 CE, it was completed and inaugurated eight years later by Titus. The structure is commonly referred to as the Colosseum – due not to its massive scale but rather to its proximity to the Colossus of Nero. Spanning over 200 metres across what was once an artificial lake in Nero's private pleasure gardens, this amphitheatre served as a venue for extravagant and often brutal spectacles, including gladiatorial combat and animal hunts. An architectural marvel and testament to ancient engineering prowess, the amphitheatre has become an emblem of Rome's grandeur and – with its baying crowds and gory spectacles – its mindboggling cruelty. It could seat (depending on which source we choose to believe) anywhere from 50,000 to 80,000 spectators, with standing room for thousands more. It featured eighty entrances, two of which were reserved for the exclusive use of the emperors and their families, and another two for the gladiators: the Porta Triumphalis (for their dramatic entrances) and the Porta Libitinaria (for the removal of their corpses) – named after Libitina, the Roman goddess of burials and funerals.

The Colosseum was a technological as well as an architectural marvel. A series of underground winches, cages and ramps dramatically propelled the lions and tigers onto the 'arena', a wooden platform covered with a layer of sand (*arena* in Latin) that absorbed the blood. Arched passageways known as *vomitoria* (from *vomere*, 'to spew') allowed the spectators easy access to the numbered sections and then their safe and efficient exit when the show was over. Spectators were distributed according to their social status, with the names of aristocrats engraved on the backs of their seats in the lower level (the 'podium'). At the top, an awning made from wood and fabric was unfurled like a giant sail to provide shade on hot summer days, the manpower supplied by brawny sailors from the fleet at Misenum. The skeletal structure we see today has been stripped not only of vast amounts of masonry (it served during the Middle Ages as a kind of architectural salvage yard) but also of its opulent decorations and special features such as the scented fountains that wafted sweet perfume over the spectators as tigers tore apart condemned criminals and the gladiators crushed each other's skulls.

Martial described most of the spectators in the Colosseum (accurately or not) as 'barbarous' foreign visitors such as Greeks, Arabs, Egyptians, Ethiopians and a people from the Danube, the Sarmatians, known for drinking the blood of their horses.[4] A typical day in the Colosseum would treat them to a slaughter of wild beasts in the morning – sometimes as many as a hundred lions – and then, during the lunchtime break, the execution of condemned criminals. Gladiatorial combat was staged in the afternoon. Gladiators (named for a short sword, the *gladius*) were often, but by no means exclusively, slaves. Most were professionals who trained in a special school (the *ludus*) under the supervision of a manager. All swore a dreadful oath: *uri, uinciri, uerberari, ferroque necari* – 'to be branded with fire, shackled in chains, whipped with rods and killed with an iron weapon'. These weapons came in various shapes and sizes, for gladiators took different, well-defined roles, with the costumes and armaments of some of them based, as we have seen, on traditional foes such as the Gauls, Samnites and Thracians. Other characters included the nautically themed Retiarius, or Net Man, who was equipped with a net and a long trident, and the Murmillo, armed with a *gladius*, a rectangular shield and a plumed helmet featuring a grilled visor and a crest decorated with the image of a fish (the *mormyrus*) from which he took his name. Contests featured asymmetrical match-ups in which, for example, the swift, unadorned Net Man would try to ensnare and harpoon the Murmillo, who was more heavily armoured but equipped with a far shorter weapon. Most gladiators fought two or three times a year, with an average life expectancy of perhaps a dozen matches. Not every contest ended in death, for a gladiator, if he had made himself popular, could earn a 'reprieve' from the crowd and live to fight another day.

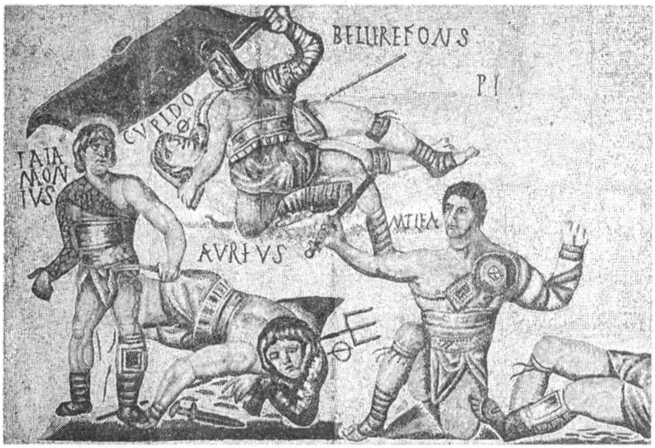

A mosaic showing the brutal aftermath of combat. On the left, the victorious gladiator stands over Net Man, whose trident is under his corpse. Another Net Man is about to meet a similar fate at the hands of a *gladius*-wielding Secutor. To the right, the Retiarius has enjoyed a better result.

While the social position of gladiators was beneath that of prostitutes and bankrupts, celebrity brought some perks: a graffito about a gladiator in Pompeii named Celadus declared that he was *suspirium puellarum* (heart-throb of the girls). A gladiator named Sergius evidently possessed a similar allure, for a noblewoman named Ennia, the wife of a senator, abandoned her family (including 'wailing children') to run off to Greece with him. Juvenal reported that Sergius made a gruesome sight, with battered features 'and the nasty condition of a constantly weeping eye'. But such disfigurements did little to deter Ennia and other women. As Juvenal bitterly observed: 'The iron is what they love.'[5]

There were even female gladiators who engaged in what a disapproving poet called 'manly combat'.[6] Their appeal seems to have been their novelty: they were rare enough that Latin did not have a word (such as *gladiatrix*) to classify or categorise them. But they are well attested in many sources, representing popular if sometimes scandalous attractions. Ancient writers mention female charioteers as well as *venatores* (beastfighters). Martial claimed to have seen women killing lions in combat in the arena, and female beastfighters during one entertainment participated in the slaying of 9,000 animals. Women also fought each other in gladiatorial battle, and they sometimes found themselves pitted against what one Roman poet called 'a bold string of midgets'.[7] Remarkably, at least some of these female gladiators appear to have come from Rome's upper classes – something that Roman writers and historians found shocking and disgraceful. Alas, we have no reports of what might have possessed a well-born Roman woman to pick up a sword, don a crested helmet and enter the 'cruel sand' of the arena.[8]

Indeed, the role of the gladiator was a desperate and unenviable one even for those, like the women of Rome, with severely limited career prospects. Few entered the profession by choice. Seneca the Younger told the story of a reluctant German gladiator who committed suicide in the arena's latrine with a *xylospongium* – the sponge-on-a-stick that Romans used to wipe their bottoms. The unfortunate warrior choked himself to death by thrusting the sponge down his throat. 'It was not a very elegant or becoming way to die,' tut-tutted Seneca, who took his own life, as we've seen, by more easeful means.[9]

*

With its majesty, technical excellence and austere beauty – and with its terrible agonies and bloody sufferings – the Colosseum was an apt emblem of the Roman Empire itself. Indeed, many of the funds for the construction of the Colosseum came from the spoils of one of Rome's most brutal conquests. A year after Vespasian was acclaimed emperor, his eldest son, Titus, then thirty years old, besieged and captured Jerusalem, massacring many of the inhabitants, enslaving others, razing the city and destroying the Second Temple. Josephus reported that more than a million Jews died in the Siege of Jerusalem. Although that number is likely inflated, the carnage was certainly sufficient for, as Josephus tells us, the Roman soldiers to grow 'weary of slaughter'.[10]

Under the Flavians, the Roman Empire continued its relentless campaign of conquest. Roman legions extended their control into northern England, made initial efforts to establish peace in Wales, ventured into Scotland and, led by the skilled general Julius Agricola, pondered the possibility of invading Ireland. In tandem with this expansion came a strategy of 'Romanisation', by which Roman culture and institutions – what one historian has summarised as 'gods, pots, and Latin'[11] – were imposed on the most distant reaches of the known world. Tacitus described how Agricola (his father-in-law) pacified the restless, warlike Britons by assisting their communities in the construction of temples, houses and marketplaces. Soon the toga came into fashion and Britons began speaking Latin, shaving their beards and enjoying public baths and the delights of a well-appointed dinner table at which, instead of beer, they served wine in elegant cups. The wealthier among them built Roman-style villas, complete with mosaics, frescoes and central heating. Tacitus observed that the 'simple natives' gave the name *humanitas* to this new style of living.[12] Coined by Cicero, the word *humanitas* described a combination of wisdom, cultural refinement, broadmindedness and benevolence. The 'simple' Britons therefore believed the Romans had elevated and humanised them – turned them into a better sort of people.

Yet the darker side of Romanisation is evident in a speech that Cassius Dio gave to Boudicca, queen of the Iceni tribe in Britannia, who led an uprising against the Romans in 60 CE. She condemned the 'imported despotism' of the Romans that left the Iceni 'stripped and despoiled like a murderer's victims'. Likewise, Tacitus puts similar sentiments into the mouth of another British leader, Calgacus. Opposing the Roman advance in Scotland in 83 CE, Calgacus urged his countrymen to fight off these plundering invaders, whom he described as the 'robbers of the world': 'To plunder, butcher, steal,' he declared, 'these things they misname empire: they make a desolation and they call it peace.'[13]

The Romans may have imposed gods, pots and Latin on conquered people. However, they failed – and indeed had no real desire or ability – to create a monoculture, whether in the provinces or in Rome itself. The historian Ramsay MacMullen has noted the many 'unromanised' people who lived in Rome, such as the Jews and Christians who wrote and spoke Hebrew and Greek rather than Latin, or the thirty-odd workers in a warehouse on the Janiculum Hill whose names and gods, inscribed on an altar, identified them as immigrants from Syria, Arabia and Lebanon. Likewise, a man named Iarhai, 'son of Haliphi', raised an altar to his gods, Aglibol and Malakbel, with inscriptions in both Greek and Palmyrene.[14] These people were what the Romans called *alienigeni* – 'born elsewhere'. Many of them, such as Iarhai, who also went by the Latin name Heliodorus, may have lived in the city for many decades and become fluent in Latin, but there seems to have been no pressure on them to abandon either their old gods or the languages of their homelands.

Moreover, the influences were sometimes reciprocal. The Romans' contacts with other people around the Empire became a matter not merely of domination but also of assimilation, a mash-up that meant 'Roman' culture was (like the 'Roman' people) a cosmopolitan fusion of various cultures and influences. We have already seen their embrace of the political and religious paraphernalia of the Etruscans, the literature, philosophy and statuary of the Greeks, the monumental architecture (obelisks and pyramids) of the Egyptians, and cults and gods from virtually everywhere around the Empire. To give an example from another culture, despite the Roman destruction of Carthage, the Romans took from the Carthaginians the word *ave*, 'hail', as in *ave Caesar* ('hail Caesar'). The word 'caesar' was likewise, as we've seen, a Punic word – and so the acclamation of a Roman conqueror was delivered in words borrowed from a conquered people.

*

By about the year 700, a saying about Rome and its architecture appeared in Anglo-Saxon England: 'So long as the Colosseum stands, so stands Rome; when the Colosseum falls, so falls Rome; and when Rome falls, so falls the world.'[15] There is some debate about whether the author was referring to the Colosseum or (perhaps more likely) the Colossus of Nero.[16] In either case, the fate of the world was somehow seen to rest on monumental Roman architecture. However, even as the Colosseum was nearing completion, the daunting power of Roman civilisation was spectacularly humbled. In 79 CE, two months after he succeeded his father as emperor, Titus was confronted by a devastating natural disaster: the eruption of Mount Vesuvius. For the victims caught in Pompeii and Herculaneum, it must have seemed that the world was indeed at an end.

The giant volcano (whose name possibly came from the portentous phrase *vae suis*, 'woe unto them') had occasionally spewed forth fire and ash, including in 216 BCE, when its ash fell as far away as China. Since this eruption came shortly before the Battle of Cannae, its smoke and flames were taken, after the fact, as a portent of the devastating loss to Hannibal (who was himself apparently given a tour of Vesuvius).[17] The quakes and eruptions were understood by the Romans to be the restless tumult of the giants defeated by Hercules, trying to free themselves from imprisonment under the mountains. Generally, the volcano's sporadic eruptions were seen as good omens, since the ash, acting as a fertiliser, ensured abundant crops, many of which were grown on its slopes. The air on the mountain was believed to be so healthy that physicians sent their patients there for treatment. Someone else who had taken refuge there, but for different reasons, was Spartacus and his band of rebels, who in 73 BCE hid in the volcano's crater.

The eruption of 24 August 79 was on a different scale from anything ever seen before.* Following a series of earthquakes

---

* The exact date of the eruption has recently become a matter of debate. Although 24 August has long been accepted, doubts have been raised by the fact that autumnal nuts and fruits such as walnuts and pomegranates, as well as heating braziers, have been found among the ruins of Pompeii; some of the victims, moreover, were wearing heavy woollen clothing. Graffiti in charcoal found in the new Regio V excavation in 2018, apparently scrawled in the middle of October 79, points to a date in autumn.

and lava flows, an eruption column rose more than 30 kilometres into the sky before collapsing and causing pyroclastic surges, in which masses of rock and poisonous gases cascaded down the mountainside at 200 kilometres per hour. One eyewitness to the spectacular explosion was the eighteen-year-old Pliny the Younger. He was some 25 kilometres away at the naval base of Misenum with his uncle, the distinguished scholar and admiral Pliny the Elder. The younger Pliny described how in the early afternoon the two of them watched a dirty cloud shaped like an umbrella pine rise into the sky above the Bay of Naples. The elder Pliny was a man with avid scientific interests, author of the massive and encyclopedic tome *Natural History*, one of the most famous of all the books written in ancient Rome. He therefore decided, in the interests of science, to set off in a boat across the bay to witness the phenomenon at closer range. However, before setting off he received by letter a plea for help from a friend living at the base of the volcano, and so instead he set sail with his fleet on a rescue mission. Pliny described his uncle's heroic voyage across the tumultuous bay through a hail of hot ashes, bits of pumice and charred stones. His ship came ashore at Stabiae, 6 kilometres south of Pompeii, as the volcano disgorged 'broad sheets of fire and leaping flames'.[18] Pliny the Elder died on the beach, under a blackened sky, either asphyxiated in the stink of sulphur or killed by a slave whom he begged to hasten his end when he was overcome by the terrible heat. In any case, he became the most famous of Vesuvius's thousands of victims.

The number of dead has been estimated at around 16,000, which in some respects is remarkably low considering that Pompeii's population might have been as high as 22,000, with another 5,000 in Herculaneum. More people died at Fidenae, 15 kilometres north of Rome, when a cheaply built wooden amphitheatre collapsed during a gladiatorial show in 27 CE, crushing 20,000 spectators to death and injuring thousands of others (still the world's worst stadium disaster). Vesuvius claimed fewer victims because people had time to flee – perhaps as much as a day or two – as the giant rumbled, smoked and shook their homes as a prelude to its explosion. The remains of some of those who left things too late have been discovered outside Pompeii, including a group found north of the city near the local necropolis, some carrying small hordes of coins and a few possessions.

Titus's short reign was troubled not only by Vesuvius but also by a fire a year later that destroyed large sections of Rome. Scarcely had this fire been extinguished before a plague devastated the city – a mysterious pestilence that, according to Suetonius, had never been known before. Titus desperately appealed for a cure, researching medicines and performing sacrifices, but in vain. It may in fact have been this plague (the exact nature of which is still unknown) that claimed his life: he died of a fever in September 81.

Titus's brother and successor, thirty-year-old Domitian, may also have been responsible. Relations between the two brothers – a dozen years apart in age – had never been cordial, beginning perhaps with Domitian refusing to marry Titus's daughter Julia, and Titus as a result refusing to name Domitian as co-emperor. According to Suetonius, Domitian was indolent and unambitious: he spent the first days of his reign shut away in a room doing nothing but stabbing houseflies with a sharpened stylus. He did eventually pursue certain goals with great vigour. First of all, he launched a building campaign, constructing a gigantic residence for himself on the Palatine, an athletics stadium on the site of what is now Piazza Navona, and, to honour his brother, the Arch of Titus (with its scenes showing loot such as the seven-branched menorah taken from Jerusalem). Second, he expanded the Empire, consolidating the conquest of Britain with the defeat of the Caledonians. Finally, adopting the title *Dominus et Deus* (Lord and God), he turned into a power-mad autocrat.

The beehive hairstyle that came into fashion during the Flavian era: a mass of curls piled high on the head. No doubt pioneered by one of the imperial wives, it quickly caught on among fashionable Roman women.

Or that, at any rate, was how ancient sources such as Tacitus, Suetonius and Cassius Dio portrayed Domitian. As always, we must be cautious about taking these sources at face value. Tacitus, a senator, was active in politics during Domitian's reign, and he, like Cassius Dio a century later, resented the encroachments of the emperors on senatorial privileges and the freedom of ordinary citizens. Domitian's high-handed behaviour certainly brought him into conflict with the Senate, as a result of which he put a number of senators to death. He also dealt harshly with the Vestal Virgins, some of whom had evidently not been faithful to their vows of chastity. Their lovers were publicly beaten to death with rods and the chief vestal, a woman named Cornelia, was executed in the time-honoured fashion: she was buried alive.

Suetonius reported that in Domitian's youth, soothsayers had predicted the day and even the hour of his demise. Their predictions were supported in the days before his assassination by a series of omens: lightning strikes, a squawking raven, unsettling dreams such as one in which Domitian saw a 'golden hump' sprout from his back (an 'infallible sign' that the Empire would flourish after his death).[19] He took desperate measures, such as putting to death a famed astrologer named Ascletarion, who had predicted his impending demise. He also lined the walkways of his palace with reflective surfaces so he could spot assassins sneaking up behind him. It was all in vain: in September 96, after he'd spent fifteen years in power, palace conspirators trapped Domitian in his bedroom as he went for his midday nap and, after a wild and unseemly struggle on the floor, stabbed him to death. The Senate voted a *damnatio memoriae* to obliterate his name from history. His coins were melted down, his name erased from public records and his statues either destroyed or recarved into images of Augustus, Titus or the man who succeeded him: Nerva.

Marcus Cocceius Nerva was the first of what history has come to know as the 'Five Good Emperors': five men in succession who ruled the Empire for the next eight decades, during the period of its greatest majesty and success. Unlike the Flavians and Julio-Claudians, these men were for the most part unrelated or, if related, like Trajan and Hadrian, then only distantly. They were chosen and advanced based on merit rather than lineage or violence. The structure would falter only when the position of emperor once more started following a hereditary succession.

The Flavian bloodline disappeared because, in addition to leaving behind no male offspring, Domitian had murdered various cousins and other potential Flavian heirs. Yet Nerva may have seemed an unlikely choice on the part of the Senate. An able operator with an amiable disposition, he hailed from the Umbrian hinterlands. Infirm and in his sixties by the time he came to power, 'Old Nerva' (as the poet Ausonius called him) was a veteran politician, a former adviser to Nero and the author of erotic poems. He soon endeared himself to the senators by issuing coins with such reassuring slogans as 'Public Freedom', 'Equity' and 'Justice'. He righted various of Domitian's wrongs by returning confiscated land and releasing prisoners charged with treason. He died early in 98, after only eighteen months in power, and with no children of his own.

A bloodbath along the lines of the 'Year of the Four Emperors' may easily have followed, but Nerva had solved the problem by means of adoption. As Pliny the Younger pointed out, 'Sons are adopted with more judgement than they are begotten.'[20] Nerva's adopted son was a tall, handsome, 45-year-old Spanish-born soldier serving as governor of Upper Germany: Marcus Ulpius Traianus, better known to us as Trajan. According to Cassius Dio, Nerva had not been bothered that Trajan was not Italian – 'for he believed in looking at a man's ability rather than at his nationality'.[21] Indeed, this Roman instinct to ignore race, ethnicity and origins in favour of talent and ability had always served Rome well.

Trajan proved the wisest of choices, becoming Rome's greatest ruler since Augustus, and arguably its greatest ever. 'The sufferings of the past are over,' Pliny the Younger exulted in a speech in 100 CE. 'Times are different.'[22] Trajan governed, he emphasised, as a first among equals rather than as an arbitrary despot. He exhibited humility, politeness and compassion, and in doing so he elicited warmth and happiness instead of – as in the case of many of his forerunners – animosity and fear. The Senate bestowed upon him the formal epithet *Optimus Princeps* (the Best of the Best), and subsequent emperors would be welcomed by senators with the phrase, *Felicior Augusto, melior Traiano* ('May you be luckier than Augustus and better than Trajan'). He enjoyed excellent press for centuries afterwards. Some 1,200 years later he would receive a stunning accolade: Dante placed him in the sixth sphere of Paradise, among the Just and Temperate Rulers – an impressive appearance for a man who was, after all, a pagan. Still later, in 1930, Trajan was chosen to represent the figure of Justice in the bas-reliefs in the entrance hall to the Supreme Court in Washington, D.C.

Under Trajan, the Roman Empire achieved its greatest and most mind-boggling territorial expanse, stretching from the north of England to the shores of both the Caspian Sea and the Persian Gulf. Rome's boundaries had been aggressively pushed outwards during the Republic, under men such as Pompey the Great and Julius Caesar. However, Augustus at his death left a directive that it should be extended no further. His own territorial ambitions had been dramatically checked in September 9 CE, in the Teutoburg Forest, in a defeat that Roman historians called the Clades Variana (the Varian Disaster). Ambushed in the dense forest by a Germanic tribe, three Roman legions under the command of Publius Quinctilius Varus were wiped out – perhaps as many as 15,000 men. The magnitude of the defeat stunned the Romans, no one more than Augustus, who went into mourning, beating his head against the wall and crying: 'Quinctilius Varus, give me back my legions!'[23]

The loss was soon avenged by Roman armies led by Tiberius and Germanicus, but during the decades that followed, the emperors largely accepted Augustus's conviction that the Empire had reached its natural and proper limits, not least because the potential taxes and resources harvested from Germania could not have offset the expenses required for its conquest. Claudius's incorporation of Britain was a rare exception. Trajan, by contrast, tore up the playbook, fighting wars that incorporated new, far-flung provinces.

Trajan's first military success came against the Dacians, a wealthy kingdom (the Carpathians were rich in gold mines) north of the River Danube, which marked one of the Empire's frontiers. To facilitate the movement of the massive invasion force of ten legions, the brilliant architect Apollodorus of Damascus constructed across the Danube what was then the world's largest bridge. In 106 CE, following a series of hard-won victories, in one of which the wounded Trajan cut up his own uniform for bandages, the new, mineral-rich province of Dacia Traiana was added to the Empire. Its 2,000-kilometre circumference included much of modern Romania, whose name alludes to the conquerors and whose national anthem, composed in 1848, states that 'Roman blood still flows' through its people, and that 'in our chests we still proudly bear a name / Triumphant in battles, the name of Trajan'. The story of this conquest is celebrated in stone, in relief sculpture that spirals around Trajan's Column in Rome, likewise constructed by Apollodorus. The victory over the Dacians was further celebrated in Rome with the mass slaughter of 11,000 animals.

Trajan next pressed farther east, like a latter-day Alexander the Great. He annexed Armenia, crossed the Euphrates, marched his legions down the Tigris, and captured the Parthian capital of Ctesiphon (30 kilometres south of modern Baghdad). The new provinces of Mesopotamia and Assyria were added to the Roman Empire. Trajan even sailed down the Tigris to the Persian Gulf, where, watching a ship bound for India, he

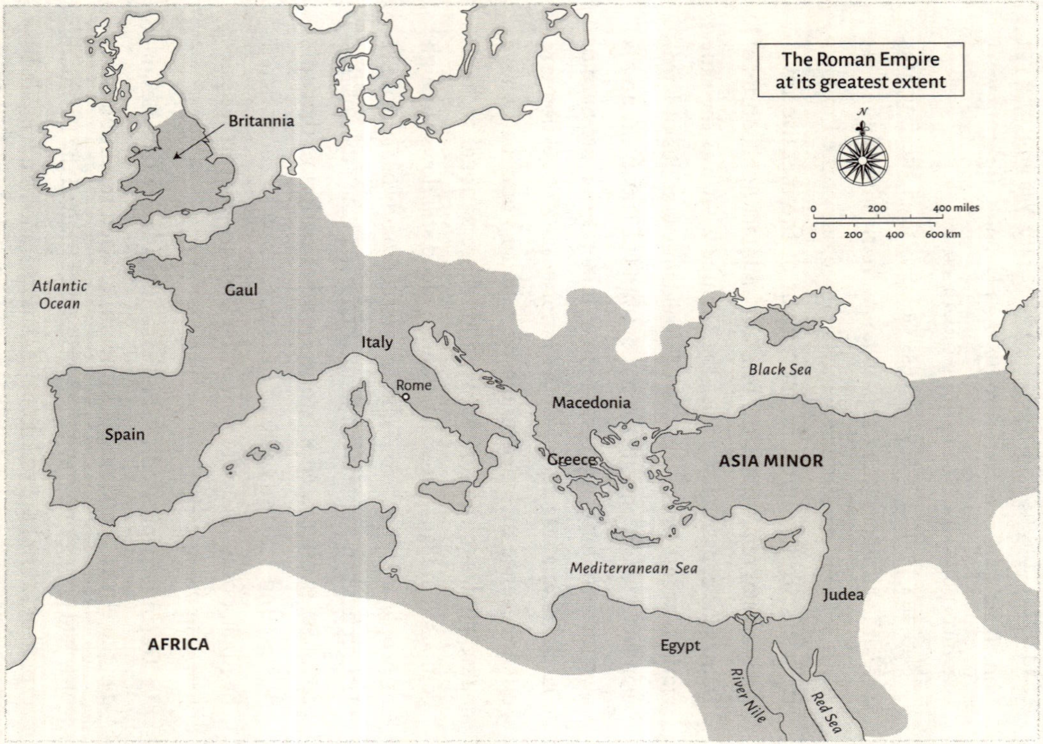
The Roman Empire
at its greatest extent
N
0
200
400 miles
0
200
400
600 km
Britannia
Atlantic
Ocean
Gaul
Italy
Rome
Spain
Macedonia
Greece
Black Sea
ASIA MINOR
Mediterranean Sea
Judea
Egypt
AFRICA
River Nile
Red Sea

lamented that at his age (he had reached his early sixties) not enough time remained for him to equal Alexander's feats. Indeed, in August 117, after falling ill on his return journey to Italy, he died at Selinus (subsequently renamed Traianopolis) on the south coast of what is now Turkey. His cremated remains, returned to Rome, were placed in a golden urn in a chamber at the bottom of his magnificent column.

Trajan's military adventures hugely enriched Rome. The conquest of Dacia brought tremendous wealth from its gold and silver mines. If loot from Jerusalem had funded the Colosseum, that from Dacia was put to use in what became Trajan's Forum, Rome's most spectacular urban development. This massive complex of bureaucratic and religious spaces was a multifunctional public building on six levels. Designed by Apollodorus and dedicated in 112 CE, it included the seat of a procurator, or judge, as well as offices for bureaucrats, three triumphal arches, a market, a temple, two libraries (one Greek, one Latin), the 38-metre-high column and dozens of statues, some aptly bearing the legend *Ex manubiis* ('from the spoils of war'). Its most important building was the Basilica Ulpia, a great law court and one of Ancient Rome's most famous monuments.

In the fourth century CE a historian called Trajan's Forum 'a construction unique under the heavens ... beggaring description and never again to be imitated by mortal men'.[24] Today, thanks to an earthquake in 801 CE and many centuries of looting, little remains but the stunted columns and zigzagging foundations that sprout from the rubble-strewn acres on the north side of Via dei Fori Imperiali.

*

Trajan and his wife, Plotina, had no children. On his deathbed, he therefore adopted as his son and heir a distant relation – a son of his father's cousin who hailed from the same town in Spain, and who in 100 CE had married another of Trajan's relatives, his great-niece Vibia Sabina. Publius Aelius Hadrianus, or Hadrian, was forty-one years old when he became emperor in 117 CE.

Hadrian was a markedly different emperor to Trajan. Instead of pushing the boundaries of the Empire outwards, he returned to the policy of marking and defending the existing ones (the most famous testament to which was Hadrian's Wall, the 4-metre-high, 118-kilometre-long frontier-wall stretching across the top of Britannia). He quickly surrendered many of the lands conquered by Trajan, returning Parthia to the Persians and withdrawing Roman garrisons from Mesopotamia and Armenia.

Hadrian had accompanied Trajan on the Dacian expedition, proving himself an excellent soldier. However, he was also a lover of music, philosophy, literature and architecture. A great admirer of Greek culture, he became known as Graeculus ('Little Greek'). He loved to philosophise and debate with friends, although they tended to concede. As one of them shrugged: 'Who could contradict the Lord of Thirty Legions?'[25] Hadrian composed verses in both Greek and Latin. He became the first emperor to wear a beard – an allusion to the Greek philosophers whose images he admired in portrait busts. He also had his hair curled with hot tongs by a team of specially trained slaves. Hadrian formed a passionate relationship with a Greek youth named Antinous, displaying immense grief when his young lover tragically drowned in the Nile under mysterious circumstances. He proclaimed Antinous a god, and the youth was thereafter commemorated in statues and worshipped across the Empire. In his honour, Hadrian founded a city on the east bank of the Nile called Antinoöpolis.

A biography by Anthony Birley called Hadrian 'the restless emperor', and he was indeed a great traveller, constantly on the move around the Empire.[26] He spent twelve of his twenty-one years as emperor travelling around the provinces and often (as in Egypt, where he visited the tomb of Alexander the Great) playing the part of a curious tourist. The Christian writer Tertullian later called him *omnium curiositatum explorator* ('explorer of all interesting things'). He climbed both Mount Etna in Sicily and Mount Casius (Jebel Aqra in modern Turkey) simply to see the sunrise. Besides Egypt, he visited Gaul, Upper Germany, Britannia and Spain. Crossing the Strait of Gibraltar, he became the first emperor to set foot in the province of Mauretania (Morocco). He made trips across Asia Minor, to Palestine and, of course, prompted by his passion for all things Greek, to Athens, where he built a magnificent library on the slopes of the Acropolis hill. The people of Ephesus, where he stayed for several happy weeks in 129 CE, enthusiastically hailed him as Zeus.[27]

As a reminder of his travels through his vast domains, Hadrian built himself an enormous palace at Tibur, in the airy foothills of the Apennines, 30 kilometres outside Rome. The whole complex was a version of the Roman Empire in architecture, a sort of Disneyesque 'Empire World'. It featured caryatids matching those Hadrian had admired on the Erechtheum in Athens, as well as copies of the Temple of Venus at Cnidus and the Temple of Aphrodite in Corinth. There was a miniature Nile, beside which squatted, for the sake of authenticity, a statue of a snapping crocodile. And he even included, for the sake of completion, a model of Hades.

Hadrian indulged his architectural interests in Rome as well, lavishing on the city more than thirty building projects. He designed Ancient Rome's largest temple, the Temple of Venus and Roma, situated on the Velian Hill at the eastern edge of the Roman Forum. To make room for this double temple, he had the Colossus of Nero moved – a task that required the pulling power of twenty-four elephants. The massive new temple led to the death of Apollodorus of Damascus, the architect behind so many of Trajan's magnificent monuments. Shown Hadrian's plans for the temple, the architect quipped that the ceiling was so low the statues of the goddesses inside would bump their heads if they rose to their feet. According to Cassius Dio, Hadrian 'was both vexed and exceedingly grieved … and he restrained neither his anger nor his grief, but slew the man'.[28]

The Temple of Venus and Roma was badly damaged by a fire in 307 CE and then an earthquake a few centuries later. Today, few visitors as they enter the Colosseum cast a glance at the battered hulk rearing a few metres behind them. Another building from Hadrian's era enjoyed better fortunes: the redesign of the Pantheon, the temple in the Campus Martius built at Marcus Agrippa's expense during the early years of Augustus's reign. Badly damaged in the fire of 80 CE, it was struck by lightning thirty years later and once again burned down. Work on the temple's next reconstruction began in the next decade, possibly during the latter part of Trajan's reign. A spectacular audience hall where Hadrian could hold court,[29] it became one of Rome's, and the world's, most audacious, unique, recognisable, influential and breathtaking buildings.

The inscription on the Pantheon's pediment caused much confusion. For many centuries the existing structure was believed to be that of Agrippa – for, after all, the large lettering reads:

*M.AGRIPPA L.F. COS TERTIVM FECIT* ('Marcus Agrippa, son of Lucius, three times counsul, made it'). But this was simply one of Hadrian's quirks: he rarely put his own name on his building projects, and he no doubt wished to pay tribute to Agrippa by preserving the original inscription. (Trajan, by contrast, put his own name on any and all buildings that he restored – with the result that he was later jokingly known as *herbam parietinam*, or 'wall grass'.) The fact that this new Pantheon was finished during Hadrian's reign was determined only in the 1890s. Roman brick founders stamped dates (as well as the name of the foundry and the foreman of the works) onto their bricks to let customers know they had been seasoned long enough, usually for a couple of years. A study of the dates on the bricks in the Pantheon by a young French architect named Georges Chedanne (later to design the Galeries Lafayettes in Paris) appeared to reveal how the structure, including the portico, was raised in the 120s CE. However, matters were complicated when a recent analysis of the evidence found that many of the brickstamps previously thought to come from Hadrian's reign are in fact datable to Trajan's, suggesting that the Pantheon was begun before Hadrian became emperor.[30]

What Agrippa's original Pantheon looked like is impossible to know for certain. But the renovation envisaged a temple of the boldest design. Cassius Dio tells the revealing story of how Apollodorus, discussing some building works with Trajan, high-handedly dismissed the young Hadrian when he tried to offer input: 'Be off and draw your melons.'[31] The remark not only hints at Apollodorus's eventual fate but also tells us about Hadrian's architectural interests – his passion for 'melons', or domes. Hadrian himself could hardly have been the architect for the Pantheon: it's far too technically sophisticated in terms of its materials and engineering for an untrained amateur (who, after all, had an empire to run). But the overall scheme and ambition – the beautiful cupola that rises skyward with no visible means of support, pierced at the top by an opening, 9 metres in diameter, that lets in sunlight and rain – was certainly inspired by Hadrian's fascination with domical structures.

The building is a visual tour de force. Its shape was as simple (a sphere on a cylinder) as its engineering was complex and challenging. The 43-metre span of its dome was not significantly surpassed until the modern age of steel and reinforced concrete. The sixteen columns of the portico, each metres high and weighing 50 tonnes, were quarried in Egypt. The rose-coloured ones came from Aswan on the Nile, the grey ones from an even more remote and inaccessible quarry at Mons Claudianus, near the shores of the Red Sea, some 4,000 kilometres from Rome. These latter columns, which took a year to carve, began their long journey with a gruelling 240-kilometre trek to the Nile across the rocky Egyptian desert. The columns' bases and capitals were carved from marble quarried near Athens on Mount Pentelicus, the source, five centuries earlier, for the columns of the Parthenon.

Yet only when a visitor passes through these monumental columns and into the rotunda does the building reveal its true grandeur. It is remarkably well preserved – the best-kept interior space from Ancient Rome, and almost certainly the most alluring visual experience ever created by the Romans. Its survival depends in part on the fact that in 609 CE it was converted into a church, having been exorcised of heathen cults and dedicated by Pope Boniface IV to Saint Mary and All Martyrs. But it also owes something, one suspects, to the looters whose pickaxes chipped away so remorselessly at the Colosseum and the Basilica Ulpia being stunned into restraint by the sheer majesty

The magnificent interior of the Pantheon, made from poured concrete. The oculus at the top is almost 9 metres across.

of the Pantheon. Michelangelo spoke for many when he called it the work of angels – something divine rather than human.

This reaction, however understandable, doesn't quite do justice to the ingenuity of the Roman builders and engineers. Roman builders were fortunate to have at their disposal volcanic rocks from the complexes of volcanoes in both the Alban Hills to the south of Rome and, to the north, the Monti Sabatini. Quarries on their slopes provided dense, heavy stones (from the lava) for their roads, tuff (from volcanic ash that hardened into solid rock) for their walls, and lightweight pumice for arches and vaults. The ash and lapilli were readily available, with an especially rich supply at Pozzuoli, or ancient Puteoli, on the north side of the Bay of Naples.

The magic ingredient in the Pantheon's spectacular vault, 'pozzolana concrete' (so named for Puteoli), was made by mixing this volcanic ash together with an aggregate of small stones, water and lime. Roman engineers had been using this ash for several centuries (including in Nero's Octagonal Room), presumably following careful observation and experimentation. Whereas simple lime mortar set only when all the water evaporated, pozzolana set by combining chemically with water. Since pozzolana concrete set very quickly, in damp conditions and even, indeed, under water, it had been used for constructing ports and harbours around the Empire, such as the ones at Caesarea (in what is now Israel), Hersonissos (Crete) and Pompeiopolis (Turkey). Volcanic ash from the hills around Naples had thus been crucial to the expansion of Rome's trade.[32]

Pozzolana concrete's rapid setting and early compressive strength meant it could also be used for structural elements in massive buildings. It was exploited most dramatically in the Pantheon, where, after mixing, it was poured over wooden formworks whose dimensions were carefully controlled. To lighten the load at the top, the architects added lightweight aggregates like pumice, as well as – in order to create 'bubbles' in the dome – empty amphorae, the clay bottles used to hold olive oil. Another ingredient in Roman concrete was animal blood, which acted as a dispersant to reduce the concrete's water content. Pliny the Elder claimed the blood of bullocks worked best of all. Like empty bottles of olive oil, animal blood was something of which the Romans had abundant supplies.

*

One of Hadrian's final architectural endeavours was his tomb – a colossal cylindrical mausoleum, today known as Castel Sant'-Angelo, that towers above the banks of the Tiber. This edifice, with its lush gardens and imposing statue of Hadrian driving a chariot, was intended to rival the one dedicated to Augustus, and to signal the arrival of a new political dynasty. Hadrian had reflected much on his mortality and on his successor in his final two years, during which he suffered so terribly from various illnesses that he begged one of his slaves to kill him (the slave killed himself instead) and asked his doctors for poison. When he finally died at the age of sixty-two, in 138 CE, he had made careful plans for a transfer of power.

Hadrian's first choice had been his great-nephew, Fuscus, but he soon switched his attentions to a young man named Lucius Aelius. He adopted Aelius as his son, anointed him as his successor, named a bridge after him – the Pons Aelius (today the Ponte Sant'Angelo) – and put Fuscus, the erstwhile favourite, to death. Aelius came from a distinguished family that boasted a long line of consuls, but one ancient historian complained that the young man's 'sole recommendation was his beauty'.[33] Hadrian's plans went awry when Aelius, still only in his early thirties, died suddenly in January 138. Hadrian then adopted 52-year-old Titus Aurelius Fulvus Boionius Antoninus, the husband of his niece. Of Antoninus's four children, only a daughter, Faustina, was still alive. Hadrian therefore stipulated that Antoninus should adopt as his own heirs both the son of Aelius – a seven-year-old boy named Lucius Verus – and another fatherless boy, a distant relation who was the great-grandnephew of Trajan, and whom Hadrian had affectionally dubbed Verissimus ('Truest One'). He was a seventeen-year-old prodigy named Marcus Aurelius.

Cheerful, thrifty, modest and kind, practical of mind and sound of judgement, Antoninus proved a worthy choice. He was warmly welcomed by the Senate, which soon christened him Antoninus Pius because of (among other admirable qualities) his loyalty and filial piety towards Hadrian, whom he deified and for whom he built a temple a short stroll from the Pantheon. (Eleven of the massive columns survive, looming over the Piazza di Pietra.) *Pietas* was a crucial Roman virtue encompassing duty, respect and devotion – qualities that Antoninus showed towards the state as well as to his adoptive father. During his long reign, the Roman Empire experienced a notable (and uncharacteristic) period of tranquillity and economic prosperity. Prior to his passing in 161 CE, following twenty-three years of rule, his parting watchword to his guards was *aequanimitatis* (equanimity), reflecting yet another of his many admirable qualities.

Hadrian had intended Lucius Verus, though the younger of Antoninus's two heirs, to take priority over Marcus Aurelius, arranging for him to marry – once she came of age – Antoninus's eight-year-old daughter, Faustina. However, Antoninus came to share a much closer bond with Marcus, a young scholar who immersed himself in Greek philosophy and dressed in Greek clothing. Lucius, by contrast, was lively and carefree, known for 'the coarseness of his character and the excess of his unrestrained life'.[34] For convenience of debauchery he even had a tavern installed in his palace. Antoninus eventually appointed Marcus as his sole heir, breaking Faustina's engagement to Lucius and, in 145 CE, marrying her to Marcus instead. However, when Marcus assumed the throne he generously elevated Lucius to the position of co-emperor. This arrangement proved effective, with the serious and solemn Marcus concentrating on administrative duties in Rome while the energetic Lucius handled military affairs. The bond between them was sealed when Lucius married Marcus and Faustina's twelve-year-old daughter, Lucilla.

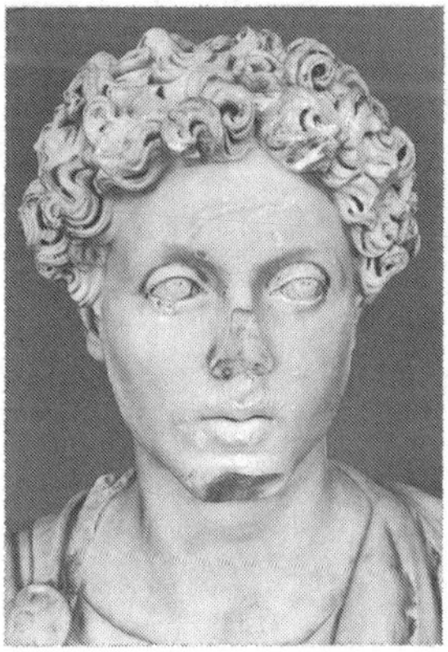

A tousle-haired young Marcus Aurelius, the solemn scholar under whom the Empire faced some of its most terrible threats. He was to be the last of the 'Five Good Emperors'.

The Roman Empire had in some ways reached its zenith at this time. The eighteenth-century historian Edward Gibbon famously declared the reign of Marcus Aurelius to be 'the period in the history of the world during which the condition of the human race was most happy and prosperous'.[35] Yet it was during this reign that Rome was struck by disasters so great that some believed the end of the world had come.

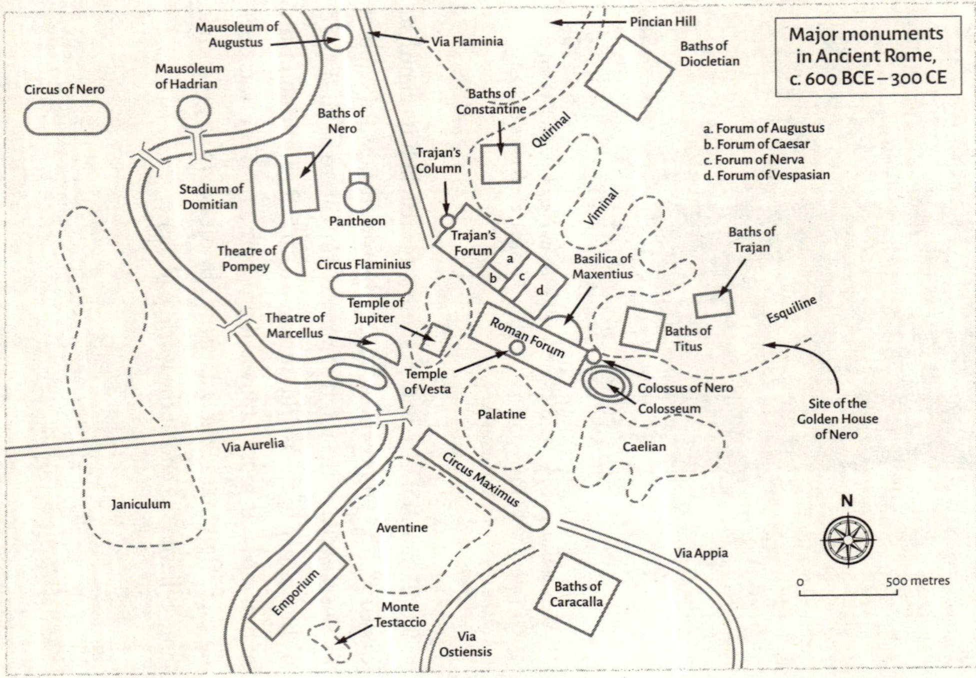
Major monuments in Ancient Rome, c. 600 BCE – 300 CE
a. Forum of Augustus
b. Forum of Caesar
c. Forum of Nerva
d. Forum of Vespasian
Pincian Hill
Baths of Diocletian
Mausoleum of Augustus
Via Flaminia
Circus of Nero
Mausoleum of Hadrian
Baths of Nero
Baths of Constantine
Quirinal
Trajan's Column
Stadium of Domitian
Pantheon
Viminal
Trajan's Forum
a
b
c
d
Theatre of Pompey
Circus Flaminius
Basilica of Maxentius
Baths of Trajan
Temple of Jupiter
Theatre of Marcellus
Roman Forum
Baths of Titus
Esquiline
Temple of Vesta
Colossus of Nero
Colosseum
Site of the Golden House of Nero
Palatine
Caelian
Via Aurelia
Circus Maximus
Janiculum
N
Aventine
Via Appia
0
500 metres
Emporium
Monte Testaccio
Baths of Caracalla
Via Ostiensis

# 8

# 'REVERE THE GODS, SAVE MANKIND': THE AGE OF THE ANTONINES

SOMETIME EARLY IN 163 CE A COIN was minted in Rome featuring Lucius Verus on horseback, dressed in a military cape and holding a spear. It commemorated Lucius's recent expedition to the East to prosecute a war against the Parthian Empire. This expedition got off to a bad start. Lucius fell ill even before he sailed, and once he crossed the Ionian Sea he dallied in the fleshpots of Antioch and then, in Smyrna, took a beautiful mistress. However, he was accompanied by capable generals and their ruthless legions who reconquered Armenia and invaded and sacked the cities of Ctesiphon and Seleucia. In the latter, a city of 600,000 on the west bank of the Tigris some 30 kilometres south of modern Baghdad, as much as half the population was put to the sword. By 165 CE the Parthians had been defeated, and the following year Lucius and the victorious legions returned home. Besides booty from the East, they unwittingly brought with them what the physician Galen called 'the great plague', and what history has come to know as the 'Antonine plague'.

Ancient historians and popular legend attributed this deadly pandemic to the pillaging of Seleucia, when Roman soldiers broke into a temple of Apollo and (according to various sources) either carried off a statue or opened a golden chest. In doing so, they released a pestilential vapour that 'polluted everything with contagion and death, from the frontiers of Persia all the way to the Rhine and to Gaul'.[1] Whatever its origins, the plague did certainly spread death across the Empire. Over the next three decades its steady outbreaks killed perhaps a tenth of the population – as many as 10 million people. It was reported at one stage to be killing 5,000 people a day in Rome, where, according to an ancient historian, 'the dead were removed in carts and wagons'. As the city filled with terror, a man clutching a stork clambered up a fig tree in the Campus Martius and declared what must have seemed the case to many – that the end of the world was nigh.[2]

The symptoms of the disease were described by Galen, the greatest physician of the age. (The pestilence is sometimes known as a result as the 'plague of Galen'.) Modern historians have attempted to identify it as smallpox because victims developed symptoms such as a dry cough, diarrhoea, delirium, inflammation of the pharynx and a rash whose eruptions turned into scabs. However, neither Galen nor anyone else mentioned the most conspicuous feature of smallpox: its disfiguring scars. The plague was graphically described as 'infiltrating pain, heavy-spiriting, flesh-wasting, melting, from the hollows of the veins' – the words inscribed in Greek on a pewter amulet worn in Roman London by a man named Demetrios and found in the Thames in 1989. Demetrios's charm begged Apollo to 'drive away the cloud of plague'. It noted that the god was urging people to refrain from kissing – no doubt a wise precaution.[3]

In the absence of a cure, many others besides Demetrios turned to religion. From Hadrian's Wall to Mauretania and Asia

Minor, people stuck on the walls and doors pleas to the gods for protection, especially to Apollo, whose anger at the looting of his temple had, many believed, unleashed the deadly plague. Those who consulted his oracle at the Temple of Apollo in Hierapolis (western Turkey) were told to put up a statue of him and sacrifice a hundred oxen.[4]

The millions of deaths during the decades of plague took on the Empire a toll whose magnitude and consequences historians still debate. The nineteenth-century German historian Barthold Georg Niebuhr saw it as a vital turning point in history: the ancient world 'never recovered from the blow inflicted upon it by the plague'.[5] Another historian, writing in the 1930s, argued that the depopulation caused by the plague 'contributed perhaps more than any other factor to the decline of the Empire'.[6] Not all historians today make such bold pronouncements, and plenty of other factors (as we shall see) were involved in the decline and fall. But the plague undeniably wreaked devastating havoc. The economy was severely affected due to the manpower shortages. Farms were abandoned, towns depopulated and government positions left unfilled. Between the 160s and the 190s CE, few new public buildings were constructed in Italy. Brick production declined, and between 166 and 172 CE no stone was quarried in Phrygia, the source of much of the marble on the interior of the Pantheon as well as of hundreds of columns and pediments throughout Italy and the Empire.[7]

One of the most drastic effects was on the Roman army. Galen claimed to have witnessed the death of most of the legions gathered at Aquileia in northern Italy. St Jerome, writing around 400 CE, was no doubt exaggerating when he claimed that by 172 CE 'the Roman army was reduced almost to extinction'.[8] But the plague inflicted such tremendous casualties that to replenish his forces, Marcus Aurelius resorted to conscripting slaves, gladiators and rural law enforcement officers (known as the *diogmitae*) whose job it was to hunt down bandits – and he even conscripted bandits as well. He also recruited warriors from among the Germanic tribes to bolster his army for an impending conflict. Because, besides the ravages of the epidemic, the Roman Empire faced another dire menace, this one on its northern borders.

*

The Romans took a dim view of the people – a tall race with red hair and fierce blue eyes – who lived east of the Rhine and north of the Danube. According to Tacitus, they occupied a harsh and wild land, one of bristling forests and unhealthy marshes that was 'pleasant neither to live in nor look upon'.[9] They included peoples such as the Ubii (on the east bank of the Rhine), the Quadi (Moravia and western Slovakia), and the Marcomanni, or 'bordermen' (in modern Czechia). The Romans knew them by the catch-all term 'Germani', possibly derived from the Celtic word *gaírmeanna*, reflecting their terrifying war cries.

The aggressive nature of these Germanic tribes had long posed a challenge to the stability and security of the Roman Empire. Julius Caesar, in an audacious stunt intended to intimidate them, had crossed the Rhine in 55 BCE. He had his legions build in ten days a 300-metre-long bridge to span the fast-flowing river and allow the passage of 40,000 legionaries. The locals fled into the forest while, over the next eighteen days, Caesar burned their villages, took hostages and, having made his point, marched back across the bridge. He then – to keep the Germans out – dismantled and destroyed it.

The Rhine remained the frontier despite Augustus's attempts – shattered in the Teutoburg Forest in 9 CE – to push beyond it. The enormous popularity of Germanicus had been down to the fact that a few years later (11–16 CE) he inflicted successive defeats on the German tribes in their own territories. But the Romans had neither the forces nor the inclination to take possession of the vast, heavily forested, swamp-infested lands beyond the Rhine and the Danube. Instead, the Romans were happy to keep themselves separated from what they called the 'barbarians', establishing a series of palisades, ditches, garrisons and watchtowers that stretched from the mouth of the Rhine to the banks of the Danube.

During the reign of Marcus Aurelius and Lucius Verus, the Germanic tribes began migrating steadily southwards and, in doing so, displaced the Celtic populations. In late 166 CE, a coalition of tribes seized the opportunity presented by the widespread pandemic afflicting the Roman legions to breach the frontier and launch a series of coordinated assaults. The Langobards and Ubii struck first, crossing the Danube to invade Pannonia, while farther north another tribe, the Chatti, crossed the Rhine. All were beaten back, but another tribe, the Iazyges, invaded Dacia, slaying the Roman governor, taking control of the gold mines and then, in battle against the Romans, killing the general Marcus Claudius Fronto. Most terrifying of all, the Marcomanni destroyed a Roman army on the Danube at Carnuntum and then, crossing the Julian Alps on the Amber Road, entered Italy and lay siege to plague-stricken Aquileia.

Marcus Aurelius, a man who would have preferred to live a life of gentle philosophical introspection, faced some of the most dangerous crises in the history of the Roman Empire. He confronted them alone because Lucius Verus died early in

169 CE, possibly from the plague. An unlikely rumour had it that Marcus murdered him with the cunning *modus operandi* of poisoning one side of a carving knife, then cutting a cooked sow's womb in half and putting the harmless portion on his own plate while serving the poisoned one to Lucius. The story probably tells us more about gruesome Roman gastronomy than the fate of Lucius. Sow's womb was a Roman favourite, especially the *vulva eiectitia*, or 'miscarried womb'. This delicacy was obtained through the horrific means of jumping on the belly of a pregnant sow, forcing her to miscarry, then slaughtering her and eating her womb, which was boiled, stuffed and served with a vinegar sauce.[10]

Marcus spent the last decade of his life fighting the Germans (in what is now known as the Marcomannic Wars) and re-establishing the northern frontier. He used politics as well as warfare, detaching various tribes from their alliances and settling them within the Empire, in part to solve the manpower problems caused by the plague. He met with some setbacks, as when a soothsayer informed him that the best way to subdue the enemy was to throw two lions into the Danube. He followed this singular advice, but when the beasts paddled to the far side they were clubbed to death by the Germans. A happier result was achieved in a desperate battle against the Quadi. The 12th Legion was outnumbered and surrounded by the enemy on a scorching summer day. All looked to be lost when a storm broke out and a thunderbolt struck the Quadi ranks while the 12th Legion was showered with cool, thirst-quenching rain. Although Cassius Dio put this 'rain miracle' down to the wiles of an Egyptian magician on Marcus's staff, Tertullian gave the credit to the many Christians in the legion who quite literally prayed for rain. However that may be, the scene was featured on the Column of Marcus Aurelius (which today stands in Piazza Colonna), along with other scenes of the Germans getting their bloody comeuppances.

A beneficent deity showers the 12th Legion with a refreshing rain. The Quadi, meanwhile, lie dead from the thunderbolt that gave the legion its new name: the Legio Fulminata (Thunderbolt Legion).

Marcus died in the spring of 180 CE while still campaigning north of the Danube near what is now Vienna. He later became famous for something utterly unknown to his contemporaries (or indeed to everyone else for many centuries thereafter): a work, composed in Greek, that we call *Meditations*, but which he simply entitled 'To Himself'. This remarkable document was a series of private and random musings that Marcus jotted down towards the end of his life, some when he was on campaign against the Quadi. He presumably had no intention of ever making them public. Their survival is as miraculous (they may originally have been written on something as perishable as wax tablets) as their contents (the candid and intimate personal thoughts of an ancient ruler) are unique. Literally hundreds of editions and translations have been published since the work was first referred to in the pages of a Greek encyclopedia produced around 900 in Constantinople.

The *Meditations* begins with acknowledgements to people from whom Marcus has learned, such as his parents, grandparents, various tutors and philosophers, and Antoninus Pius. What follows are reflections and injunctions in which he consoles, commands and sometimes upbraids himself in a series of philosophical pep talks. He tells himself, for example, to beware of becoming 'Caesarified', and to remember that his purple-edged imperial robe 'is nothing but sheep's wool steeped in the blood of a shellfish' (Tyrian purple came, in fact, from the snot of a carnivorous sea snail). Fairness, thrift, temperance, truth and justice – those are the orders of the day. 'Keep yourself a simple and good man,' he instructs himself, 'uncorrupt, dignified, plain, a friend of justice ... Revere the gods, save mankind.'[11] These exhortations show how far we have come from the days of Caligula, Nero and Domitian.

Marcus was haunted by the transience of life and of the fickle and fleeting nature of fame. Think of all the great men from the past, he wrote, who made such an 'extraordinary blaze in the world': they were all enfolded soon enough 'in absolute oblivion'.[12] Yet the enduring fame of Marcus Aurelius is assured. It is a pleasant irony that the man who wrote these words about the fugitive nature of worldly renown is remembered not for any 'Caesarifying' but rather for his introspective, late-night ruminations on how to become a better person.

*

Marcus Aurelius's death, probably from the plague, marked the end of the era of the Five Good Emperors. According to Cassius Dio, the Roman Empire thereafter descended from 'a kingdom of gold to one of iron and rust'.[13]

In Cassius's opinion, the rust began with Marcus Aurelius's successor, his son Lucius Aurelius Commodus. Not yet nineteen, Commodus had been the beneficiary of Rome's finest teachers of Greek and Latin. However, despite his father's best efforts to educate and cultivate him, Commodus proved to be – as another ancient historian claimed – 'disgraceful, dishonorable, cruel, and lecherous'. He was accused by the historians of all the usual vices: gambling, drinking, cavorting with unsuitable companions, racing the streets in chariots, keeping a harem of beautiful women, kissing a male lover in public and allowing himself 'to be sexually violated, both anally and orally'.[14] At the age of twelve, enraged by bathwater too cool for his liking, he supposedly ordered the imperial bathkeeper to be thrown into a furnace.

Commodus has certainly received extremely bad press, especially from Cassius Dio, who, as a senator during Commodus's time, was fiercely biased against him. Two other historians with critical accounts, Herodian of Antioch (writing in about the 230s) and the anonymous author of the *Historia Augusta* (compiled around 400 CE), were as notoriously unreliable as they were luridly sensationalist. Commodus also served, memorably, as the villain of Ridley Scott's 2000 film *Gladiator*, which – thanks to the screenwriter's careful but uncritical reading of these sources – depicts his obsession with gladiatorial battles. Dio described how, not content as a spectator, Commodus participated in combats of his own. He underwent rigorous coaching from a personal trainer, a wrestler named Narcissus, before stepping into the Colosseum under the fearsome moniker

Hercules Romanus. He fought both men (first making sure their swords were made of wood) and beasts. Exotic animals were shipped from all over the known world for him to kill: giraffes, gazelles, elephants and a rhinoceros. One of his showpieces was to shoot lions and bears from the safety of an elevated walkway: a demonstration of marksmanship, if not of courage. When not dealing death to animals, he lounged in the emperor's box in the Colosseum, swilling alcohol and wearing women's clothing. The contrast with his father was so extreme that rumour hinted he was the result of his mother's adulterous liaison with a gladiator.

Commodus posing as his hero, Hercules. The emperor wears the skin of the Nemean lion over his head and holds in his left hand the golden apples retrieved by Hercules from the garden of the Hesperides.

The sources recount a megalomania that would have given pause even to Nero, whose head Commodus removed from the top of the Colossus and replaced with his own. He gave himself a dozen names – Lucius Aelius Aurelius Commodus Augustus Hercules Romanus Exsuperatorius Amazonius Invictus Felix Pius – with which he christened the twelve months. Rome itself he renamed Colonia Commodiana. The Roman legions became the Commodianae. For good measure, in 192 CE he had the Senate declare him a god.

If we can credit half of what the sources say, the days of the 'bad emperors' had well and truly returned. Commodus's reign of terror recalled the worst excesses of previous centuries, with proscription lists and scores of executions. His murders were not always politically motivated. He sometimes amused himself with vicious and homicidal pranks, such as cutting a fat man open so his entrails came gushing out, or amputating people's feet and gouging out their eyes simply so he could mock them for their disabilities. A dinner invitation from Commodus was not one to be envied, given his habit of mixing human excrement into the delicacies – 'and he did not refrain from tasting them'.[15] On one memorable occasion he served up on a platter, smeared in mustard, a live pair of *gibbos retortos* ('twisted hunchbacks').

At least these unfortunates were amply rewarded for their service, as was a faithful attendant with a gigantic penis ('larger than that of most animals') on whom Commodus showered a small fortune.[16] He was obsessed with the malformed and disproportionate – although so too were many other Romans. Ancient Rome might conjure in our minds images of marble statues of gods and goddesses with shapely limbs and perfect profiles and proportions. But for centuries the Romans had been attracted to the aesthetic flipside of these ideals of physical beauty – to whatever they regarded as ugly or misshapen. Both the excessively large (such as the pair of 3-metre-high giants whose bones could be seen displayed in a garden in Rome) and the fantastically small (the pair of 1-metre-tall Roman men whose bodies Pliny the Elder saw preserved in coffins) were sources of great fascination. Plutarch claimed that Rome even had a special 'monster market' where one could purchase slaves with deformed arms or legs, three eyes or 'ostrich heads'.[17] A great demand existed for these unfortunates since, like Commodus's hunchbacks on their platter, they were used by rich Romans for ornamental purposes. One writer related the disturbing story that slaves were sometimes purposely disfigured: they were locked in cages with their limbs bound, stunting their growth and enfeebling and deforming their arms and legs. Such indeed may have been the origins of Commodus's hunchbacks.[18]

Commodus ultimately went the way of his fellow bad emperors. Several assassination attempts miscarried, but in December 192, following a dozen years in power, he made the fatal mistake of leaving unattended a writing tablet on which he had scratched the names of the people he was planning to execute – everyone from various senators to his mistress, Marcia. Herodian tells the story that the tablet was picked up by Commodus's catamite, a boy nicknamed Philocommodus, who customarily trotted about the palace naked and bedecked in jewels. After plucking up the tablet, Philocommodus bumped into the unsuspecting Marcia. She took the tablet from the boy and – in a tense and dramatic sequence befitting a Hollywood thriller – discovered her name topping the hit list. Wisely deciding to strike first, she served Commodus a cup of poisoned wine and then, for good measure, summoned Narcissus. In exchange for a large reward, the brawny wrestler strangled his star pupil in his bedchamber.

*

Commodus's death was followed by the homicidal rotation known as the 'Year of the Five Emperors'. His immediate successor was Pertinax, a wise and capable general who had risen from the humblest of beginnings (his father was a freed slave). He lasted less than three months on the throne. His plan to reform the riotous and drunken behaviour of the Praetorian Guard (indulged by the riotous and drunken Commodus) reaped its predictable reward when he was cut to pieces in the imperial palace. Ultimately a 48-year-old named Lucius Septimius Severus emerged victorious, defeating his rivals in battle and then killing them.

The first emperor born outside of Europe, Septimius Severus came from Leptis Magna, a city near Tripoli in modern Libya. Swarthy and dark-haired, he was the son of a Roman mother and a father of Carthaginian (and perhaps also Berber) blood. His mother was one of the Fulvii, an ancient Roman family that over the centuries had provided numerous consuls and other distinguished figures. Although he became the first in what historians called the Severan Dynasty, Septimius promoted himself as one of the Antonines, for in 195 CE he declared himself the adopted son of Marcus Aurelius (who had died fifteen years earlier). The fictitious adoption was intended to legitimise Septimius's reign – to present him as a natural and obvious successor to the Antonines. Marcus Aurelius had promoted a similarly bogus imperial genealogy for himself: an inscription from early in his reign celebrated him as the son of Antoninus Pius, the grandson of Hadrian, the great-grandson of Trajan, and the great-great-grandson of Nerva. There was more wishful thinking than accuracy in the family tree thus sketched out, but it meant the 'Five Good Emperors' could all seem to be related. Septimius Severus was eager to graft himself onto this esteemed genealogical tree.[19]

In truth, Septimius was a military adventurer from the provinces who crushed the opposition on the battlefield and then slaughtered the dozens of senators who had favoured his rivals. Since his position depended on the support of the army, he treated the soldiers well, giving them their first pay rise in more than a hundred years. He raised three more legions, bringing the total to thirty-three and basing one of them at Albano, conveniently near Rome. Under Septimius, the Roman army numbered as many as 475,000 men (compared with 330,000 under Augustus and his immediate successors).[20] But he then confronted the enormous difficulty of paying these extra wages.

The Roman Empire had long faced a basic but dire financial problem. Its expansion thanks to the conquests of Pompey, Julius Caesar and Augustus had brought tremendous wealth from the booty of conquered territories, but since the Empire had ceased expanding, the emperors needed to pay for its upkeep – for its administrative and, most importantly, its military costs – out of its own resources. Since high taxes were unpopular, for the previous century emperors had instead debased the currency: they reduced the silver content of the denarius, the standard coin (first minted around 217 BCE) that was worth roughly a day's wages for a labourer. In the time of Augustus the denarius contained 4.5 grams of silver, essentially making it pure silver (apart from an alloy to harden and preserve it). By the time of Marcus Aurelius, the silver content had dropped to roughly 3.4 grams. Faced with vast military expenditures, Septimius continued its debasement, reducing the silver content to as little as 2 grams. Although this policy meant the emperor received as revenue the difference between the face value of the coin and its intrinsic silver value, it brought the disadvantage of inflation, which during the second half of the 200s ran at a rate of about 3.65 per cent per annum – not enough, perhaps, to trouble the dreams of today's central bankers, but a major problem when, unchecked, it continued over four or five decades. The policy of debasing the coinage at the expense of inflation would bring the Roman Empire to the brink of ruin.

Septimius died in Britannia, at Eboracum (modern York), in February 211 while on a military campaign to reinforce Roman authority and control over the province. With him were his two sons, aged twenty-three and twenty-two, whom he had named as his heirs and successors, hoping they would rule together. The elder of the pair, Lucius Septimius Bassianus, had other ideas. As a child he had been charming, respectful, courteous and kindly. So sensitive was he to violence that he wept or averted his gaze whenever he saw condemned criminals ripped apart by wild beasts. Indeed, he seemed to be living up to the new name that his father gave him, 'Marcus Aurelius Antoninus' – yet another attempt to forge a link with the great Marcus Aurelius of beloved memory. Within a few years, however, the young man altered his behaviour, becoming stern and even savage – as his wife and father-in-law discovered: both were murdered on his orders. Next to feel his wrath was his brother, Geta, with whom, following their father's death and despite their mother's pleas, he had no plans of sharing imperial power. Geta too was murdered at his command, in their mother's arms – yet another Roman fratricide.

The new emperor may have been named after Marcus Aurelius, but he was far better known by the nickname he earned because of the hooded, ankle-length, Celtic-style cloak, known as a *caracallus*, that he always wore. Caracalla therefore became the second emperor, after Caligula, to be named for a fashion accessory.

Busts of Caracalla show him with a menacing scowl.

Caracalla appeared to fit the bill as the latest in Rome's depressing roster of bad emperors. However, as always, a good deal of critical and salacious testimony comes from his political enemies. In particular, we have the account of Cassius Dio, a senator during Caracalla's reign and an ambitious political operator who found himself excluded from Caracalla's inner circle – leaving him an embittered and anything but impartial observer. He presented Caracalla as almost uniformly hostile to the senators, choosing instead to consult and carouse with soldiers and other boon companions. In one memorable passage he described how Caracalla decapitated an ostrich and then waggled the head at the senators, 'indicating that he would treat us in the same way'.[21]

It is difficult to either refute or confirm many of Cassius's charges against Caracalla, who appears to have possessed all of the grisly caprices of his fellow bad emperors. His own singular preoccupation revolved around Alexander the Great. He hero-worshipped Alexander to the extent that he founded a

16,000-strong 'Macedonian phalanx': men from Macedonia whom he kitted out with the same equipment used in Alexander's day, more than 500 years earlier – something that must have made them look more like a historical re-enactment society than a modern fighting force. His generals were obliged to address him as Alexander, and to a startled Senate he proclaimed himself Alexander's reincarnation.

Lunatic reveries about Alexander proved one of the reasons for the end of Caracalla's short, bloody reign. Determined to push eastwards in emulation of his hero, he mounted a campaign against the Parthian Empire. While fighting in Mesopotamia in 217 he took a detour to pay his respects at a temple in Carrhae (in what is now southern Turkey). Suffering stomach trouble en route, he dismounted to make an urgent and ill-fated pit stop. The Romans were generally less inhibited about bodily functions than we are today. Their public toilets, known as *foricae*, featured unpartitioned, side-by-side holes in a marble slab laid over a trough of running water – which meant, depending on how crowded the *forica*, one potentially defecated in close proximity to (indeed, a matter of inches from) similarly occupied friends or strangers (with whom one then shared the bottom-wiping sponge-on-a-stick that sat handily nearby in its bucket of water). Elite Romans, however, were accustomed to the splendid isolation of their *latrinae*, the private toilets in their palaces. That may have been why, as Caracalla hitched up his toga, the rest of the company 'turned their faces away ... out of respect for the emperor's dignity and his modesty while in the act'.[22] Their consideration meant that Caracalla, in the midst of his business, could be stabbed to death by one of his Praetorians, probably on orders from their head, Marcus Opellius Macrinus, who succeeded him as emperor.

A public toilet in Ostia Antica. The Romans were casual about their bathroom habits, relieving themselves in close proximity to – and in clear view of – their neighbours.

Caracalla left behind a multitude of portrait busts that portrayed him with a short-cropped, military haircut and an intimidating scowl. He also left behind one of the greatest, and among the last, architectural treasures of Ancient Rome: the Baths of Caracalla. This sprawling bathing and leisure complex – the stupefyingly gigantic stone husks of which can still be seen to the southwest of the Circus Maximus – was constructed between 211 and 216, using a daily workforce of 9,000 men (many of them slaves). Besides hot and cold baths that could accommodate 6,000 visitors at any given time, it featured a gymnasium, gardens, an open-air swimming pool, a library of Greek and Latin works, a temple to the god Mithras (the largest ever built within the Empire), underfloor heating and rooms for saunas, massages and the plucking of body hair. It was beautifully decorated with hundreds of marble columns, statues, fountains, mosaics and polychrome marble floors and pavements.

The Baths of Caracalla were constructed in one of Ancient Rome's poorer districts. For a small fee, the working-class residents could share in the same physical recreations, sensual bliss and aesthetic beauties as Rome's wealthiest classes. Such a democratisation of luxury and pleasure might strike us today as admirable and worthy of emulation. Other civilisations, however, from the early Christians through to the Victorians, regarded Rome's baths as places of indulgence and dissipation, and as one of the leading causes of the Empire's decline. 'The habits of luxury and inertia which were introduced with the magnificent baths of the emperors', the author of a Victorian guidebook primly declared, 'were among the principal causes of the decline and fall of Rome.'[23] This same aversion to the spectacle of Romans frittering away their time on massage tables in steamy rooms serviced by towel-bearing slaves may have lurked behind the early Christian belief that uncleanliness was a virtue. 'He who has once bathed in Christ,' wrote St Jerome, who studied in Rome, 'has no need of a second bath.' The Roman Empire was certainly in peril by Caracalla's time, when there were almost 900 other public baths also available in Rome. But bathing and massages had little to do with its problems.[24]

Caracalla's other great legacy was the Constitutio Antoniniana, known as the Edict of Caracalla. The decree was issued in 212, soon after (and perhaps intended to distract people from) the murder of Geta. It gave all free inhabitants across the Roman Empire the same rights and privileges as Italians, thereby dissolving the legal and political distinctions between Italians and the *peregrini* (as foreigners were known). Caracalla's edict took to the limit the generous enfranchisement policies of Romulus and Claudius. Coming from such a ruthless despot, this liberal edict appears paradoxical. Historians have long harboured suspicions that Caracalla's motive was financial, since extending Roman citizenship vastly expanded the tax base. However, regardless of Caracalla's brutal reputation or any underlying economic motivations, the significance of his action remains remarkable. In theory, the edict bestowed equal citizenship rights upon millions of individuals throughout Europe and beyond, fostering a sense of legal equality under Roman law that transcended all previous distinctions.

Testament to the impact of Caracalla's edict was that the most popular name in the East became, at a stroke, Aurelius (for the emperor was known, of course, as Marcus Aurelius Antoninus). The name was given or adopted in gratitude for what one of the proud bearers, Aurelius Zosimus (formerly Zosimus Leonidou), called Caracalla's 'sacred gift'.[25]

# 9

# THE EMPIRE IN CRISIS

ROME'S HISTORY BEGINS WITH THE EXPOSURE of the infants Romulus and Remus. We have seen how the stories of such abandonments (and the miraculous rescues therefrom) formed part of a thriving folkloric tradition in the ancient world. The tradition flourished in part, no doubt, because the actual practice of infant exposure was widespread. In Ancient Rome, it was used as a crude and cruel means of birth control. Unwanted children were abandoned by their parents in the street or on the edge of the city, from where they might be claimed by a slave dealer; another fate was, according to one writer, to be 'devoured by dogs'.[1] Often they were abandoned for economic reasons: too expensive as another mouth to feed. One Roman writer marvelled that not only the poor abandoned children for this reason but also 'those who have an abundance of things'[2] – for parents did not want to spread the family inheritance too thinly. Deformed children were also exposed or worse, for a Roman law stated bluntly: 'A notably deformed child shall be killed immediately.'[3] But children were sometimes rejected by their parents simply because (as an astrologer explained) they had been born under an unlucky star – when, for example, 'Mars and Saturn are in the seventh house'.[4]

Whether many Romans paid such heed to these astrological superstitions is an open question. Financial considerations were no doubt more acute. Female children were regarded as financial burdens because, among other things, they required dowries. As one husband wrote to his pregnant wife in what must have been a tragically common refrain: 'If it is a boy keep it, if a girl discard it.'[5] Indeed, so many girls were abandoned or victims of infanticide that by the third century CE, Rome began experiencing demographic problems: Rome had 131 men for every 100 women, a ratio contributing to a falling population. The situation on the peninsula outside Rome, as well as in Egypt and the rest of North Africa, was even worse, with 140 men for every 100 women.[6]

This demographic problem contributed to what historians call the 'Crisis of the Third Century' of the Roman Empire – a political, military, economic and demographic plight that threatened the integrity and even the existence of the Empire. One historian has called this prolonged crisis a 'watershed between the Ancient World and the European Middle Ages'.[7] Its causes were multiple: everything from bad governance and financial woes to barbarian invasions, further outbreaks of plague and a powerful new enemy rising in the East. In the end, the Empire would be preserved only thanks to the actions taken at the end of the century by one of Rome's last great emperors: Diocletian.

The Crisis of the Third Century took place, technically, during the decades between 235 and the accession of Diocletian in 284. But the years following the death of Caracalla were fraught and turbulent. Caracalla's successor, Macrinus, lasted little more than a year before he, too, died by the sword when some of the legions, irked by their pay and conditions, mutinied in support of a rival whom they proclaimed emperor. This opponent was an unlikely candidate, a fifteen-year-old based in Emesa (modern

Homs) in Syria who held the hereditary position of high priest in the temple of the local sun-god. His mother, however, was Caracalla's first cousin, and the family promoted the flimsy story that the boy – born Varius Avitus Bassianus – was actually Caracalla's illegitimate son. To make his case more compelling, young Varius changed his name to Marcus Aurelius Antoninus, the name Caracalla was given in his youth. His mother added a further inducement, and clinched the deal, by offering massive bribes to the Roman legions.

In 219, the boy-emperor arrived in Rome. He had probably been born and raised in or near Rome before moving with his family to foreign parts such as Numidia, where his father, a Roman aristocrat, had served as governor. But young Marcus Aurelius Antoninus had about him strong whiffs of the exotic and, indeed, the bizarre. He brought with him from Emesa the cult of his sun-god, Elagabalus Deus Sol Invictus ('Invincible Sun-god Elagabalus'), whose sacred symbol, likewise conducted to Rome, was a cone-shaped black stone. Berobed in what one senator called the 'barbaric dress' of a Syrian priest, the new emperor soon earned the nickname 'The Assyrian'. History would later know him, after his sun-god, as Elagabalus – possibly the craziest and certainly the most inept and ill-suited of all the emperors.

Ancient historians famously portrayed Elagabalus in a negative light, starting with Cassius Dio, who witnessed the boy-emperor in action. In his history of Rome, Cassius referred to him scathingly as the 'False Antoninus' and repeated malicious stories – especially about the young man's sexual habits and profligate lifestyle – for which the details are as lewd as the evidence is slight. It does seem clear, however, that Elagabalus quickly managed to alienate the Senate, the army, the people of

Rome and even his mother. He sold offices of state to the highest bidder, and often (according to another ancient historian) bestowed them on those with the largest penises: a collection of chariot-drivers, barbers, mule-drivers, locksmiths and dancers. A recent historian has made the remarkable suggestion that this penis-based promotion constituted 'an early form of affirmative action'.[8]

Like many other emperors, Elagabalus married and divorced multiple times in rapid succession. He entered seven marriages in the space of a few years, with five women (including a Vestal Virgin) and, like Nero before him, two men. Most outrageous of all to the Romans was his treatment of their religion. The Romans, as we've seen, generally welcomed foreign cults, including many from the East, and there was nothing especially odd about Elagabalus's devotion to his sun-god: both Caligula (on coins) and Nero (on his Colossus) had themselves depicted as the Novus Sol ('new sun-god'), with rays radiating from their heads. Nor was there anything odd about venerating a lump of rock. The worship of unusual-looking stones (most of them meteorites) was common enough in the ancient world, especially in the East. The Minoans, Phoenicians, Hittites and Greeks had all possessed sacred stones, such as the one at Delphi that each day was reverently anointed with olive oil.

Elagabalus constructed a special temple, the 'Elagabalium', to house his own stone, around which, in his duties as priest, he danced to the music of flutes. He took to parading the stone through the streets of Rome in a chariot driven by a team of brightly caparisoned white horses. He himself walked backwards before the chariot, gazing in adoration at his rock. Of course, Rome had come to expect such eccentricities from its emperors, but Elagabalus overstepped the mark when he replaced the traditional religions with worship of the Invincible Sun-God. He even dared assert that the Invincible Sun-God out-ranked Jupiter, the city's supreme deity since time immemorial. Jupiter suddenly disappeared from Roman coins, replaced by an image of the all-pervasive stone in a chariot drawn by four horses, or else carried by an eagle with a crown in its beak. Elagabalus appeared on the obverse, with a penis sprouting from his forehead – a representation of the desiccated bull's pizzle he donned whenever he performed sacrifices to the Invincible Sun-God.[9]

Elagabalus's end was as unbecoming as his reign. Told by Syrian priests that he would meet a violent death, he tried to cheat the prophecy by carefully preparing for a more elegant quietus: a silk scarf with which to hang himself; beautiful poisons mixed with sapphire and emeralds; gold swords on which to impale himself; even a high tower, its floorboards gilded and bejewelled, from which to take a final, fatal swan dive. But his plans for a sumptuous suicide came to naught. In March 222 he was slain by his Praetorians in a latrine, after which his headless corpse was dragged through the streets, taken on mocking laps round the Circus Maximus, thrust into a sewer, and finally tossed from a bridge into the Tiber. He had not yet turned nineteen. As for his stone, it was never seen again.

*

Elagabalus was succeeded by his fourteen-year-old cousin, Severus Alexander, another great-nephew of Septimius Severus. Alexander's reign saw two significant and challenging events: further incursions of barbarian tribes from the North, and of the Sassanids from the East. The Sassanids had defeated their fellow Persians, the Parthians, taken over their empire and, motivated by geopolitical ambitions and religious fervour (Zoroastrianism), begun encroaching on Roman territory. With the Empire's frontiers crumbling on two fronts, Alexander fought against both invaders, managing to keep control of Mesopotamia in the East but dying at the hands of his own mutinous legionaries while campaigning on the banks of the Rhine in 235.

Alexander's death marked the start of the Crisis of the Third Century, a prominent characteristic of which was the political instability of a dizzyingly fast turnover of emperors. Between 235 and the arrival of Diocletian in 284, some thirty emperors (depending on which are counted as true emperors rather than pretenders) held power, many only for a few months before their various deaths by assassination, suicide, plague or enemy action. There was even, in 238, the bloody successions of the 'Year of the Six Emperors'. The nadir perhaps arrived in 260 when the emperor Valerian was captured and then humiliated by the Sassanid ruler Shapur I. This 'King of Kings' displayed Valerian in chains and used him as a footstool to mount his horse before having him murdered and his flayed skin dyed crimson, stuffed with straw and displayed as a trophy in his palace in Ctesiphon.

Even more persistent and dangerous than the Sassanids were the Germanic tribes. In 250 the Goths, who had migrated down the Vistula River from Scandinavia, invaded the Roman province of Moesia (modern Serbia and Bulgaria); at the same time, in a concerted attack, another tribe, the Carpi, overran Dacia (Romania). The Roman emperor Decius mounted against them a military campaign that ended disastrously in the summer of 251, some 80 kilometres south of the Danube in modern Bulgaria, with the shattering defeat of three Roman legions. Decius and his son both died on the field of battle (while Decius's other son and successor, the emperor Hostilian, died a few months later from the plague). The shocking debacle was on par with the Roman defeats at Cannae and in the Teutoburg Forest. The Goths then expanded their raids into Asia Minor, sacking Ephesus in 262 and destroying the Temple of Diana, one of the Seven Wonders of the World.

Even Rome itself came under threat. In 271 the Juthungi – yet another Germanic tribe – crossed into northern Italy and sacked the city of Placentia (Piacenza). Roman soldiers sent to avenge the attack were ambushed and suffered a stunning defeat in the woods outside Piacenza – 'such a defeat', lamented one ancient historian, 'that the empire of Rome was almost destroyed'.[10] The Juthungi marched down Via Aemilia towards Rome, sending the city into panic. Only the intervention of the emperor Aurelian salvaged the situation. Known as *Manu ad Ferrum* (Hand on Hilt), Aurelian was a brilliant general and one of the few capable rulers during the decades-long crisis. He defeated the Juthungi at the Battle of Fano before pursuing the survivors as they fled north and destroying them at the Battle of Pavia. The Senate bestowed on him the title Germanicus Maximus, and coins were issued with the triumphant inscription *Victoria Germanica*. However, the near disaster of a barbarian army descending on Rome compelled Aurelian to take measures unheard-of in Rome for almost 700 years.

Rome had long outgrown the fortifications constructed in the aftermath of the city's sack by the Gauls at the beginning of the fourth century BCE. These ancient walls were already crumbling and neglected by the time of Augustus, and Rome's nonchalance about its defensive structures offered testimony of its confidence in the might of the legions and the expanse of its Empire. But his chastening experience with the Juthungi forced Aurelian to rethink the city's defences. He therefore began a new and larger series of fortifications: what has become known as the Aurelian Wall. Built from brick between 271 and 275, this new wall rose to a height of 6.5 metres and ran for almost 20 kilometres around the seven hills (and also encompassed an eighth, the Pincian). On its circuit around the city it incorporated many pre-existing structures, as can still be seen along a stretch of the Aqua Claudia at the Porta Maggiore on Rome's eastern side and at the Pyramid of Cestius, the Egyptian folly built during the reign of Augustus.

Aurelian earned the title *Restitutor Orbis* – Restorer of the World. However, in 275, in what had long been the greatest occupational hazard for an emperor, he was murdered by his Praetorian Guard. History then repeated itself with one of his successors less than a decade later. In 284, while he was campaigning against the Sassanids, the reigning emperor, Marcus Aurelius Numerianus, was murdered by the prefect of the Praetorian Guard, Lucius Flavius Aper, who also happened to be his father-in-law. The Roman legions then proclaimed as their new emperor a forty-something Dalmatian cavalry commander named Gaius Valerius Diocles. His first act was to take out his sword and, in full view of the troops, kill Aper. It was a typically violent transition of power during the Crisis of the Third Century. However, the new emperor, who would soon be known more grandly as Diocletianus, or Diocletian, was the man who would try to bring a measure of order and stability to the faltering Empire.

*

Diocletian came from humble origins. His father had been a slave, and Diocletian himself was illiterate. His improbable ascent to power was forecast when he was a young soldier and a Celtic soothsayer named Driada, encountered in a tavern, predicted that he would become emperor after slaying a wild boar. Since the word for boar in Latin is *aper*, Diocletian came to regard his slaying of Lucius Flavius Aper as a fulfilment of the prophecy. Although the story is of the most dubious authenticity, the murder of the treacherous Aper brought to power someone who would attempt to bolster and safeguard the Roman Empire.

One of Diocletian's initiatives involved implementing a system of power-sharing similar to the arrangement observed during the reign of Marcus Aurelius and Lucius Verus. Recognising the impracticality of governing the vast Empire alone, in 286 he appointed a co-emperor: Maximian, a fellow soldier of humble origins. Their duties were parcelled out according to geographical regions: Maximian, stationed in Mediolanum (Milan), oversaw the governance of the Western territories and monitored activities along the German frontiers. Diocletian, stationed in Nicomedia (located in modern-day Turkey), administered the Eastern territories and kept a watchful eye on the Sassanids. A further decentralisation of power attempted to address the ever-present problem of imperial succession. In 293, each of these two senior emperors (or 'augustuses') appointed a junior emperor, known as a 'caesar', to assist him and eventually inherit his position. Constantius, stationed in Trier on the northern frontier, was appointed by Maximian, while Galerius, stationed in Sirmium (in modern Serbia), was selected by Diocletian. The allegiances were reinforced when Constantius and Galerius divorced their wives and married the daughters of Maximian and Diocletian respectively, each of whom then adopted his caesar as his son.

So was born the Tetrarchy, or rule of four – what came to be known as the *Quattuor Principes Mundi* ('Four Princes of the World'). Diocletian remained, however, the dominant personality. He ruled with great pomp, robing himself in purple silk and forcing everyone either to stand in his presence or, if they approached him, to prostrate themselves – the latter probably intended to foil the sort of opportunistic assassins who had eliminated so many of his predecessors.

All for one, and one for all. This statue, from about 300 CE, represents the four tetrarchs demonstrating solidarity.

None of the four tetrarchs was an aristocrat, and none had been born in Italy. All of them hailed, rather, from the Balkans. Diocletian came from Salona (near present-day Split in Croatia), the capital of the Roman province of Dalmatia. Maximian, son of a shopkeeper, and Constantius (whose son later invented a bogus genealogy to cover up his humble origins) had both been born in what is now Serbia. Galerius started life herding sheep in Dacia, though he did claim to have been conceived when his mother had sex with Mars (which, as the Christian writer Lactantius sneered, meant that his mother was an adulteress). The other thing the tetrarchs had in common was their tremendous prowess as generals. A document drawn up in 301 listed their numerous credentials as conquerors of the Germans, the Sarmatians, the Medes, the Persians, the Britons, the Carpi, the Armenians and the Adiabeni – the latter a kingdom in Mesopotamia.

Crucially, none of the Four Princes of the World was based in Rome, which after 286 had been supplanted as the capital in the West by Mediolanum. Diocletian's only visit to Rome came in 303, nearly two decades into his rule, indicating the diminishing significance of the Eternal City and its traditional institutions. He did bestow on the Roman people a magnificent new set of baths that rivalled those of Caracalla in size and magnificence.

Diocletian implemented numerous administrative changes primarily intended to decentralise political authority, establish an effective bureaucracy and distinguish between civil and military governance. He wished in particular to mitigate the political influence of the legions, which had played such a significant role in the rise and fall of emperors during the preceding decades of military anarchy. His bureaucracy ultimately became so massive that, according to one estimate, half the population of the Empire was employed in the civil service.[11] Not that Diocletian neglected the army. On the contrary: he virtually doubled it in size, to perhaps as many as 600,000 men, adding some thirty-five new legions to the forty-two that existed at the beginning of his reign. Not relying on sheer force of numbers, he also undertook an enormous program of building and repairing defensive fortifications along the frontiers.

All of these measures, which now included the upkeep of four ostentatious imperial courts, came at a huge financial cost. To increase revenue, Diocletian attempted a more efficient system of taxation, assessing land based on its productivity rather than its size. However, taxes could not easily be paid in cash because of the debasement of the coinage (the denarius had dropped to a minuscule 0.02 per cent silver), which meant money was next to worthless. Landowners in the countryside were thus forced to pay tax by means of agricultural products such as wheat, and merchants were reduced to bartering goods and services.

The debasement of the coinage had, as we've seen, another detrimental effect. By 300, inflation reached 35 per cent per annum, causing eyewatering price rises: some commodities cost seventy times as much as they had in the days of Augustus.[12] Compounding the problem was hoarding and profiteering. Diocletian deplored the enormous profits made by greedy individuals who cornered and controlled the markets. He attempted to deal with both hyperinflation and the profiteers by means of the Edict of Maximum Prices, promulgated in the autumn of 301. It was the world's first experiment with wage and price control, establishing price ceilings for more than a thousand products: everything from radish seeds, snails and pork sausages to peacock feathers, gazelle and lion skins, racehorses and slaves. Of the latter, the most expensive – 'of the masculine sex, from sixteen years to forty years' – cost 30,000 denarii, the same as a camel ('female, with two humps') and less than a third of the price of a good racehorse. The most expensive item on the list was a male lion from Africa, which required an outlay of 150,000 denarii.[13]

Diocletian's edict promised severe punishments for black marketeers and anyone selling above the approved rates. It also set maximum salaries for approximately 125 different occupations, including camel drivers and water carriers (25 denarii for each day of work), scribes (25 denarii for every 100 lines of 'the best writing') and tailors (25 denarii for cutting and finishing a *caracallus*). Barbers could earn two denarii for each shave, armourers six denarii for every axe they sharpened – and a further two if the weapon was double-edged. The approved monthly rates for teachers offer an insight into the educational priorities of the late Roman world. Teachers of arithmetic or shorthand could charge 75 denarii per month, those of geometry or Greek or Latin literature 200, and teachers of rhetoric – the art of public speaking – 250 per month.

Diocletian also undertook another initiative aimed at propping up the tottering Empire. In 302 he had been in Antioch watching a haruspex examine the entrails of a dead animal – the ancient Etruscan art of divining the future. But when the entrails failed to reveal anything, an anxious Diocletian consulted the local oracle of Apollo. Here he was informed that the haruspex's reading failed because Christian courtiers present for the ceremony had crossed themselves, an act that frightened off the divine beings who inscribed signs of the future on the livers of animals. Diocletian promptly had the courtiers flogged and all Christians dismissed from the Roman legions in the East (actions that attest to the presence of Christians both at the imperial court and in the Roman army). Then, on 23 February 303, back in Nicomedia and suspicious about a fire in his palace that Galerius blamed on the Christians, he unleashed the Great Persecution.

*

The number of Christians had been growing steadily. By Diocletian's time the Christian population of Rome was about 50,000. They accounted for perhaps 10 per cent of the Empire's population, with the greatest number in the East. However, Rome was the seat of the papacy thanks to (as we have seen) Peter and Paul, the two chief apostles, having been martyred and interred in the city, and Peter – since Christ gave him 'the keys to the Kingdom of Heaven' – being regarded as the Bishop of Rome and the first pope. Christianity was technically illegal, punishable by death, from the reign of Trajan forward.[14] As a religion fixated on the afterlife rather than the pursuit of personal glory and worldly gain, it was deeply subversive of Rome's values and institutions. Yet for the most part Romans grudgingly tolerated Christians, as they did Jews (who had a full legal right to their own worship) and indeed many of the other cults and religions imported into Italy. Nero persecuted Christians in the 60s CE, but not until the third century, when the Empire was in crisis, did the persecutions of Christians become more widespread and systematic. In 250 the emperor Decius ordered all citizens around the Empire, with the exception of Jews – who enjoyed certain exemptions thanks to the pragmatic and often tolerant approach of Roman authorities – to burn incense to the Roman gods. Since refusal to do so amounted to treason, Christians who disdained the Roman gods were either imprisoned or executed. Pope Fabian was among the first victims. Over the next few years two of his successors, Cornelius and Stephen, were likewise martyred, with Stephen decapitated (according to one legend) as he celebrated Mass. In the summer of 258 a Spanish-born archdeacon named Laurentius (the future St Lawrence) was executed in Rome by the emperor Valerian, supposedly roasted slowly on a red-hot *craticula*, or gridiron. With impressive gallows humour, Laurentius quipped to his executioners that he was done on one side and therefore they should flip him over. (St Lawrence is now – thanks to the sardonic wit of the faithful – the patron saint of cooks.)

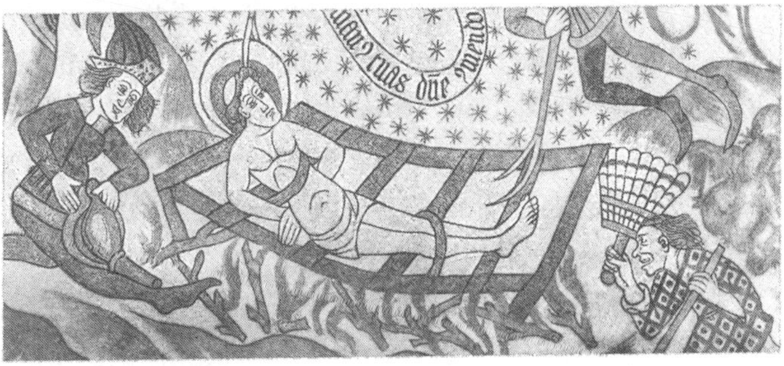

A fifteenth-century fresco showing St Lawrence (martyred under Valerian) strapped to a gridiron as his persecutors eagerly fan the flames.

However unlikely the story of the gridiron, Valerian's persecutions were real and harsh enough. He decreed that all bishops and deacons should be punished, that Christians who were senators and other public figures should lose their positions, and that if they persisted in their faith they should lose their heads. There was an economic as well as a religious motive behind these persecutions. In the old days, Roman emperors had filled their coffers by confiscating the property of their political enemies; now it was the turn of the Christians to be shaken down, their property looted and claimed by the treasury.

The wave of persecutions in the 250s had ended with Valerian's capture, humiliation and execution two years later at the hands of (as we've seen) the Sassanid King of Kings. The grisly fates of Decius and Valerian, the two emperors who so aggressively persecuted Christians, must have strengthened Christian arguments about the workings of divine providence.

Christianity certainly benefited from the anarchy and misery of the third century. At a time when the old gods seemed as devalued and unreliable as the currency, Christianity offered to Roman citizens reassuring messages about how the things of the Earth were to be despised, there was nobility in suffering, and better things awaited in the hereafter. Intriguingly, Christian converts during the first few centuries were disproportionately female. Christianity appealed to women because it accorded them a higher status, including the possibility of occupying positions of authority such as that of deaconess. This prominence of women in the Church is reflected in the large number of female saints and martyrs.[15]

Christians at first fared well under Diocletian's reign. Eusebius of Caesarea, born about 260, praised Diocletian for his indulgence of Church officials as well as of the Christians in his household, which included both his wife, Prisca, and his daughter, Valeria (further examples of the appeal of Christianity to women). The emperor instead took a firm hand against a different religion, burning alive the Manichaeans, members of a cult from Persia that had recently appeared in Europe and North Africa. But then, in 303, he came for the Christians. Galerius is the one blamed by Lactantius for turning Diocletian against the Christians. Although Galerius was married to Valeria, his mother was a fanatical pagan who, according to Lactantius, became furious with her Christian servants when they refused to eat the meat she had sacrificed to her primitive and vengeful mountain gods. She therefore urged Galerius to unleash the persecution.

Whatever the cause, over the following decade the repressions came swiftly and brutally: churches and cathedrals were demolished, the Holy Scriptures burned, and any Christians in positions of authority were required on penalty of death to renounce their faith. Eusebius enumerated the particular punishments meted out around the Empire: in Arabia they were killed with axes, in Cappadocia their legs were broken, in Antioch they were roasted on heated gridirons, and the Mesopotamians strung them upside-down by their feet and kindled a fire beneath. Martyrs included St Sebastian, a young captain in the Praetorian Guard originally from Mediolanum. After assisting persecuted Christians in Rome, he was marched before a firing squad of Mauretanian archers (a scene beloved of many fifteenth-century artists). He recovered from his arrow wounds after being tended by St Irene (another favourite scene), only to be clubbed to death and buried in an abandoned pozzolana mine south of Rome on Via Appia.

This disused mine was one of the underground labyrinths in which – following the example of the city's Jews, who did not cremate their dead – the Christians of Rome had been interring their loved ones, wrapping them in shrouds and placing them in niches (*loculi*) cut into the volcanic rock and sealed with slabs of marble or terracotta. The most prestigious and coveted sites for burial were the niches in positions known as *retro sanctos* ('behind the saints'). A wealthy Christian might be interred not in a niche but in a table-tomb beneath a semicircular arch; the arches and walls were often painted with decorations – some of the earliest surviving Christian art.

Today we refer to all of these subterranean cemeteries that honeycomb the outskirts of Rome as catacombs (a word whose original meaning is much debated). In Roman times this term was reserved only for the cemetery where St Sebastian was buried inside an ancient stone quarry. All of the other below-ground passages were known as *coemeteria*, from the Greek κοιμητήριον (koimitírion), which means 'sleeping place' or 'dormitory' – a reference to the belief that the dead would 'awaken' with the Resurrection. With literally hundreds of kilometres of passageways, the *coemeteria* served, from the late second century through to the early 400s, as the last resting place of at least 500,000 bodies – evidence of how populous the Christian community in Rome would ultimately become. Because within a year of Diocletian's death in 311, the fortunes of Christians in the Roman Empire underwent a drastic transformation.

*

The Tetrarchy ultimately failed to ensure the smooth transfers of power envisaged by Diocletian. Rivalry, ambition and an unwillingness to cooperate put paid to his best laid plans. He and his fellow augustus, Maximian, retired in 305, to be succeeded, as planned, by their caesars, Galerius and Constantius. When Constantius died in Eboracum (York) in the summer of 306, his legions proclaimed his 34-year-old son, Constantine, as augustus – a position that Galerius granted instead to his own caesar, Severus. Even more disgruntled than Constantine was Maximian's son Maxentius, who in 307, with the support of the Senate and the Praetorian Guard, declared himself augustus. What followed were various battles, treacherously shifting alliances and executions. In 311 Galerius died in Serdika (Sofia) following a horrific illness that Christian authors were delighted to report: ulcers on his privates led to putrefying flesh and worms consuming his intestines; the stench supposedly enveloped the entire city. The way was clear for a showdown between Constantine and Maxentius.

In the spring of 312 Constantine crossed the Alps through the Mont Cenis Pass with an army of 40,000 men. He quickly captured the Alpine town of Segusium (Susa) before moving on to take the larger city of Augusta Taurinorum (Turin) and then Verona, both times heavily defeating the forces of Maxentius. He then began his descent through Italy to Rome, preparing for a momentous final confrontation.

Maxentius remained hunkered down in Rome because soothsayers foretold that he would perish if he left the city. He hoped to resist Constantine's assault thanks to the robust Aurelian Walls (which he had recently strengthened) and his numerically superior forces: some 100,000 troops, including the elite force of the Praetorian Guard. He may well have prevailed had he not, as his enemy descended Via Flaminia, ordered the Sibylline Books to be inspected. Made bold by their pronouncement that 'the enemy of the Romans' would perish in battle, he marched his men through the Porta Flaminia on Rome's north side. His army crossed the Tiber using not the Milvian Bridge – which Maxentius had knocked down, along with other bridges, to hamper Constantine's progress – but a pontoon bridge he cobbled together from barges and rafts.

While Maxentius consulted the Sibylline Books, Constantine received a different kind of omen on the eve of the battle. Two authors, Lactantius and Eusebius, both Christians with close ties to Constantine, recounted the event, although each presented a slightly different version. According to Lactantius, writing three years later, Constantine had a dream in which he was instructed to utilise a specific symbol, the Chi-Rho, which consisted of the Greek letters X and P, representing the first two letters of ΧΡΙΣΤΟΣ ('Christ'). Constantine duly had the emblem painted onto the shields of his soldiers as they prepared for battle.

Eusebius, writing thirty years later, asserted that Constantine's vision was not merely a personal dream but rather a celestial phenomenon witnessed by him and his entire army. On the eve of a battle two years earlier, Constantine had received a vision of the Invincible Sun-God, and on this occasion he was on the alert for any other such portents. Instead of offering sacrifices to the traditional Roman deities – which he observed had consistently failed previous emperors – he chose to pray to the Christian God. In the midst of his prayer, he and his troops witnessed a luminous cross in the sky alongside the Greek inscription ἐν τούτῳ νίκα (Latinised as *In hoc signo vinces* – 'In this sign you shall conquer'). Constantine therefore had the symbol of the cross depicted not on shields but, with the hasty assistance of artisans using gold and precious stones, on his battle standard. The following day – 28 October 312 – he confronted the troops of Maxentius as they crossed the Tiber River.

Maxentius's army bested Constantine's in their first engagement, at Saxa Rubra, or Red Rock, some 10 kilometres north of the Porta Flaminia. But they failed to press their advantage, and as Constantine led the cavalry charge Maxentius's troops found themselves exposed with their backs to the Tiber. The auxiliaries panicked and attempted to flee across the pontoon bridge, which collapsed under their weight, drowning many of them and taking the life of Maxentius himself. After his body was fished from the waters, he was decapitated and his head impaled on a spear. The Praetorian Guard fought through the night, but the cause was lost: Constantine's victory was absolute. The next day, he marched into Rome as the undisputed ruler of the Western Empire, attributing his triumph to the divine intervention of the Christian God.

He then sought to show his gratitude. In 313, he convened with Licinius, the Eastern augustus, in Mediolanum, where they jointly issued the Edict of Toleration, granting Christians unrestricted freedom of worship. He also made other magnanimous gestures, restoring property confiscated from Christians during Diocletian's persecutions, exempting the Church and its clergy from taxes, and providing land on which Christians might construct churches. He prudently preserved the ceremonial heart of Rome, with its abundance of ancient monuments, while overseeing the construction of two new Christian basilicas on the outskirts: St Peter's in the west – on the site where it was believed St Peter had been interred – and St John Lateran in the southeast. To commemorate his victory, he raised a triumphal arch beside the Colosseum, the Arch of Constantine, one of whose scenes showed Maxentius and his army drowning in the Tiber. An inscription at the top asserted that Constantine delivered Rome from its tyrant because he was 'divinely inspired' – though it failed to specify which divinity had inspired the victory.

Constantine did not remain long in Rome, which, after all, was not one of the Empire's capitals. He departed shortly after his triumph and revisited the city only on two other occasions, in 315 and again in 326. On the latter occasion he angered the locals by refusing to take part in a pagan ceremony. These were the briefest of stays, and indeed throughout his long reign (he died in Nicomedia in 337) he spent less than six months in total in Rome. His son and successor, Constantine II, never once set foot in the city.

Maxentius proved to be the last emperor of any importance to live in Rome, and the last to embellish it with grandiose architectural dreams. During his six-year reign he had bolstered his precarious claim to power and legitimacy through a magnificent building program that recalled the days of Augustus and Trajan. A fire in 306 offered him the opportunity both to restore damaged temples and to add new attractions, including public baths on the Quirinal. An earthquake that caused part of the Circus Maximus to collapse, killing 13,000 people, inspired him to build a new circus on Via Appia, just outside Rome.

Maxentius's most spectacular contribution to Rome's architecture stood at the heart of the city: a gigantic new basilica intended to serve as a law court and imperial audience hall. Running the length of a football pitch, with vaults 22 metres wide and soaring 10 storeys high, it offers testimony to the fact the Roman architects and engineers of the early fourth century were every bit as adept and ambitious as those of Trajan and Hadrian two centuries earlier. Alas for Maxentius, unfinished in October 312, it's known today as the Basilica of Maxentius and Constantine – for the latter hijacked various of the former's building works (including his baths) and attached his name to them. Even the Arch of Constantine appears to have been begun by Maxentius and then claimed by Constantine following his victory.[16]

Constantine was as determined as Maxentius to leave his stamp on Rome. However, he was the emperor who led to its decline in importance as he shifted the Empire's centre of gravity eastwards. Tensions between him and his co-emperor in the East, Licinius, contributed to several armed confrontations before, in 324, he defeated Licinius at the Battle of Chrysopolis, on the east side of the Bosporus Strait. He reigned thereafter as the sole augustus, with his son Constantius II as caesar. During his campaign against Licinius he had noticed on the west side of the Bosporus a city, Byzantium, whose strategic importance – its impregnability as well as its quick access to the frontiers of both the Danube (where lurked hostile Germanic tribes) and Mesopotamia (the Sassanids) – did not escape him.

On 8 November 324, he therefore founded on the site a new capital, Nova Roma, which after his death became known as Constantinople. This 'New Rome' would thrive and flourish as the old one continued to wane in political significance.

Even so, we must not be too hasty in proclaiming the end of Rome's importance. By the middle of the fourth century its population still stood as high as perhaps 800,000 people, and a document of the time, a catalogue of the buildings and landmarks of Rome, listed nineteen aqueducts, twenty-eight libraries and 254 bakeries. Catering to all needs, it could also boast forty-six brothels and 144 public latrines.[17]

# 10

# 'THERE WILL NEVER BE AN END TO THE POWER OF ROME'

BY THE TIME OF CONSTANTINE'S DEATH in 337, perhaps half the Empire was Christian, and Christianity was on its way to becoming an integral part of the Roman state. By 400, Christians probably accounted for at least 90 per cent of the population, not least because in 391 Theodosius, the emperor at the time, prohibited pagan sacrifices and banned access to pagan temples. The fourth century was therefore one of mass conversions, and of Christian churches supplanting pagan temples. The Roman aristocracy and intelligentsia, with their reverence for the old gods, remained among the few holdouts. The others came from the opposite end of the social spectrum: poorer people living in the countryside, or the *pagus* (a Roman term for village communities). They therefore became known as 'pagans' (*paganus* originally meant a villager or rustic).

If many pagans believed that Rome had erred drastically by abandoning the gods of their forefathers and embracing Christianity, their fears seemed horribly realised when, in the year 410, Rome was invaded and sacked by a Visigothic army led by Alaric. The city was pillaged for three days, with both Christian and pagan buildings stripped of their valuables and, in some cases, destroyed. The invasion was an earth-shattering event. After all, in Virgil's great epic, *The Aeneid*, Rome was said to be an 'an empire without end', bounded by neither time nor space, stretching to lands lying 'under no mapped stars'. For centuries, Latin literature had reverberated with the notion of Rome as the 'Eternal City' – an epithet (*urbs aeterna*) first found in the work of the poet Tibullus, a younger contemporary of Virgil. Four centuries later, around the year 400, the poet Claudianus confidently proclaimed: 'There will never be an end to the power of Rome.' The capture of Rome by the Visigoths therefore left both pagans and Christians alike dumbstruck and aghast. St Jerome, in Bethlehem at the time, spoke for many when he wrote that 'the brightest light on the whole earth was extinguished', and that 'the whole world perished in one city'.[1]

The Empire must fall. An 1890 French painting imagines the barbarian Visigoths sacking Rome in 410 as King Alaric calmly watches.

Reports of Rome's death at this time were greatly exaggerated. But who or what was to blame for the disappearance of Rome's grandeur? The finger-pointing began before the dust had even settled on the sack of 410, and has continued unabated ever since. The pagans, naturally, blamed the Christians for this latest calamity. As a result, a few years after the sack a former pagan of Berber stock named Aurelius Augustinus, originally from Thagaste (Souk Ahras in Algeria), felt compelled to defend his adopted religion. St Augustine (as he became) attempted to refute the critics in his magnum opus, *The City of God Against the Pagans*. This work reveals the broad chasm opening between Christian teaching and the classical outlook. Augustine disparaged the way the Romans had expended all their efforts 'pursuing earthly joys and gaping after transitory things'.[2] The Roman way of life had indeed been a relentless pursuit of worldly glory. The Roman political class had traditionally been – or at least saw itself as – public spirited. Romans were encouraged by writers such as Cicero to practise civic values and virtues, to dedicate themselves to the common welfare, and thereby to achieve honour for both their country and themselves. Roman religion was directed towards the achievement of these goals: the gods were venerated and sacrifices performed not to safeguard the fate of the soul in the afterlife but to grant favours and advantages in the here and now – a kind of contractual relationship summed up in the legal phrase *do ut des* ('I give so that you will give'). The only immortality that a Roman desired was, as Cicero wrote, 'the remembrance of our names', preferably for heroic deeds performed on behalf of the fatherland.[3]

Roman civic values and the desire for earthly glory were severely undermined by Christianity. A wide fissure separated the 'earthly city' of the Romans – with its hankering after prestige, honour and glory – and the Christian 'city of God', to which an individual gained access through prayer, contemplation and a renunciation of worldly ambition. Early Christianity was impregnated with an otherworldliness that advocated an apathy about, even a scorn for, the terrestrial world. The fate of the soul in the hereafter was the important thing, not material gain or the pursuit of glory in the service of Rome and the Empire. As a distinguished modern historian has written, Christian society 'failed notably to find an honourable place for the Roman soldier'.[4] Pride of place was given, rather, to ecclesiastics. The highest expression of the repudiation of earthly rewards was monasticism, in which people removed themselves from the wider political community for spiritual contemplation. Indeed, the word 'monk' comes from the Greek μόνος (*monos*), meaning 'alone'.[5]

The theory that the Roman Empire declined and fell because of the mass conversion of its people to Christianity has enjoyed a long and durable currency. It was most famously and influentially expressed by the eighteenth-century English historian Edward Gibbon, who lamented that Roman military vigour had been entombed within the religious cloister, that the clergy preached 'patience and pusillanimity', and that vast sums were diverted from the army to nuns and monks, 'the useless multitudes of both sexes, who could only plead the merits of abstinence and chastity'. A more recent English historian, A.H.M. Jones, argued along similar lines, pointing out that Christianity created too many 'idle mouths' – nuns and monks who devoted themselves to spiritual duties rather than military or economic ones. The Church, claimed Jones, not only helped itself to a larger share of the national wealth than the imperial bureaucracy ever did, but also proved equally adept at fleecing the poor.[6]

The 'decline and fall' of Rome was not attributable to any single cause or event but, rather, to diverse and intricate processes. Christianity is only one of the – according to a tally given in 1984 by a German historian – 210 reasons given over the centuries for the fall of the Empire.[7] This list covers everything from earthquakes and plagues to hypothermia. It includes challenges caused by labour shortages and incursions by Germanic tribes; health issues like gout, malaria and both lead and mercury poisoning; environmental concerns such as deforestation, drought and soil degradation; social issues like poor education, racial discrimination, gender equality and the emancipation of slaves; perceived moral decay including gluttony, hedonism, homosexuality and prostitution; and characteristics such as militarism, individualism and the desire for fame. Additionally, contrasting attributes have been blamed, such as passivity, sluggishness, celibacy and even impotence – the latter purportedly caused by excessive time spent in the hot baths of Roman spas.

Many of these theories reveal as much about the anxieties and sympathies of the times in which they were written as they do about the Roman Empire itself. For example, in 1916, as theories about differences in racial characteristics were promoted in physical anthropology and the social sciences (and soon adopted in certain dangerous political circles), an American historian speculated that Rome's decline may have been linked to the fact that it had become 'a nation of ex-slaves and their offspring' – immigrants from foreign parts who lacked the sturdy Roman virtues of old.[8] A decade later, a distinguished Russian historian who had fled the Bolshevik Revolution determined the cause to have been the destruction of the urban 'bourgeoisie' by means of a class-conscious alliance between Roman soldiers and the rural 'proletariat'.[9] In 1940 a scholar, witnessing the rise of 'New Women' in America following World War I, pointed to the 'unbridled wantonness, dissoluteness, profligacy, and immorality' of Roman women as a contributing factor.[10] Then in 1950, an eminent French historian who had twice witnessed the Germans overrun his country argued that the Roman Empire had been 'murdered' by 'bands of Germans who had succeeded in living on the borders of the empire for centuries without being civilised'.[11]

These first three theories – those pointing their fingers at racial impurity, the proletariat and women – found little traction. In more recent decades, many historians have vigorously challenged the fourth one – German barbarians rampaging across borders – so ingrained in the popular imagination. Instead they offer a picture not of relentless barbarian onslaughts, but of a 'transformation' of the Empire in which new immigrants from beyond the Rhine and the Danube were 'accommodated' by the Roman authorities.[12] Such histories reflect the values of multiculturalism and cultural relativism prevailing in academia as well as the postwar political consensus in Europe that did not wish to be reminded of heavily armed Germans storming across foreign borders in search of *Lebensraum*. More recently, a number of English historians have revisited this darker scenario, documenting the violence and brutality of these invasions and emphasising the loss of the literacy, prosperity and cultural values on which Roman civilisation was based – not to mention material comforts such as baths, roof tiles and well-made cooking pots.[13]

The causes of Rome's fall were clearly multiple, but the barbarian invasions proved an undeniably crucial factor. Indeed, their role was emphasised by A.H.M. Jones in his magisterial three-volume, 1,500-page treatise on the later Roman Empire, first published in 1964.[14] His conclusion was the 'simple but rather unfashionable view' that 'barbarian attacks probably played a major part in the fall of the West'. The Germanic tribes of the late 300s and 400s differed politically and militarily from the scattered and disunited bands that had probed the frontiers a few centuries earlier. More intensive and efficient agriculture led to greater populations and a more formidable military organisation that, in turn, lent themselves to larger tribal groups, or what the historian Peter Heather calls 'supergroups'.[15] Into this mix, sometime in the 370s, swept the Huns – 'the seed and origin of all the ruin and various disasters', according to the ancient historian Ammianus Marcellinus.[16] A nomadic people from the steppes of central Asia, the Huns were skilled horsemen armed with a devastating weapon: a powerful bow whose arrows could penetrate iron. These ferocious warriors displaced Gothic tribes from their lands along the Dnieper, triggering a mass migration. The Roman emperor in the East, Valens, allowed the fleeing Goths to cross the Danube and settle in Thrace. This short trip across the rain-swollen Danube by numberless 'barbarian hordes' brought about, Ammianus believed, 'the ruin of the Roman world'.[17]

A humanitarian crisis ensued. Famine led to starvation. Desperate families sold their children into slavery for dog meat: the going rate was one dog for one child. Ill-treatment by the Romans led to an uprising by the Goths and, in the summer of 378, a battle near Hadrianopolis (modern Edirne in Turkey) that ended in a catastrophic defeat for the Romans and the death of Valens on the battlefield. The Goths then lay waste to Thrace before, pacified by Valens' successor, Theodosius, they settled south of the Danube, inside the Empire – an example of the 'accommodation' of the Goths by the Romans.

The next few decades would witness the collapse of the imperial frontiers that for so many centuries the Romans had so assiduously marked, guarded and defended. In the winter of 406–407, Germanic tribes such as the Vandals and the Suevi crossed the Rhine in vast numbers, likewise fleeing the irresistible westward expansion of the Huns. The Huns themselves, under Attila, crossed the Rhine in 451, but were defeated at Châlons by an army of Romans and Visigoths. Attila then swept into Italy, intent on claiming for his bride the sister of Emperor Valentinian III and, as a dowry, half the Western Empire. (Valentinian's free-spirited sister, Honoria, to save herself from an undesirable marriage, had sent a ring to Attila – a gesture that he interpreted, not unreasonably, as a marriage proposal.) Rebuffed by Valentinian, Attila (like an 'indignant lover', as Gibbon called him) rampaged through northern Italy, plundering a dozen cities, including (to give their modern names) Padua, Pavia, Bergamo, Vicenza, Verona and Milan. For three months he besieged Aquileia, known as *Roma Secunda*, one of the largest and richest cities on the Adriatic coast with a population of around 100,000. He was about to raise the siege and depart when he caught sight of storks flying from one of the city's towers. It was, in fact, the start of their annual migration to Africa but, to Attila, it seemed a favourable omen: the birds, he reasoned, were abandoning a doomed city. He therefore renewed the siege, breached one of the walls and razed the city to the ground.

*

One reason the invasion theory has been revived is because it dovetails with recent scientific research into the role played by climate change in Rome's fate. Studies of tree rings, ice cores, glaciers, stalactites, pollen deposits in marine sediments and fluctuations in solar activity detectable in the radiocarbon record: all suggest that the Empire waxed and waned according to climatic conditions, and that adverse and unpredictable weather events led to Rome's uncontrollable economic and political problems.[18]

For its first few centuries the Roman Empire enjoyed, for the most part, fair weather. Optimum conditions for agricultural production generally prevailed between 100 BCE and 200 CE, when the weather was warm and wet with few major fluctuations or disruptive events (apart from the eruption of Vesuvius). Evidence shows that the glaciers in the Alps retreated, as did the sea ice in Greenland, while the stalactites in caves in Austria and Turkey record relatively stable temperatures and precipitation. July temperatures in Roman Britain hovered 1 degree Celsius above what they were in the 1950s, allowing the Romans to make wine.

If today we are concerned about catastrophic warming trends, the Romans had urgent reasons to worry about the opposite. The thickening of the pack ice in Greenland and the expansion of the Great Aletsch glacier in Switzerland indicate a change, early in the third century, to cooler, drier and more unpredictable weather. This changing climate – and in particular a severe drought in the late 240s – may have led to yet another of the third century's multiple crises. In 252 the bishop of Carthage, Cyprian, in a sermon to the faithful, recorded in horrifying detail the symptoms of a new and dreadful pestilence. Now known as a result as the Plague of Cyprian, this highly contagious infection caused fever, vomiting, bloody diarrhoea, putrefying limbs and a haemorrhaging in the eyes – dreadful symptoms that have led modern historians to speculate that the culprit may have been a filovirus such as Ebola or Marburg.[19] Although the mortality rate is impossible to estimate given the lack of reliable sources, the pandemic lasted for more than a dozen years. At one point as many as 5,000 people were dying each day in Rome, and the population of Alexandria may have halved.

While this deadly pathogen came, in all likelihood, from sub-Saharan Africa, a drought a century later caused a different kind of terror to emerge, this time from the East. Just as warmer temperatures began returning to western Europe in the second half of the fourth century, a climatic disaster struck in central China, where the tree rings from junipers reveal periods of extreme drought prevailing for several decades. Douglas firs in New Mexico and kauri trees in New Zealand both appear to point the finger at the El Niño-Southern Oscillation in the Pacific Ocean. Whatever the case, a series of major droughts and famines in central Asia were almost certainly the catalyst that sent the Huns storming out of the Eurasian Steppe. What followed were the panicked mass migrations of Goths across eastern Europe and, ultimately, terrible problems that the Romans struggled, desperately and unsuccessfully, to solve.

*

Attila's descent into Italy ended before the Huns reached Rome. As he moved south, the embassy arriving to negotiate with him was led not by Emperor Valentinian, who had fled, but by a sixty-something Roman-born aristocrat: Pope Leo I, later known as Leo the Great.

Clad in ceremonial attire, Leo encountered Attila at Ambuleium, close to Ravenna, the capital of the Western Empire since 402 (its marshlands and watercourses rendered it safer from attack than Rome or Mediolanum). Leo's priestly garments and persuasive oratory left a strong impression on the Hunnic king, as did the substantial amount of money he gave Attila in exchange for leaving Italy. Leo had slightly less success a few years later, in 455, when Gaiseric, King of the Vandals, appeared before the gates of Rome. Leo went to meet him and managed to extract a promise that the Vandals would refrain from killing people or burning buildings – which, by and large, they obeyed during the leisurely two weeks they spent carting off statues and stripping gold, silver and precious stones from Rome's buildings.

In these invasions, the pope rather than the emperor assumed the leadership role in Italy. Over the ensuing decades and centuries, the power and significance of the pope and the Church grew. Revered and influential figures that embodied political as well as religious authority, the popes would spearhead governance and, along with their bishops, assume roles previously held by the emperors and other Roman officials. The Roman Catholic Church, meanwhile, became the largest landowner in Western Europe after the state as, in the words of one historian, 'the nobility got poorer and the Church grew richer'.[20]

The Eastern Empire endured until the Ottoman Turks conquered Constantinople in 1453 – an event marking the definitive end of the Roman Empire. However, the Western Empire collapsed on a September day in 476 in Ravenna, with the downfall of the last emperor of the West. In an ironic twist, he was named Romulus. Only sixteen, he was known by the title Augustulus, or 'Little Augustus'. He had been elevated to the throne by his father, a Roman general named Flavius Orestes who in 475 overthrew the reigning emperor of the West with the assistance of Germanic mercenaries to whom, in return, he offered lands in Italy. When Orestes reneged on his promise, the mercenaries rebelled.

Led by a soldier named Odovacar, they defeated and killed Orestes. On 4 September 476, Odovacar and his troops seized control of Ravenna and removed Romulus Augustus from power. The boy-emperor was treated with the sort of leniency experienced by few of his predecessors: Odovacar pensioned him off to spend the rest of his days in a luxurious villa in southern Italy.

Odovacar was declared king but not, notably, emperor, a title and position in which he appears to have shown no interest. He signed documents as *Regis Odoacris* and *Odovacer Rex*, identifying himself simply as Odovacar the King (although he did incorporate a Roman touch to his name, sometimes referring to himself as Flavius Odovacar). A coin minted the following year in Ravenna portrayed him without imperial regalia, titles or symbols. Instead, he is depicted with a distinctive bowl hairstyle and a moustache. The latter was such a rarity among Romans that no word for it existed in Latin.

Minted in Ravenna in 477, this silver coin shows the Gothic chieftain who deposed the last emperor in the West. Odovacar's moptop and moustache clearly identify him as a barbarian.

*

The Empire in the West may have collapsed in 476, but in many respects Rome never fell, and not just in the sense that the Empire would continue in the East, headquartered in Constantinople, until 1453. The legacy of Rome is still with us today. It lingers in the law codes of most European countries, in the stadiums in which we watch sporting events and in the thousands of words (candidate, circus, curator, ovation, spectator, triumph) that have entered our vocabulary. In fact, some 60 per cent of English words have Latin roots, many having come via French, which has an even higher rate. It has left the deepest of imprints on the political culture of the West. In the 1400s, especially in Florence, intellectuals revived ancient notions of patriotism, liberty, civic virtue and the common good – the values of the 'earthly city' of the Romans that had been submerged for so many centuries beneath the Christian 'city of God'. This rediscovery of the importance of the earthly city, of how to live in the here and now, and not simply for the sake of an afterlife – of how to educate, adjudicate and legislate in secular society – led to the birth of the modern world.

The 'Renaissance' of the fifteenth century meant, above all, a rebirth of many political, aesthetic and philosophical values of the ancient Romans. These ideas and values, especially ones of liberty, equality and democracy, would be galvanised again during both the American and the French revolutions. As Hannah Arendt once wrote, without the classical example of the Greeks and Romans, 'none of the men of the Revolution on either side of the Atlantic would have possessed the courage for what then turned out to be unprecedented action'.[21] The overthrow of Tarquin the Proud may have been, at best, an exaggeration and, at worst, complete fiction; but for anyone hoping to throw off the yoke of monarchy and establish a republic, it was an inspiring feat to be emulated.

The debt of the United States to Roman prototypes and examples can be found not just in the architecture of so many 'Federal-style' buildings, such as the State Capitol of Virginia, which Thomas Jefferson based on an Augustan-era temple, the Maison Carrée in Nîmes. It is also shown in the way the Founding Fathers cleaved to the heroes and principles of what John Adams called 'immortal Rome'. The spirit of the Eternal City was reborn beside Boston Harbor and along the banks of the Potomac and the Delaware. Samuel Adams proudly declared that his countrymen had discovered 'the Spirit of Rome', while George Washington boasted that his troops were acting on 'the same principles that actuated the arms of Rome in the days of her glory'. Few in America could have been taken aback when politicians and journalists adopted classical pseudonyms such as Cicero, Atticus and Publius, when Jenkins Hill in Washington

The Virginia State Capitol, pictured in the 1860s. The word 'capitol' refers to the Capitoline Hill, the strategic, symbolic and religious heart of Rome. The Roman Senate opened each new session '*in Capitolio*' – at the top of the Capitoline.

was renamed Capitol Hill or when, turning up to deliver a speech at the Old South Meeting House in Boston in March 1775, Dr Joseph Warren sported a toga.[22]

Yet there was also, we have seen, a darker side to Rome, and that legacy, too, has been handed down. The United States during the eighteenth and nineteenth centuries followed the Roman example of owning slaves – and in fact the 1:3 ratio of slaves to citizens in Augustan Rome almost exactly matched that of the United States in 1820.[23] What separated Roman slavery from more recent forms in the United States, the Caribbean and Brazil was, however, race and colour. Today's white supremacists and far-right activists see their aspirations having been realised in the 'white' civilisation of the Romans; hence the Roman insignia on display at the 'Unite the Right' rally in Charlottesville, Virginia, in August 2017, and the Roman helmets worn by alt-right demonstrators in Washington during the storming of the Capitol in January 2021.

To be sure, the ancient Romans were, like most ancient societies, patriarchal and misogynistic. Even so, concepts such as 'whiteness' and racial purity held little or no significance for the Romans. Their statues and portrait busts were not intended to convey images (as one misguided theory maintains) of pale complexions: such statues were, in fact, almost always painted. There is no indication that the Romans placed a high value on pale skin. Quite the contrary in some cases, for pale skin might suggest that someone was feeble and soft – and Julius Caesar's fair skin was, like his thin physique and 'distemper in the head', one of the things that Plutarch counted to his disadvantage.[24] Nor was pale skin necessarily seen as physically appealing. Certainly, poets like Ovid sometimes wrote fondly of a lover's 'snow-white skin', but they also acclaimed 'a dusky hue'.[25] 'You're nothing but white skin,' sniffs a female character to her rival in a play by the second-century satirist Lucian. 'Nobody thinks much of that.'[26] Meanwhile, Juvenal mocked the Germans for their 'blue eyes and yellow hair twisting into points with ... greasy curls'.[27]

If the Romans held few negative views about different racial types, it was because they were themselves racially and ethnically mixed. As we've seen, Rome was, from the time of its mythical origins, heterogeneous and multiethnic – an 'open society' based, in large part, on tolerance and pluralism. As one demographic study maintained, only a very small percentage of people walking the streets of Rome 'could prove unmixed Italian descent'.[28] That ethnic variation reached all levels of Roman society and government. Septimius Severus was, on his father's side, of North African descent, and in 139 CE Quintus Lollius Urbicus, a Berber from the Roman province of Numidia in modern-day Algeria, became governor of Britannia. Further, Rome's success was based (as we've also seen) on an open-door immigration policy and an embrace of people of different ethnicities, such as Samnites, Gauls, Greeks and Goths. Being a 'Roman' ultimately had nothing to do with ethnic origins – it was an absorbent and wide-ranging legal and cultural identity (as finally enshrined by the Edict of Caracalla). The Romans even practised their own form of political correctness: Augustus did away with gladiators dressed as Samnites and Gauls because these former enemies had, like so many other foes, become Romans.

Indeed, if much of the world had become Roman under Augustus and his heirs, then so too, in multiple ways, have we. In many places and in many respects, cultural, legal and political, the *orbis Romanus* lives on. The proud boast of Claudianus – 'There will never be an end to the power of Rome' –

can therefore be read not as a pronouncement uttered, ironically, as the Empire was on the verge of collapse, but as a prophecy of a future in which Roman culture, politics and ideas would survive and flourish for millennia to come.

## Acknowledgements

I am grateful to Livia Galante and Paul Chrystal for reading and commenting on large chunks of the manuscript. Much earlier and more abbreviated versions were read by Paul Erdkamp and Scott Perry. Natasha Broad offered helpful stylistic advice, and George Blumenthal provided assistance with the notes. Any errors or infelicities that inevitably remain are, alas, mine alone.

I am indebted once again to the team at Black Inc. for their enthusiasm and expertise in seeing the book through from manuscript to book: Chris Feik, Jo Rosenberg, Sophy Williams, Marilyn de Castro and Amelia Willis. Thanks also to Rebecca Bauert for proofreading and Garry Cousins for the index.

Two people, as always, deserve special thanks. I am deeply grateful to Melanie for her unwavering love and support: *Ubi tu Gaia, ego Gaius.* This book is dedicated to Christopher Sinclair-Stevenson, whose wisdom and guidance have been invaluable to me, as has his friendship, for the past thirty years.

# Image Credits

Maps and illustrations on pages 8, 90 and 177 by Alan Laver.

Map on page 158 by John Gilkes.

p. viii: Romulus, Remus and the wolf: Cebas / iStock; Samnite warrior: Sunny Celeste / Alamy Stock Photo; Hannibal: Collection of National Archaeological Museum of Naples. Image by Fratelli Alinari via Wikimedia Commons; Sulla: Collection of Glyptothek, room 11, Inv. 309. Image via Wikimedia Commons; Caesar: Collection of Musei Vaticani. Image via Wikimedia Commons.

p. ix: Ara Pacis (detail): piola666 / iStock; Trajan's column: Photograph by Matthias Kabel. Image via Wikimedia Commons; Baths of Caracalla: Photograph by the author.

p. x: Ian Dagnall / Alamy Stock Photo.

p. 6: Cebas / iStock.

p. 11: Collection of the Met Museum. Dimensions: Other: 29.4 x 36.2 cm, Fletcher Fund, 1938. Public domain.

p. 19: Artemisia Gentileschi, *Lucretia*, c. 1627, Oil on canvas. Collection of the J. Paul Getty Museum, Los Angeles, 2021.14.

p. 26: Collection of Naples National Archaeological Museum. Image by Shonagon via Wikimedia Commons.

p. 28: Collection of Naples National Archaeological Museum. Image by Marie-Lan Nguyen via Wikimedia Commons, CC-BY 2.5.

p. 33: Jacopo Ripanda, *Hannibal Crossing the Alps* (detail), fresco, c. 1510. Collection of Palazzo dei Conservatori (Capitoline Museum), Rome. Image by José Luiz Bernardes Ribeiro via Wikimedia Commons, CC BY-SA 4.0.

p. 39: Photograph courtesy of Capitoline Museums.

p. 44: Photograph by Carlo Dell'Orto. Image via Wikimedia Commons.

p. 47: Bartolomeo Pinelli, *The Death of Tiberius Gracchus*, 1818, paper, etching, 315 mm × 424 mm. Penta Springs Limited / Alamy Stock Photo.

p. 54: Photograph by Didier Descouens. Collection of Museo Archeologico Nazionale, Venice. Image via Wikimedia Commons CC 4.0.

p. 66: J.C. Armytage engraving after the painting by Jean-Léon Gérôme, *Cleopatra and Caesar*, 1866 reprinted in *Art Journal*, 1877. Charles Walker Collection / Alamy Stock Photo.

p. 69: Elisabetta Sirani, *Portia Wounding Her Thigh*, 1664, oil on canvas, 101 x 138 cm. Collezioni d'Arte e di Storia della Fondazione della Cassa di Risparmio, Bologna. Public domain.

p. 71: Grafissimo / iStock.

p. 75: Photograph by Ángel M. Felicísimo. Image via Flickr.

p. 78: Collection of the Vatican Museums. Image via Wikimedia Commons.

p. 80: Photograph by the author.

p. 83: Collection of Paestum, National Archaeological Museum of Spain, Madrid. Image by Carole Raddato via Wikimedia Commons.

p. 84: © The Trustees of the British Museum.

p. 99: Sergey Sosnovskiy / Flickr.

p. 107: Collection of Farnese Collection, Naples National Archaeological Museum. Photograph by Marie-Lan Nguyen. Image via Wikimedia Commons.

p. 111: Photograph by the author.

p. 122: Photograph by Carole Raddato. Image via World History Encyclopedia.

p. 125: Sunny Celeste / Alamy Stock Photo.

p. 129: Julius Schnorr von Carolsfeld, Woodcut for 'Die Bibel in Bildern', 1860.

p. 133: Tommaso Masaccio, *Predella panel from the Pisa Altar – Crucifixion of St Peter* (detail), 1426. Collection of Gemäldegalerie, Berlin. Image via Wikimedia Commons.

p. 135: Print by Simon Francois Ravenet, 18th century, Classic Image / Alamy Stock Photo.

p. 145: © Galleria Borghese / Mauro Coen.

p. 153: Unknown artist. Collection of Capitoline Museums, Gift of Father Joseph Maria Fonseca. Image via Wikimedia Commons.

p. 165: Fokkebok / iStock.

p. 169: Photograph by the author.

p. 177: Adam Eastland / Alamy Stock Photo.

p. 180: Photograph by the author.

p. 186: Photograph by Jean-Pol Grandmont. Image via Wikimedia Commons.

p. 188: Photograph by Fubar Obfusco. Image via Wikimedia Commons.

p. 200: Collection of Piazza San Marco. Image via Wikimedia Commons.

p. 205: Stigalenas / iStock.

p. 215: Joseph-Noël Sylvestre, *The Sack of Rome in 410 by the Barbarians*, 1890, oil on canvas. Collection of Musée Paul Valéry. Image via Wikimedia Commons.

p. 225: © The Trustees of the British Museum. Image via Wikimedia Commons, CC 4.0.

p. 227: United States Library of Congress. Image via Wikimedia Commons.

# Notes

**CHAPTER 1**

1. Seneca, *Natural Questions*, trans. Thomas H. Corcoran, Loeb Classical Library 457 (Cambridge, MA: Harvard University Press, 1972), 6.8. Seneca's account is confused as he seems to place the 'two rocks' with the waterfall within the swamp. For a discussion of the problem, see Giovanni Vantini, 'Da Dove Viene l'Acqua del Nilo? Ricerche e Risposte di Antichi Scienziati', *Piroga*, vol. 8 (2004), pp. 89–90.
2. Cassius Dio, *Roman History*, trans. Earnest Cary and Herbert B. Foster, Loeb Classical Library 175 (Cambridge, MA: Harvard University Press, 1924), 60.19.2.
3. For the lead pollution, see Joseph R. McConnell et al., 'Lead Pollution Recorded in Greenland Ice Indicates European Emissions Tracked Plagues, Wars, and Imperial Expansion During Antiquity', *PNAS*, vol. 115, no. 22 (2018); and idem., 'Pervasive Arctic Lead Pollution Suggests Substantial Growth in Medieval Silver Production Modulated by Plague, Climate, and Conflict', *PNAS*, vol. 116, no. 30 (2019). For shipwrecks, see A.J. Parker, *Ancient Shipwrecks of the Mediterranean and the Roman Provinces* (Oxford: Tempus Reparatum, 1992), fig. 3.
4. Polybius, *The Histories*, vol. 1, trans. W.R. Paton, revised F.W. Walbank and Christian Habicht, Loeb Classical Library 128 (Cambridge, MA: Harvard University Press, 2010), 1.1.5.
5. See Donald B. Redford, 'The Literary Motif of the Exposed Child', *Numen*, vol. 14 (November 1967), pp. 209–28.
6. See T.J. Cornell, 'Aeneas and the Twins: The Development of the Roman Foundation Legend', *Proceedings of the Cambridge Philological Society*, new series, no. 21 (1975), pp. 1–32.
7. Livy, *History of Rome*, vol. 1, trans. B.O. Foster, Loeb Classical Library 114 (Cambridge, MA: Harvard University Press, 1919), preface and 1.4.
8. See Plutarch, 'Romulus', *Lives*, vol. 1, trans. Bernadotte Perrin, Loeb Classical Library 46 (Cambridge, MA: Harvard University Press, 1914), 59.1.
9. Livy, *History of Rome*, 1.8.
10. Livy, *History of Rome*, 1.9.
11. Quoted in Cornell, 'Aeneas and the Twins', p. 8, note 3.
12. See Hermann Strasburger, *Zur Sage von der Gründungs Roms* (Sitz. d. Heidelberger Akad. d. Wiss., Philos.-Hist. Kl., Heidelberg: Universitätsverlag Winter, 1968). The theory is discussed and dismissed in Cornell, 'Aeneas and the Twins', pp. 8–9.

13. Livy, *History of Rome*, 1.9.
14. Andrea Carandini, *Rome: Day One*, trans. Stephen Sartarelli (Princeton: Princeton University Press, 2018).
15. On the tricky question of life expectancy, see Keith Hopkins, 'On the Probable Age Structure of the Roman Population', *Population Studies*, vol. 20 (1966), p. 264; Richard P. Saller, *Patriarchy, Property and Death in the Roman Family* (Cambridge: Cambridge University Press, 1994); and Walter Scheidel, 'Progress and Problems in Roman Demography', in Walter Scheidel, ed., *Debating Roman Demography* (Leiden: Brill, 2000), p. 42. I am grateful to Livia Galante for her help with this question.

**CHAPTER 2**

1. Livy, *History of Rome*, 5.21.
2. Heinz Bellen, *Metus Gallicus-Metus Punicus: Zum Furchtmotiv in der Römischen Republik* (Stuttgart: Franz Steiner, 1985); and Veit Rosenberger, 'The Gallic Disaster', *The Classical World*, vol. 96 (Summer 2003), pp. 365–73.
3. Livy, *History of Rome*, 8.8.
4. H.H. Scullard, *A History of the Roman World, 753 to 146 BC*, 4th edn. (Abingdon, Oxon: Routledge, 1980), p. 151.
5. Plutarch, 'Gaius Marius', *Lives*, 21.9.
6. Polybius, *The Histories*, 1.10.
7. *The Histories*, 1.13.
8. *The Histories*, 1.20.
9. Livy, *History of Rome*, 21.4.
10. Polybius, *The Histories*, 3.17.
11. Polybius, *The Histories*, 3.34.
12. See H.H. Scullard, *The Elephant in the Greek and Roman World* (Cambridge: Cambridge University Press, 1974), p. 174–7.
13. John F. Shean, 'Hannibal's Mules: The Logistical Limitations of Hannibal's Army and the Battle of Cannae, 216 BC', *Historia: Zeitschrift für Alte Geschichte*, vol. 45 (1996), p. 75.
14. Polybius, *The Histories*, 9.24.
15. Polybius, *The Histories*, 3.55.
16. Silius Italicus, *Punica*, vol. 1, trans. J.D. Duff, Loeb Classical Library 277 (Cambridge, MA: Harvard University Press, 1934), 1.50.
17. Livy, *History of Rome*, 22.57. The Romans also sacrificed a Greek and a Gallic couple in 228 BCE and in 113 BCE. For these puzzling episodes, see Paul Erdkamp, 'War, Vestal Virgins, and Live Burials in the Roman Republic', in Matthew Dillon and Christopher Matthew, eds., *Religion and Classical Warfare*, vol. 2: *The Roman Republic* (Barnsley: Pen & Sword, 2020), pp. 180–215.
18. Livy, *History of Rome*, 22.51.

19. *History of Rome*, 22.54.
20. R.T. Ridley, 'To Be Taken with a Pinch of Salt: The Destruction of Carthage', *Classical Philology*, vol. 81, no. 2 (April 1986), pp. 140–6.
21. Plutarch, 'Marcellus', *Lives*, 21.1.
22. Horace, *Epistles*, trans. H. Rushton Fairclough, Loeb Classical Library 194 (Cambridge, MA: Harvard University Press, 1926), 2.1.156–7.
23. Quoted in Alan E. Astin, *Cato the Censor* (Oxford: Oxford University Press, 1978), p. 172.
24. Plutarch, 'Marcus Cato', *Lives*, trans. Bernadotte Perrin, Loeb Classical Library 47 (Cambridge, MA: Harvard University Press, 1914), 23.2.

**CHAPTER 3**

1. Livy, *History of Rome*, 3.48.
2. Polybius, *The Histories*, 6.53.
3. Appian, *Roman History*, trans. Brian McGing, Loeb Classical Library 5 (Cambridge, MA: Harvard University Press, 2020), 1.34 and 35.
4. Appian, *Roman History*, 1.39.
5. Velleius Paterculus, *Compendium of Roman History*, trans. Frederick W. Shipley, Loeb Classical Library 152 (Cambridge, MA: Harvard University Press, 1924), 2.16.
6. Appian, *Roman History*, 1.60.
7. Appian, *Roman History*, 1.60.
8. Valerius Maximus, *Memorable Doings and Sayings*, vol. 2, ed. and trans. D.R. Shackleton Bailey, Loeb Classical Library 493 (Cambridge, MA: Harvard University Press, 2000), 7.6.
9. Plutarch, 'Caesar', *Lives*, 17.2.
10. Suetonius, 'The Deified Julius', *Lives of the Caesars*, vol. 1, trans. J.C. Rolfe, Loeb Classical Library 31 (Cambridge, MA: Harvard University Press, 1914), 1.6.
11. Suetonius, 'The Deified Julius', *Lives of the Caesars*, 1.49.
12. Cassius Dio, *Roman History*, 43.20.
13. See Ruth Mazo Karras, 'Active/Passive, Acts/Passions: Greek and Roman Sexualities', *The American Historical Review*, vol. 105 (October 2000), pp. 1250–65; and Judith P. Hallett and Marilyn B. Skinner, eds., *Roman Sexualities* (Princeton: Princeton University Press, 1997), especially the essays by Jonathan Walters (pp. 29–44), Holt N. Parker (pp. 47–65) and Anthony Corbeill (pp. 99–128).
14. Suetonius, 'The Deified Julius', *Lives of the Caesars*, 1.7.
15. Suetonius, 'The Deified Julius', *Lives of the Caesars*, 1.74.
16. Suetonius, 'The Deified Juluis', *Lives of the Caesars*, 1.51.
17. Cicero, *Pro Sestio*, trans. R. Gardner, Loeb Classical Library 309 (Cambridge, MA: Harvard University Press, 1958), 45.96–8.

18. Plutarch, 'Caesar', in *Lives*, 14.1–2.
19. Plutarch, 'Crassus', in *Lives*, 16.5.
20. Plutarch, 'Crassus', in *Lives*, 32.3.
21. Julius Caesar, *Civil War*, ed. and trans. Cynthia Damon, Loeb Classical Library 39 (Cambridge, MA: Harvard University Press, 2016), 1.7.1.
22. Plutarch, 'Caesar', *Lives*, 32.5.
23. Appian, *Roman History*, 2.35.
24. Suetonius, 'The Deified Julius', *Lives of the Caesars*, 32.1.
25. Plutarch, 'Pompey', *Lives*, 1.32.
26. Julius Caesar, *Civil War*, 1.15.
27. Plutarch, 'Pompey', *Lives*, 60.3.
28. Plutarch, 'Pompey', *Lives*, 63.2.
29. Plutarch, 'Pompey', *Lives*, 77.4.
30. Suetonius, 'The Deified Julius', *Lives of the Caesars*, 40.1.
31. Cicero, *Philippics 1–6*, ed. and trans. D.R. Shackleton Bailey, revised by John T. Ramsey and Gesine Manuwald, Loeb Classical Library 189 (Cambridge, MA: Harvard University Press, 2010), 3.5.12.
32. Plutarch, 'Caesar', *Lives*, 57.3 (translation slightly modified).
33. Plutarch, 'Caesar', 62.5.
34. Plutarch, 'Brutus', 23.4 and 13.11.
35. Plutarch, 'Caesar', 63.6.
36. Plutarch, 'Caesar', 66.13.

**CHAPTER 4**

1. Suetonius, 'The Life of Augustus', *Lives of the Caesars*, 2.15.
2. Sabine Grebe, 'Augustus' Divine Authority and Vergil's "Aeneid"', *Vergilius*, vol. 50 (2004), pp. 35–62.
3. Ronald Syme, *The Roman Revolution* (Oxford: Oxford University Press, 1960), p. 11.
4. The theory is that of Edmund Buchner in works such as 'Solarium Augusti und Ara Pacis', in *Mitteilungen des Deutschen Archäologischen Instituts, Römische Abteilung*, vol. 83 (1976), pp. 319–65. The theory has recently been challenged: see Bernard Frischer, 'Edmund Buchner's *Solarium Augusti*: New Observations and Simpirical Studies', *Rendiconti: Atti della Pontificia Accademia Romana di Archeologia*, vol. 89 (2017), pp. 1–73.
5. Strabo, *Geography*, vol. 2, trans. Horace Leonard Jones, Loeb Classical Library 50 (Cambridge, MA: Harvard University Press, 1923), 5.3.8.
6. *Roman Antiquities*, vol. 1, trans. Earnest Cary, Loeb Classical Library 319 (Cambridge, MA: Harvard University Press, 1937), 3.68.
7. Suetonius, 'Gaius Caligula', *Lives of the Caesars*, 23.2.
8. Credit for the market and portico often goes to Augustus, who is said to have built them in Livia's name. But for Livia's involvement, see Marleen

Boudreau Flory, '*Sic Exempla Parantur*: Livia's Shrine to Concord and the Porticus Liviae', *Historia*, vol. 33 (1984), pp. 309–30; and Nicholas Purcell, 'Livia and the Womanhood of Rome', *Proceedings of the Cambridge Philological Society*, new series, vol. 32 (1986), p. 89 and p. 102, notes 64 and 65.

9. Keith Bradley, *Slavery and Society at Rome* (Cambridge: Cambridge University Press, 1994), p. 12.
10. Mary L. Gordon, 'The Nationality of Slaves under the Early Roman Empire', *The Journal of Roman Studies*, vol. 14 (1924), p. 108.
11. Seneca, *Epistles*, vol. 2, trans. Richard M. Gummere, Loeb Classical Library 76 (Cambridge, MA: Harvard University Press, 1920), 80.9; and Pliny the Elder, *Natural History*, vol. 7, trans. W.H.S. Jones with A.C. Andrews, Loeb Classical Library 393 (Cambridge, MA: Harvard University Press, 1956), 24.22.
12. Strabo, *Geography*, 14.5.
13. Bradley, *Slavery and Society at Rome*, p. 59.
14. For Livia's slaves, see Bradley, *Slavery and Society at Rome*, p. 60. For Gaius Caecilius Isidorus: Pliny the Elder, *Natural History*, 33.135.
15. See Alexander Szakats, 'Slavery as a Social and Economic Institution in Antiquity with Special Reference to Roman Law', *Prudentia*, vol. 7 (May 1975), pp. 33–45, especially pp. 37–8.
16. Horace, *Satires*, trans. H. Rushton Fairclough, Loeb Classical Library 194 (Cambridge, MA: Harvard University Press, 1926), 1.6.76–8.
17. Cicero, *Letters to Friends*, vol. 2, ed. and trans. D.R. Shackleton Bailey, Loeb Classical Library 216 (Cambridge, MA: Harvard University Press, 2001), 123.3.
18. Horace, *Epistles*, 47.5.
19. Petronius, *Satyricon*, ed. and trans. Gareth Schmeling, Loeb Classical Library 15 (Cambridge, MA: Harvard University Press, 2020), 28.7–8.
20. Horace, *Epistles*, 47.7.
21. See Jennifer Trimble, 'The Zoninus Collar and the Archaeology of Roman Slavery', *The American Journal of Archaeology*, vol. 120 (July 2016), p. 447.
22. See Jennifer A. Glancy, 'Slaves and Slavery in the Matthean Parables', *Journal of Biblical Literature*, vol. 119 (Spring 2000), p. 67.
23. Seneca, *Epistles*, 114.6.
24. Horace, *Epistles*, 1.7.14–15.
25. Virgil, *Georgics*, trans. H. Rushton Fairclough, revised by G.P. Goold, Loeb Classical Library 63 (Cambridge, MA: Harvard University Press, 1916), 1.70–1.
26. Tacitus, *Annals*, trans. Clifford H. Moore and John Jackson, Loeb Classical Library 249 (Cambridge, MA: Harvard University Press, 1931), 1.10. For the 'Lucretia story', see Christina S. Kraus, '"*Initium Turbandi Omnia a Femina Ortum Est*": Fabia Minor and the Election of 367 BC', in *Phoenix*, vol. 45 (Winter 1991), pp. 314–25. For the 'abduction' of Livia in this context: Thomas E. Strunk, 'Rape and Revolution: Livia and Augustus in Tacitus' *Annals*', *Latomus*, vol. 73 (2014), pp. 126–48.

27. Tacitus, *Annals*, 1.10.
28. Cassius Dio, *Roman History*, 57.12.

**CHAPTER 5**

1. Tacitus, *Annals*, 1.10.
2. Suetonius, 'Tiberius', *Lives of the Caesars*, 3.23.
3. Suetonius, 'Tiberius', 3.24.
4. Suetonius, 'Gaius Caligula', *Lives of the Caesars*, 4.2–3.
5. Tacitus, *Annals*, 2.69.
6. Tacitus, *Annals*, 4.3.
7. Tacitus, *Annals*, 4.67.
8. Suetonius, 'Tiberius', *Lives of the Caesars*, 3.62.
9. Suetonius, 'Gaius Caligula', *Lives of the Caesars*, 4.13.
10. Cassius Dio, *Roman History*, 59.3.
11. Tacitus, *Annals*, 1.1.
12. For a good summation, see Barbara Sidwell, 'Gaius Caligula's Mental Illness', *The Classical World*, vol. 103 (Winter 2010), pp. 183–206.
13. Cassius Dio, *Roman History*, 59.10.
14. Suetonius, 'Gaius Caligula', *Lives of the Caesars*, 4.29 and 33.
15. Cassius Dio, *Roman History*, 59.10.
16. Cassius Dio, *Roman History*, 59.15.
17. Cassius Dio, *Roman History*, 59.21.
18. Suetonius, 'Gaius Caligula', *Lives of the Caesars*, 4.25.
19. *Roman History*, 59.29.
20. *Roman History*, 59.1.
21. Suetonius, 'Claudius', *Lives of the Caesars*, 5.10.
22. Suetonius, 'Claudius', *Lives of the Caesars*, 5.3.
23. Cassius Dio, *Roman History*, 60.2.5.
24. Suetonius, 'Claudius', *Lives of the Caesars*, 5.32.
25. Cassius Dio, *Roman History*, 60.19.2.
26. See Michael B. Charles and Michael Singleton, 'Claudius, Elephants and Britain: Making Sense of Cassius Dio 60.21.2', *Britannia*, vol. 43 (November 2022), pp. 173–84.
27. See Tacitus, *Annals*, 1.24–7.
28. Suetonius, 'Claudius', *Lives of the Caesars*, 5.26.
29. Cassius Dio, *Roman History*, 60.14.3.
30. Tacitus, *Annals*, 11.26.
31. Juvenal, *Satires*, ed. and trans. Susanna Morton Braund, Loeb Classical Library 91 (Cambridge, MA: Harvard University Press, 2004), 6.23.
32. Suetonius, 'Claudius', *Lives of the Caesars*, 5.40.

## CHAPTER 6

1. Cassius Dio, *Roman History*, 61.2.3–4.
2. 'Eclogue IV', *Minor Latin Poets*, vol. 1, trans. J. Wight Duff and Arnold M. Duff, Loeb Classical Library 284 (Cambridge, MA: Harvard University Press, 1934), 138–9.
3. Cassius Dio, *Roman History*, 62.19.4.
4. Cassius Dio, *Roman History*, 61.5.1–2.
5. Cassius Dio, *Roman History*, 62.13.1–2.
6. Quoted in William N. Eskridge, Jr., 'A History of Same-Sex Marriage', *The Virginia Law Review*, vol. 79 (October 1993), p. 1445.
7. Juvenal, *Satires*, 2.129.
8. Suetonius, 'Nero', *Lives of the Caesars*, 6.29.
9. Tacitus, *Annals*, 13.13.
10. Tacitus, *Annals*, 13.14.
11. Cassius Dio, *Roman History*, 62.13.5.
12. Cassius Dio, *Roman History*, 62.14.3.
13. M.I. Finley, quoted in Joe-Marie Claassen, 'The Familiar Other: The Pivotal Role of Women in Livy's Narrative of Political Development in Early Rome', *Acta Classica*, vol. 41 (1998), p. 72.
14. Livy, *History of Rome*, 34.3.
15. These reports from Cato are given in Aulus Gellius, *Attic Nights*, 10.23. Cato was writing around 200 BCE, and Gellius, writing in the second century CE, notes that it refers to *mulierum veterum* ('women of ancient times').
16. Dionysius of Halicarnassus, *Roman Antiquities*, trans. Earnest Cary, Loeb Classical Library 319 (Cambridge, MA: Harvard University Press, 1937), 2.15; and Maureen Carroll, *Infancy and Earliest Childhood in the Roman World* (Oxford: Oxford University Press, 2018), p. 4.
17. Plutarch, *Moralia: Advice to Bride and Groom*, trans. Frank Cole Babbitt, Loeb Classical Library 222 (Cambridge, MA: Harvard University Press, 1928), 48.48.
18. Plutarch, 'Life of Pompey', 55.1; Juvenal, *Satires*, 6.95.445.
19. Cornelius Nepos, *On Great Generals*, trans. J.C. Rolfe, Loeb Classical Library 467 (Cambridge, MA: Harvard University Press, 1929), preface, 6.
20. Horace, *Satires*, 6.86.398–9.
21. See Celia E. Schultz, *Women's Religious Activity in the Roman Republic* (Chapel Hill: University of North Carolina Press, 2006), p. 59.
22. Horace, *Satires*, 6.60.3178.
23. Suetonius, 'Nero', *Lives of the Caesars*, 6.38.
24. Tacitus, *Annals*, 15.44.
25. Quoted in Martin Goodman, *Judaism in the Roman World: Collected Essays* (Leiden: Brill, 2007), p. 108. Goodman notes the ambiguity and undependability of the few sources on this expulsion.

26. Josephus, *Jewish Antiquities*, trans. Louis H. Feldman, Loeb Classical Library 433 (Cambridge, MA: Harvard University Press, 1965), 18.81.5.
27. On this inscription (which has since disappeared), see T.A. Wayment and M.J. Grey, 'Jesus Followers in Pompeii: The Christianos Graffito and "Hotel of the Christians" Reconsidered', *Journal of the Jesus Movement in Its Jewish Setting*, vol. 2 (2015), pp. 102–46. The connection of the inscription with Christianity has been questioned, as in Peter Lampe, *Christians at Rome in the First Two Centuries: From Paul to Valentinus*, trans. Michael Steinhauser, ed. Marshall D. Johnson (London: Continuum, 2003), p. 8.
28. Tacitus, *Annals*, 15.47.
29. For a discussion, see Brent D. Shaw, 'The Myth of the Neronian Persecution', *The Journal of Roman Studies*, vol. 105 (2015), pp. 73–100.
30. Shaw, 'The Myth of the Neronian Persecution', p. 76. See also M.D. Goulder, 'Did Peter Ever Go to Rome?', *Scottish Journal of Theology*, vol. 57 (November 2004), pp. 377–96.
31. *The Apocryphal New Testament, being the Apocryphal Gospels, Acts, Epistles, and Apocalypses*, trans. M.R. James (Oxford: Clarendon Press, 1924), pp. 332–6.
32. Tacitus, *Histories*, trans. Clifford H. Moore, Loeb Classical Library 111 (Cambridge MA: Harvard University Press, 1925), p. 9.
33. Cassius Dio, *Roman History*, 63.37.2.
34. Suetonius, 'Nero', *Lives of the Caesars*, 6.49.1.
35. Suetonius, 'Nero', 6.57.2.
36. Cassius Dio, *Roman History*, 61.33.1.3c.
37. For this capacity, see H. Chanson, 'Hydraulics of Roman Aqueducts: Steep Chutes, Cascades, and Dropshafts', *American Journal of Archaeology*, vol. 104 (January 2000), Table 3, p. 52.
38. Quoted in Jason Urbanus, 'Rome's Imperial Port', *Archaeology*, vol. 68 (March–April 2015), p. 33.
39. Tacitus, *Annals*, 15.42.
40. Martial, *Epigrams*, vol. 2, ed. and trans. D.R. Shackleton Bailey, Loeb Classical Library 95 (Cambridge, MA: Harvard University Press, 1993), 7.34.4–5.

**CHAPTER 7**

1. Tacitus, *Histories*, 1.2.
2. Suetonius, 'Vespasian', *Lives of the Caesars*, 8.23.
3. Suetonius, 'Vespasian', *Lives of the Caesars*, 8.23.
4. Martial, *Epigrams*, 1.3.1, 4.
5. Juvenal, *Satires*, 6.112 (translation modified).
6. Statius, *Silvae*, ed. and trans. D.R. Shackleton Bailey, revised by Christopher A. Parrott, Loeb Classical Library 206 (Cambridge, MA: Harvard University Press, 2015), 1.6.54. On female gladiators,

see Anna McCullough, 'Female Gladiators in Imperial Rome: Literary Context and Historical Fact', *The Classical World*, vol. 101 (Winter 2008), pp. 197–209.

7. Statius, *Silvae*, 1.6.57.
8. Statius, *Silvae*, 2.6.26.
9. Seneca, *Epistles*, 70.20.
10. Josephus, *The Jewish War*, vol. 3, trans. H. St. J. Thackeray, Loeb Classical Library 210 (Cambridge, MA: Harvard University Press, 1928), 6.414.2.
11. Ramsay MacMullen, 'Notes on Romanization', *The Bulletin of the American Society of Papyrologists*, vol. 21 (1984), p. 170.
12. Tacitus, *Agricola*, trans. M. Hutton and W. Peterson, revised by R.M. Ogilvie, E.H. Warmington and Michael Winterbottom, Loeb Classical Library 35 (Cambridge, MA: Harvard University Press, 1914), 21.2.
13. Cassius Dio, *Roman History*, 62.3.1, 4; Tacitus, *Agricola*, 30.4.
14. Ramsay MacMullen, 'The Unromanized in Rome', in Shaye J.D. Cohen and Ernest S. Frerichs, *Diasporas in Antiquity* (Providence: Brown Judaic Studies, 1993), pp. 47–64.
15. *Bedae Opera Omnia* (Cologne, 1612), p. 482 (my translation).
16. For a discussion, see Howard Vernon Canter, 'The Venerable Bede and the Colosseum', *Transactions and Proceedings of the American Philological Association*, vol. 61 (1930), pp. 150–64.
17. For the portent and Hannibal's tour, see Silius Italicus, *Punica*, trans. J.D. Duff, Loeb Classical Library 277 (Cambridge, MA: Harvard University Press, 1934), 8.654–62; and 12.152–4.
18. Pliny the Younger, *Letters*, vol. 1, trans. Betty Radice, Loeb Classical Library 55 (Cambridge, MA: Harvard University Press, 1969), 6.13.
19. Suetonius, 'Domitian', *Lives of the Caesars*, 8.23.2.
20. Pliny the Younger, 'Panegyricus', *Letters*, 7.7.
21. Cassius Dio, *Roman History*, 68.4.2.
22. Pliny the Younger, 'Panegyricus', 2.3.
23. Quoted in Suetonius, 'Augustus', *Lives of the Caesars*, 2.23.2.
24. Ammianus Marcellinus, *History*, vol. 1, trans. J.C. Rolfe, Loeb Classical Library 300 (Cambridge, MA: Harvard University Press, 1950), 16.10.15.
25. Quoted in Anthony R. Birley, 'Hadrian', in Simon Hornblower and Antony Spawforth, eds., *The Oxford Companion to Classical Civilization* (Oxford: Oxford University Press, 2004), p. 356.
26. Anthony R. Birley, *Hadrian: The Restless Emperor* (London: Routledge, 1997).
27. For Hadrian as Zeus, see Stefan Weinstock, *Divus Julius* (Oxford: Clarendon Press, 1971), pp. 304–5.
28. Cassius Dio, *Roman History*, 69.4.5.
29. On the Pantheon as an audience hall, see Paul Godfrey and David Hemsoll, 'The Pantheon: Temple or Rotunda', in *Pagan Gods and Shrines of the Roman*

*Empire*, ed. Martin Henig and Anthony King (Oxford: Oxford University Committee for Archaeology, 1986), pp. 195–209.

30. See Lise M. Hetland, 'New Perspectives on the Dating of the Pantheon', in Tod A. Marder and Mark Wilson Jones, ed., *The Pantheon: From Antiquity to the Present* (Cambridge: Cambridge University Press, 2015), pp. 79–98.
31. Cassius Dio, *Roman History*, 62.4.2.
32. On the Roman ports, see Nikhil Swaminathan, 'Built to Last: How Roman Harbors Have Stood the Test of Time', *Archaeology*, vol. 67 (March–April 2014), pp. 44–7.
33. *Historia Augusta*, vol. 1, trans. David Magie, Loeb Classical Library 139 (Cambridge, MA: Harvard University Press, 1921), 23.11.
34. *Historia Augusta*, 1.4 and 3.6.
35. Edward Gibbon, *The History of the Decline and Fall of the Roman Empire* (New York: Harper & Brothers, 1879), vol. 1, p. 95.

**CHAPTER 8**

1. Ammianus Marcellinus, *History*, 23.24.
2. *Historia Augusta*, 4.13.6. For an estimate of the mortality: R.J. Littman and M.L. Littman, 'Galen and the Antonine Plague', *American Journal of Philology*, vol. 94 (Autumn 1973), pp. 243–55.
3. R.S.O. Tomlin, '"Drive Away the Cloud of Plague": A Greek Amulet from Roman London', in Rob Collins and Frances McIntosh, eds., *Life in the Limes* (Oxford: Oxbow Books, 2014), pp. 197–205.
4. See C.P. Jones, 'Ten Dedications "To the Gods and Goddesses" and the Antonine Plague', *Journal of Roman Archaeology*, vol. 18 (2005), pp. 293–301.
5. *Lectures on the History of Rome*, ed. Leonhard Schmitz, vol. 3 (London: Taylor, Walton and Maberly, 1849), p. 251.
6. H.M.D. Parker, *A History of the Roman World from A.D. 138 to 337* (London: Methuen, 1935), p. 20.
7. R.P. Duncan-Jones, 'The Impact of the Antonine Plague', *Journal of Roman Archaeology*, vol. 9 (1996), pp. 108–36.
8. Quoted in Duncan-Jones, 'The Impact of the Antonine Plague', p. 120.
9. Tacitus, *Germania*, trans. M. Hutton and W. Peterson, revised by R.M. Ogilvie, E.H. Warmington and Michael Winterbottom, Loeb Classical Library 35 (Cambridge, MA: Harvard University Press, 1914), 2.3–4.
10. See Andrew Dalby, *Food in the Ancient World from A to Z* (London: Routledge, 2003), p. 360.
11. Marcus Aurelius, 'Meditations', in *Marcus Aurelius*, ed. and trans. C.R. Haines, Loeb Classical Library 58 (Cambridge, MA: Harvard University Press, 1916), 6.30.
12. 'Meditations', 4.33.
13. Cassius Dio, *Roman History*, 72.36.4.

14. 'Commodus Antoninus', in *Historia Augusta*, 1.8.
15. 'Commodus Antoninus', *Historia Augusta*, 11.1–2.
16. 'Commodus Antoninus', *Historia Augusta*, 10.9.
17. Plutarch, *Moralia*, vol. 6, trans. W.C. Helmbold, Loeb Classical Library 337 (Cambridge, MA: Harvard University Press, 1939), 520.C.
18. Longinus, *On the Sublime*, in *Aristotle, Longinus, Demetrius*, trans. Stephen Halliwell, W. Hamilton Fyfe, Doreen C. Innes, W. Rhys Roberts; revised by Donald A. Russell, Loeb Classical Library 199 (Cambridge, MA: Harvard University Press, 1995), 44.5–6.
19. Brian K. Harvey, 'Two Bases of Marcus Aurelius Caesar and the Roman Imperial Succession', *Historia: Zeitschrift für Alte Geschichte*, vol. 53 (2004), p. 47.
20. Kenneth W. Harl, *Roman Economy, 300 BC to AD 700* (Baltimore: Johns Hopkins University Press, 1996), p. 216.
21. Cassius Dio, *Roman History*, 73.21.2. See also Caillan Davenport, 'Cassius Dio and Caracalla', *The Classical Quarterly*, vol. 62 (December 2012), pp. 796–815.
22. Herodian, *History of the Empire*, trans. C.R. Whittaker, Loeb Classical Library 454 (Cambridge, MA: Harvard University Press, 1969), 4.13.
23. Augustus J.C. Hare, *Walks in Rome* (London: George Allen, 1893), vol. 1, p. 235.
24. For the number of baths, see Anne Hrychuk Kontokosta, 'Building the Thermae Agrippae: Private Life, Public Space, and the Politics of Bathing in Early Imperial Rome', *American Journal of Archaeology*, vol. 123 (January 2019), p. 46.
25. See Benet Salway, 'What's in a Name? A Survey of Roman Onomastic Practice from c. 700 B.C. to A.D. 700', *The Journal of Roman Studies*, vol. 84 (1994), pp. 133–4.

**CHAPTER 9**

1. Firmicus Maternus, *Ancient Astrology: Theory and Practice*, trans. Jean Rhys Bram (Park Ridge, NJ: Noyes Press, 1975), p. 235.
2. Musonius Rufus, quoted in Jeremiah T. Johnston, 'Hilarion's Letter to His Wife, Child Exposure, and Early Christianity', in Craig A. Evans and Jeremiah H. Johnston, eds., *Scribes and Their Remains* (London: T&T Clark, 2020), p. 155.
3. Quoted in Johnston, 'Hilarion's Letter to His Wife', p. 154.
4. Maternus, *Ancient Astrology*, p. 234.
5. Quoted in Rodney Stark, 'Reconstructing the Rise of Christianity: The Role of Women', *Sociology of Religion*, vol. 56 (Autumn 1995), p. 232.
6. J.C. Russell, 'Late Ancient and Medieval Population', *Transactions of the American Philosophical Society*, vol. 48 (1958), p. 13.

7. W.H.C. Frend, *Martyrdom and Persecution in the Early Church* (Oxford: Blackwell, 1965), p. 389.
8. Leonardo de Arrizabalaga y Prado, *The Emperor Elagabalus: Fact or Fiction* (Cambridge: Cambridge University Press, 2010), p. 271.
9. For this particular accessory, see Martijn Icks, 'Priesthood and Imperial Power: The Religious Reforms of Heliogabalus', in Lukas de Blois, Peter Funke and Johannes Hahn, eds., *The Impact of Imperial Rome on Religions, Ritual and Religious Life in the Roman Empire: Proceedings from the Fifth Workshop of the International Network Impact of Empire* (Leiden: Brill, 2006), pp. 173–4.
10. *Historia Augusta*, 26.21.1–2.
11. Henry C. Montgomery, 'Diocletian's Ceiling Prices', *The Classical Outlook*, vol. 21 (February 1944), p. 45.
12. For the rate of inflation, see Alfred Wassink, 'Inflation and Financial Policy Under the Roman Empire to the Price Edict of 301 A.D.', *Historia: Zeitschrift für Alte Geschichte*, Bd. 40 (1991), pp. 468. For the increased price of commodities: Richard Duncan-Jones, *The Economy of the Roman Empire: Quantitative Studies* (Cambridge: Cambridge University Press, 1982), p. 375.
13. Antony Kropff, trans., 'An English Translation of the Edict on Maximum Prices, also Known as the Price Edict of Diocletian', available online at http://kark.uib.no/antikk/dias/priceedict.pdf
14. T.D. Barnes, 'Legislation against the Christians', *The Journal of Roman Studies*, vol. 58, Parts 1 and 2 (1968), pp. 32–50.
15. See Stark, 'Reconstructing the Rise of Christianity: The Role of Women', pp. 229–44.
16. R. Ross Holloway, *Constantine and Rome* (New Haven: Yale University Press, 2004), pp. 50 and 163.
17. Arvast Nordh, ed., *Libellus de Regionibus Urbis Romae* (Lund: C.W.K. Gleerup, 1949).

**CHAPTER 10**

1. Virgil, *The Aeneid*, 1.180. Claudianus and St Jerome are both quoted in Theodor E. Mommsen, 'St Augustine and the Christian Idea of Progress: The Background of *The City of God*', *Journal of the History of Ideas*, vol. 12 (June 1951), pp. 346 and 347. For the 'Eternal City', see Tibullus, *Elegies*, trans. F.W. Cornish, J.P. Postgate and J.W. Mackail; revised G.P. Goold, Loeb Classical Library 6 (Cambridge, MA: Harvard University Press, 1913), 2.5.23.
2. *The Works of Aurelius Augustine, Bishop of Hippo*, vol. 1, *The City of God*, trans. Marcus Dods (Edinburgh: T & T Clark, 1871), 4.1.
3. Cicero, *Pro Archia*, trans. N.H. Watts, Loeb Classical Library 158 (Cambridge, MA: Harvard University Press, 1923), 11.29.
4. Peter Brown, 'The Later Roman Empire', *The Economic History Review*, vol. 29 (August 1967), p. 331.

5. For a discussion of some of these issues, see A.H.M. Jones, 'The Decline and Fall of the Roman Empire', *History*, vol. 40 (October 1955), pp. 209–26.
6. Edward Gibbon, *The History of the Decline and Fall of the Roman Empire*, ed. William Smith (London: John Murray, 1862), vol. 4, p. 404; A.H.M. Jones, 'The Decline and Fall of the Roman Empire', p. 219; and idem., *The Later Roman Empire, 284–602: A Social, Economic and Administrative Survey*, 3 vols. (Oxford: Basil Blackwell, 1964), vol. 2, pp. 894–94, 933–4 and 1045.
7. Alexander Demandt, *Der Fall Roms: Die Auflösung der Römischen Reiches im Urteil der Nachwelt* (Munich: C.H. Beck, 1984).
8. Tenney Frank, 'Race Mixture in the Roman Empire', *The American Historical Review*, vol. 21 (July 1916), pp. 689–708.
9. Michael Rostovtzeff, *The Social and Economic History of the Roman Empire* (Oxford: Oxford University Press, 1926).
10. Edwin W. Bowen, 'The New Woman in Ancient Rome', *The Classical Outlook*, vol. 18 (November 1940), p. 21.
11. André Piganiol, 'The Causes of the Fall of the Roman Empire', *Journal of General Education*, vol. 5 (October 1950), p. 69.
12. See, for example, Walter Goffart, *Barbarians and Romans AD 418–584: The Techniques of Accommodation* (Princeton: Princeton University Press, 1980).
13. See Peter Heather, *The Fall of the Roman Empire: A New History of Rome and the Barbarians* (Oxford: Oxford University Press, 2006), and Bryan Ward-Perkins, *The Fall of Rome and the End of Civilization* (Oxford: Oxford University Press, 2005).
14. A.H.M. Jones, *The Later Roman Empire, 284–602: A Social, Economic and Administrative Survey*, 3 vols. (Oxford: Basil Blackwell, 1964), vol. 2, p. 1027.
15. Heather, *The Fall of the Roman Empire*, p. 220.
16. Ammianus Marcellinus, *History*, 31.2.1.
17. Ammianus Marcellinus, *History*, 31.4.6.
18. The literature is vast and ever-growing, but for a good summation of the evidence (on which I rely for what follows), see Michael McCormick et al., 'Climate Change During and After the Roman Empire: Reconstructing the Past from Scientific and Historical Evidence', *The Journal of Interdisciplinary History*, vol. 43 (Autumn 2012), pp. 169–220.
19. For Ebola, see Kyle Harper, *The Fate of Rome: Climate, Disease and the End of an Empire* (Princeton: Princeton University Press, 2017), pp. 143–4; and for Marburg: Mark Orsag, Amanda E. McKinney and DeeAnn M. Reeder, *Interdisciplinary Insights from the Plague of Cyprian: Pathology, Epidemiology, Ecology and History* (Abindon: Palgrave Macmillan, 2023), pp. 87–111.
20. Peter Brown, *Through the Eye of a Needle: Wealth, the Fall of Rome, and the Making of Christianity in the West* (Princeton: Princeton University Press, 2012), p. 468.

21. Hannah Arendt, *On Revolution*, 2nd edn. (New York: Penguin Putnam 1963), p. 196.
22. See Carl J. Richard, *The Founders and the Classics: Greece, Rome, and the American Enlightenment* (Cambridge, MA: Harvard University Press, 1994), pp. 83–4; and Eran Shalev, *Rome Reborn on Western Shores: Historical Imagination and the Creation of the American Republic* (Charlottesville: University of Virginia Press, 2009).
23. Bradley, *Slavery and Society at Rome*, p. 12.
24. Plutarch, 'Caesar', *Lives*, 17.2.
25. Ovid, *Amores*, trans. Grant Showerman, revised by G.P. Goold, Loeb Classical Library 41 (Cambridge, MA: Harvard University Press, 1914), 2.4.40.
26. Lucian, *Dialogues of the Sea-Gods*, trans. M.D. MacLeod, Loeb Classical Library 431 (Cambridge, MA: Harvard University Press, 1961), 1.290.
27. Juvenal, *Satires*, 13.164–5.
28. Frank, 'Race Mixture in the Roman Empire', p. 690.

# Index

Page numbers in **bold** refer to images.